The Tragedie of Anthony and Cleopatra
Antonius und Cleopatra

Steckels Shake-Speare

William Shakespeare

The Tragedie of
Anthony and Cleopatra

Antonius und Cleopatra

Titel: Barbara Petritsch (Cleopatra), Peter Roggisch (Antonius)
Schauspielhaus Bochum, Spielzeit 1986/87
Regie Frank-Patrick Steckel
Foto Klaus Lefebvre

Rückseite:
»Die Weltdummheit macht jede Arbeit
– außer an Shakespeare – unmöglich.«
Karl Kraus, Postskriptum zum letzten Brief
an Sidonie Nádherny vom 15./16.5.1936
aus: Karl Kraus, Briefe an Sidonie Nádherny von Borutin 1913-1936
Hg. von Friedrich Pfäfflin © Wallstein Verlag, Göttingen 2005
Reproduktion mit freundlicher Genehmigung
des Brenner-Archivs, Universität Innsbruck

Bühnenrechte beim Verlag der Autoren

© Verlag Uwe Laugwitz,
D-21244 Buchholz in der Nordheide, 2013

ISBN 9783-933077-34-9

Inhalt

The Tragedie of Anthony and Cleopatra

Antonius und Cleopatra

Actus Primus. Scœna Prima.

Enter Demetrius and Philo.

Philo. NAy, but this dotage of our Generals
    Ore-flowes the measure: those his goodly eyes
    That o're the Files and Musters of the Warre,
    Haue glow'd like plated Mars:
    Now bend, now turne
    The Office and Deuotion of their view
    Vpon a Tawny Front. His Captaines heart,
    Which in the scuffles of great Fights hath burst
    The Buckles on his brest, reneages all temper,
    And is become the Bellowes and the Fan
    To coole a Gypsies Lust.
      Flourish. Enter Anthony, Cleopatra, her Ladies, the
        Traine, with Eunuchs fanning her.
    Looke where they come:
    Take but good note, and you shall see in him
    (The triple Pillar of the world) transform'd
    Into a Strumpets Foole. Behold and see.
Cleo. If it be Loue indeed, tell me how much.
Ant. There's beggery in the loue that can be reckon'd
Cleo. Ile set a bourne how farre to be belou'd.
Ant. Then must thou needes finde out new Heauen,
    new Earth.
        Enter a Messenger.
Mes. Newes (my good Lord) from Rome.
Ant. Grates me, the summe.
Cleo. Nay heare them *Anthony*.
    Fuluia perchance is angry: Or who knowes,

ERSTER AKT
Erste Szene

Demetrius, Philo.

PHILO Nein, diese Liebschaft unsres Generals
Bricht alle Schranken: sein berühmtes Auge,
Das über Kriegen und Paraden glühte
Wie das des ehrnen Mars, verdreht sich, senkt
Den Feldherrnblick in schielendem Gehorsam
Auf eine dunkle Stirn: sein Heldenherz,
Das sonst im Kampfgewühl der Schlachten ihm
Die Rüstung sprengte, es verleugnet sich
Und kühlt als Blasebalg und Fächer nun
Die Brunst einer Zigeunerin.

Antonius, Cleopatra, Gefolge.

                      Da sind sie.
Gebt acht und sehen werdet ihr, wie er,
Von den drei Säulen dieser Welt die eine,
Den Narren einer Hure macht.
CLEOPATRA Wenn es denn Liebe sein soll, sag, wieviel.
ANTONIUS Liebe, die sich rechnen läßt, geht betteln.
CLEOPATRA Ich setz ein Zeichen, wie weit Liebe gehn muß.
ANTONIUS Dann brauchst du neuen Himmel, neue Erde.

Ein Diener.

DIENER Neues, Herr, aus Rom.
ANTONIUS   Stört mich, machs kurz.
CLEOPATRA Nein, du hörst zu, Antonius:
Vielleicht ist Fulvia böse; oder, weiß mans,

If the scarse-bearded *Cæsar* haue not sent
His powrefull Mandate to you. Do this, or this;
Take in that Kingdome, and Infranchise that:
Perform't, or else we damne thee.

Ant. How, my Loue?

Cleo. Perchance? Nay, and most like:
You must not stay heere longer, your dismission
Is come from *Cæsar*, therefore heare it *Anthony*
Where's *Fuluias* Processe? (*Cæsars* I would say) both?
Call in the Messengers: As I am Egypts Queene,
Thou blushest *Anthony*, and that blood of thine
Is *Cæsars* homager: else so thy cheeke payes shame,
When shrill-tongu'd *Fuluia* scolds. The Messengers.

Ant. Let Rome in Tyber melt, and the wide Arch
Of the raing'd Empire fall: Heere is my space,
Kingdomes are clay: Our dungie earth alike
Feeds Beast as Man; the Noblenesse of life
Is to do thus: when such a mutuall paire,
And such a twaine can doo't, in which I binde
One paine of punishment, the world to weete
We stand vp Peerelesse.

Cleo. Excellent falshood:
Why did he marry Fuluia, and not loue her?
Ile seeme the Foole I am not. *Anthony* will be himselfe.

Ant But stirr'd by *Cleopatra*.
Now for the loue of Loue, and her soft houres,
Let's not confound the time with Conference harsh;
There's not a minute of our liues should stretch
Without some pleasure now. What sport to night?

Cleo. Heare the Ambassadors.

Der flaumbärtige Caesar sendet dir
Allmächtigen Befehl, ›Tu dies, tu das;
Besetze dieses Land und räume jenes;
Gehorche oder sei verdammt.‹
ANTONIUS   Wie, Liebste?
CLEOPATRA Vielleicht, nein, höchst wahrscheinlich:
Du darfst nicht länger bleiben, wirst verlegt,
Das läßt dich Caesar wissen, also höre.
Bringt Fulvias Order! Caesars, mein ich. Beide!
Ruf die Boten nur herein! So wahr
Ich Königin Ägyptens bin, Antonius
Du wirst rot, und dies dein Blut ist Caesars
Vasall: wenn nicht, zahlt deine Wange
Mit Scham für Fulvias Gezänk. Die Boten!
ANTONIUS Zerschmilz im Tiber, Rom, der Riesenbau
Der Weltmacht falle hin! Mein Platz ist hier,
Reiche sind Staub: der Kot der Erde nährt
Wie Tier, so Mensch; des Lebens Krone trägt
Allein das Paar, das sich erkennt in Liebe
Wie du und ich, und nichts als dies, das soll
Die Welt bei schwerer Strafe wissen, ist es,
Was einzigartig macht.
CLEOPATRA   Brillant gelogen!
Nahm er nicht Fulvia auch und liebte nicht?
Mich macht er zur Närrin, und Antonius
Bleibt er treu.
ANTONIUS   Nicht bei Cleopatra.
Der Liebe zulieb, ihren sanften Stunden,
Laß uns nicht Zeit mit spitzen Reden töten:
Jede Minute unsres Lebens soll
Nun ein Vergnügen füllen. Welches heute?
CLEOPATRA Botschafter anzuhören.

Ant. Fye wrangling Queene:
   Whom euery thing becomes, to chide, to laugh,
   To weepe: who euery passion fully striues
   To make it selfe (in Thee) faire, and admir'd.
   No Messenger but thine, and all alone, to night
   Wee'l wander through the streets, and note
   The qualities of people. Come my Queene,
   Last night you did desire it. Speake not to vs.
                                          Exeunt with the Traine.
Dem. Is *Cæsar* with *Anthonius* priz'd so slight?
Philo. Sir sometimes when he is not *Anthony*,
   He comes too short of that great Property
   Which still should go with *Anthony*.
Dem. I am full sorry, that hee approues the common
   Lyar, who thus speakes of him at Rome; but I will hope
   of better deeds to morrow. Rest you happy.   *Exeunt*

Enter Enobarbus, Lamprius, a Southsayer, Rannius, Lucilli-
us, Charmian, Iras, Mardian the Eunuch,
and Alexas.

Char. L. *Alexas*, sweet *Alexas*, most any thing *Alexas*,
   almost most absolute *Alexas*, where's the Soothsayer
   that you prais'd so to'th'Queene? Oh that I knewe this
   Husband, which you say, must change his Hornes with
   Garlands.
Alex. Soothsayer.
Sooth. Your will?
Char. Is this the Man? Is't you sir that know things?
Sooth. In Natures infinite booke of Secrecie, a little I

ANTONIUS   Schlimme Fürstin!
    Der alles gut bekommt, das Streiten, Lachen,
    Weinen: alle Leidenschaften suchen
    In dir gleich schön zu sein und gleich bewundert!
    Wenn Botschaft, dann von dir, und nur für mich:
    Heut Nacht durchwandern wir die Straßen, lauschen
    Menschenstimmen. Königin, so komm,
    Vergangne Nacht war es dein Wunsch. Sprecht nicht.
                            Ab.
DEMETRIUS Gilt Caesar bei Antonius so wenig?
PHILO Sir, er ist Antonius und ist's nicht,
    Und immer dann zeigt er uns dies Gesicht,
    Wenn's Marcus an Antonius gebricht.
DEMETRIUS Bedauerlich, daß er Gerüchten Recht gibt,
    Die man in Rom ausstreut: doch ich will hoffen,
    Morgen ist ein neuer Tag. Gut Nacht.

                    Zweite Szene

    Enobarbus, Lamprius (ein Wahrsager), Rannius, Lucillius,
        Charmian, Iras, Mardian (Eunuch),
                    Alexas.

CHARMIAN Lord Alexas, süßer Alexas, liebster Allesalexas,
    allerliebster Überalexas, wo ist der Wahrsager, von dem Ihr
    der Königin vorgeschwärmt habt? O wüßte ich den Gatten,
    der sich, wie Ihr meint, Girlanden um die Hörner wickeln
    kann!
ALEXAS Wahrsager!
WAHRSAGER Ihr befehlt?
CHARMIAN Ist er der Mann? Seid Ihr das, Sir, der Dinge weiß?
WAHRSAGER In der Natur verborgen tiefem Buch

can read.

Alex. Shew him your hand.

Enob. Bring in the Banket quickly: Wine enough,
   Cleopatra's health to drinke.

Char. Good sir, giue me good Fortune.

Sooth. I make not, but foresee.

Char. Pray then, foresee me one.

Sooth. You shall be yet farre fairer then you are.

Char. He meanes in flesh.

Iras. No, you shall paint when you are old.

Char. Wrinkles forbid.

Alex. Vex not his prescience, be attentiue.

Char. Hush.

Sooth. You shall be more belouing, then beloued.

Char. I had rather heate my Liuer with drinking.

Alex. Nay, heare him.

Char. Good now some excellent Fortune: Let mee
   be married to three Kings in a forenoone, and Widdow
   them all: Let me haue a Childe at fifty, to whom *Herode*
   of Iewry may do Homage. Finde me to marrie me with
   Octauius Cæsar, and companion me with my Mistris.

Sooth. You shall out-liue the Lady whom you serue.

Char. Oh excellent, I loue long life better then Figs.

Sooth. You haue seene and proued a fairer former fortune, then that which is to approach.

Char. Then belike my Children shall haue no names:
   Prythee how many Boyes and Wenches must I haue.

Sooth. If euery of your wishes had a wombe, & foretell euery wish, a Million.

Kann ich ein wenig lesen.

ALEXAS Zeig ihm deine Hand.

ENOBARBUS Tragt schleunig das Bankett auf; Wein vor allem,
Um auf das Wohl Cleopatras zu trinken.

CHARMIAN Lieber Sir, sagt mir was Liebes wahr.

WAHRSAGER Ich mache nichts, ich sehe es vorher.

CHARMIAN Dann bitte, seht mir so etwas vorher.

WAHRSAGER Ihr werdet schöner werden als Ihr seid.

CHARMIAN Er meint runder.

IRAS Nein, er meint, du bemalst dich, wenn du alt wirst.

CHARMIAN Falten verboten!

ALEXAS Lenkt ihn nicht vom Hellsehn ab, gebt Ruhe.

CHARMIAN Pst!

WAHRSAGER Du wirst mehr Liebe geben als empfangen.

CHARMIAN Lieber soll mir Trinken das Blut erhitzen.

ALEXAS Nein, hört ihn an.

CHARMIAN Es reicht, irgendwas Großes jetzt! Macht mich zur
Gattin dreier Könige und danach zu ihrer Witwe, alles an
einem einzigen Vormittag: laßt mich mit fünfzig einen
Sohn bekommen, vor dem selbst Herodes kniet. Lest, daß
ich Octavius Caesar eheliche und stellt mich der Herrin
gleich.

WAHRSAGER Ihr werdet Eure Herrin überleben.

CHARMIAN O sehr gut, mir ist ein langes Leben lieber als ein
Korb mit Feigen.

WAHRSAGER Hinter Euch liegt Schöneres als vor Euch.

CHARMIAN Also sollen meine Kinder keine Väter haben: ach
bitte, wieviele solcher Jungen und Mädchen muß ich kriegen?

WAHRSAGER Wenn jeder Eurer Wünsche fruchtbar wäre
und gebären könnte, eine Million.

Char. Out Foole, I forgiue thee for a Witch.

Alex. You thinke none but your sheets are priuie to
your wishes.

Char. Nay come, tell *Iras* hers.

Alex. Wee'l know all our Fortunes.

Enob. Mine, and most of our Fortunes to night, shall
be drunke to bed.

Iras. There's a Palme presages Chastity, if nothing els.

Char. E'ne as the o're-flowing *Nylus* presageth Fa-
mine.

Iras. Go you wilde Bedfellow, you cannot Soothsay.

Char. Nay, if an oyly Palme bee not a fruitfull Prog-
nostication, I cannot scratch mine eare. Prythee tel her
but a worky day Fortune.

Sooth. Your Fortunes are alike.

Iras. But how, but how, giue me particulars.

Sooth. I haue said.

Iras. Am I not an inch of Fortune better then she?

Char. Well, if you were but an inch of fortune better
then I: where would you choose it.

Iras. Not in my Husbands nose.

Char. Our worser thoughts Heauens mend.

Alexas. Come, his Fortune, his Fortune. Oh let him
mary a woman that cannot go, sweet *Isis*, I beseech thee,
and let her dye too, and giue him a worse, and let worse
follow worse, till the worst of all follow him laughing to
his graue, fifty-fold a Cuckold. Good *Isis* heare me this
Prayer, though thou denie me a matter of more waight:
good *Isis* I beseech thee.

CHARMIAN Verschwinde, du Narr! Ich vergebe dir deine faulen Tricks.

ALEXAS Du glaubst, nur deine Laken kennen deine Wünsche.

CHARMIAN Nein, warte, sag Iras was voraus.

ALEXAS Wir alle wollen unser Schicksal wissen.

ENOBARBUS Heut Abend lautet meins und das der meisten hier – bezecht ins Bett.

IRAS Diese Handfläche weissagt auf jeden Fall Keuschheit.

CHARMIAN Wie der fette Nilschlamm Hunger.

IRAS Verzieh dich, du Betthase, was weißt du schon.

CHARMIAN Sehr wahr, stellt so eine Schwitzhand keine Fruchtbarkeitsprognose vor, dann kann ich mir nicht das Ohr kratzen. Bitte sagt ihr ein ganz normales Frauenschicksal voraus.

WAHRSAGER Eure Schicksale gleichen sich.

IRAS Aber worin, worin? Einzelheiten!

WAHRSAGER Wie ich sage.

IRAS Mir soll es kein Stück besser ergehn als ihr?

CHARMIAN Und falls es dir ein Stück besser erginge, wo darfs sein?

IRAS Nicht an meines Mannes Nase.

CHARMIAN Ihr Himmel, bewahrt uns vor Schlimmerem! Alexas – kommt, sein Schicksal noch, sein Schicksal! O, laß ihn eine Frau heiraten, die keine Treue kennt, große Isis, ich flehe dich an, und laß sie sterben, und dann gib ihm eine schlimmere, und der schlimmeren laß eine noch schlimmere folgen, bis die schlimmste von allen lachend seinem Sarg folgt mit dem fünfzigfachen Hahnrei darin. Große Isis, erhöre mein Gebet, auch wenn du mir Wichtigeres verheimlichst: große Isis, ich flehe dich an!

Iras. Amen, deere Goddesse, heare that prayer of the
   people. For, as it is a heart-breaking to see a handsome
   man loose-Wiu'd, so it is a deadly sorrow, to beholde a
   foule Knaue vncuckolded: Therefore deere *Isis* keep decorum, and Fortune him accordingly.

Char. Amen.
Alex. Lo now, if it lay in their hands to make mee a
   Cuckold, they would make themselues Whores, but
   they'ld doo't.
                    Enter Cleopatra.
Enob. Hush, heere comes *Anthony.*
Char. Not he, the Queene.
Cleo. Saue you, my Lord.
Enob. No Lady.
Cleo. Was he not heere?
Char. No Madam.
Cleo. He was dispos'd to mirth, but on the sodaine
   A Romane thought hath strooke him.
      Enobarbus?
Enob. Madam.
Cleo. Seeke him, and bring him hither: wher's *Alexias?*
Alex. Heere at your seruice.
   My Lord approaches.
               Enter Anthony, with a Messenger.
Cleo. We will not looke vpon him:
   Go with vs.   *Exeunt.*

Messen. *Fuluia* thy Wife,
   First came into the Field.
Ant. Against my Brother *Lucius?*
Messen. I: but soone that Warre had end,

IRAS Amen, große Göttin, erhöre dies schlichte Gebet des
   einfachen Volks! Denn ist es auch herzzerreißend, einen
   schönen Mann locker beweibt zu sehn, so bringt es uns
   direkt um, wenn ein Plumpsack hörnerlos davonkommt:
   darum, große Isis, wahre den Anstand, und beschicksale
   ihn wie's ihm gebührt.
CHARMIAN Amen.
ALEXAS Sieh einer an, läge es in ihren Händen, mich zum
   Hahnrei zu machen, nähmen sie es auf sich, Huren zu
   werden.
ENOBARBUS Still, Antonius kommt.
                        Cleopatra.
                              Vielmehr die Königin.
CLEOPATRA Ihr saht den Herrn?
ENOBARBUS   Nein, Lady.
CLEOPATRA   Er war nicht hier?
CHARMIAN Nein, Madam.
CLEOPATRA Er war zu Scherzen aufgelegt; und plötzlich
   Packt ihn ein römischer Gedanke. Enobarbus!

ENOBARBUS Madam.
CLEOPATRA Such ihn, bring ihn her. Wo ist Alexas?
ALEXAS Zu Euren Diensten. Da, der Feldherr naht.

CLEOPATRA Wir werden ihn nicht ansehn: ihr geht mit. *Ab.*

                  Antonius, 1. Bote.
1. BOTE Erst rückte Fulvia, deine Gattin, vor.

ANTONIUS Gegen meinen Bruder Lucius?
1. BOTE   Ja.

And the times state
Made friends of them, ioynting their force 'gainst *Cæsar*,
Whose better issue in the warre from Italy,
Vpon the first encounter draue them.

Ant. Well, what worst.

Mess. The Nature of bad newes infects the Teller.

Ant. When it concernes the Foole or Coward: On.
Things that are past, are done, with me. 'Tis thus,
Who tels me true, though in his Tale lye death,
I heare him as he flatter'd.

Mes. *Labienus* (this is stiffe-newes)
Hath with his Parthian Force
Extended Asia: from Euphrates his conquering
Banner shooke, from Syria to Lydia,
And to Ionia, whil'st———

Ant. *Anthony* thou would'st say.

Mes. Oh my Lord.

Ant. Speake to me home,
Mince not the generall tongue, name
Cleopatra as she is call'd in Rome:
Raile thou in *Fuluia's* phrase, and taunt my faults
With such full License, as both Truth and Malice
Haue power to vtter. Oh then we bring forth weeds,
When our quicke windes lye still, and our illes told vs
Is as our earing: fare thee well awhile.

Mes. At your Noble pleasure.   *Exit Messenger.*

        Enter another Messenger.

Ant. From *Scicion* how the newes? Speake there.

1. *Mes.* The man from *Scicion*,
Is there such an one?

2. *Mes.* He stayes vpon your will.

Ant. Let him appeare:

Doch war der Zwist rasch aus, und kurz darauf
Erschienen sie verbündet gegen Caesar,
Dessen Kriegsglück sie beim ersten Treffen
Vom Festland warf.
ANTONIUS   Schön. Das Nächstschlimmre?
1. BOTE Die üble Nachricht schadet ihrem Boten.
ANTONIUS Geht sie an wen, der dumm ist oder feige.
Sprich: Dinge sind, getan, vergangne Dinge.
Wer mir die Wahrheit sagt, und sei sie Tod,
Den hör ich an wie andre Leute Schmeichler.
1. BOTE Labienus – es ist hart zu hören – nahm
Mit seinem Partherheer ganz Asien ein:
Vom Euphrat weht, von Syrien sein Banner
Bis Lydien und Ionien: währenddessen –

ANTONIUS Antonius, willst du sagen –
1. BOTE   O, Mylord!
ANTONIUS Sprich offen, würz nicht böse Zungen zuckrig:
Red von Cleopatra, wie mans in Rom tut;
Schimpf ruhig in Fulvias Stil, und meine Schwächen
Geißle ganz mit dem Recht, welches Wahrheit
Für sich in Anspruch nimmt genau wie Bosheit.
O in uns wuchert Unkraut, legen wir
Vernunft still, und uns kritisieren heißt,
Uns jäten. Zieh dich nun zurück.
1. BOTE Ganz wie Ihr wünscht.
                              2. Bote.
ANTONIUS Was gibts aus Sikyon? Sprich, du da.
1. BOTE Aus Sikyon ein Mann – ist einer da?

2. BOTE Er harrt Eures Befehls.
ANTONIUS   Laßt ihn erscheinen.

These strong Egyptian Fetters I must breake,
Or loose my selfe in dotage.

Enter another Messenger with a Letter.

What are you?

3. Mes. *Fuluia* thy wife is dead.

Ant. Where dyed she.

Mes. In *Scicion*, her length of sicknesse,
With what else more serious,
Importeth thee to know, this beares.

Antho. Forbeare me
There's a great Spirit gone, thus did I desire it:
What our contempts doth often hurle from vs,
We wish it ours againe. The present pleasure,
By reuolution lowring, does become
The opposite of it selfe: she's good being gon,
The hand could plucke her backe, that shou'd her on.
I must from this enchanting Queene breake off,
Ten thousand harmes, more then the illes I know
My idlenesse doth hatch.

Enter Enobarbus.

How now *Enobarbus*.

Eno. What's your pleasure, Sir?

Anth. I must with haste from hence.

Eno. Why then we kill all our Women. We see how
mortall an vnkindnesse is to them, if they suffer our de-
parture death's the word.

Ant. I must be gone.

Eno. Vnder a compelling an occasion, let women die.
It were pitty to cast them away for nothing, though be-

Ägyptens starke Fessel muß ich lösen,
Sonst bringt mich diese Liebschaft um mich selbst.

3. Bote, mit einem Brief.

ANTONIUS Was hast du?

3. BOTE   Fulvia ist tot, die Gattin.

ANTONIUS Wo starb sie?

3. BOTE   In Sikyon.

Die Dauer ihres Siechtums und was sonst noch
Für dich von Wichtigkeit, steht hier.

ANTONIUS   Nun laßt mich.

Da schied doch eine große Seele! Zwar
Hab ich mir gewünscht, was nun geschehn:
Doch was wir mit Verachtung von uns stoßen,
Kaum ist es fort, solls wieder unser sein.
Was uns im Augenblick Vergnügen macht,
Die bloße Wiederholung zieht es nieder,
Bis es zu seinem Gegenteil geworden:
Ich liebe sie, nun, da sie starb. Die Hand,
Die ihr den Stoß gab, risse sie zurück.
Ich muß mit dieser Zauberkön'gin brechen,
Zehntausend Übel, weit mehr als ich ahne,
Brütet mein Müßiggang. He, Enobarbus!

Enobarbus.

ENOBARBUS Sir, Eure Wünsche?

ANTONIUS Ich muß hier weg und schnell.

ENOBARBUS Schön, dann bringen wir eben alle unsre Weiber
um. Wir sehn ja, wie hart eine kleine Unhöflichkeit
ihnen zusetzt; man braucht sie nur zu verlassen, schon ist
vom Sterben die Rede.

ANTONIUS Ich muß weg.

ENOBARBUS Gut, in dringenden Fällen muß man sie sterben
lassen: schade wärs nur, sie für nichts wegzuwerfen, ob-

tweene them and a great cause, they should be esteemed nothing. *Cleopatra* catching but the least noyse of this, dies instantly: I haue seene her dye twenty times vppon farre poorer moment: I do think there is mettle in death, which commits some louing acte vpon her, she hath such a celerity in dying.

Ant. She is cunning past mans thought.

Eno. Alacke Sir no, her passions are made of nothing but the finest part of pure Loue. We cannot cal her winds and waters, sighes and teares: They are greater stormes and Tempests then Almanackes can report. This cannot be cunning in her; if it be, she makes a showre of Raine as well as Ioue.

Ant. Would I had neuer seene her.

Eno. Oh sir, you had then left vnseene a wonderfull peece of worke, which not to haue beene blest withall, would haue discredited your Trauaile.

Ant. *Fuluia* is dead.

Eno. Sir.

Ant. *Fuluia* is dead.

Eno. *Fuluia?*

Ant. Dead.

Eno. Why sir, giue the Gods a thankefull Sacrifice: when it pleaseth their Deities to take the wife of a man from him, it shewes to man the Tailors of the earth: comforting therein, that when olde Robes are worne out, there are members to make new. If there were no more Women but *Fuluia*, then had you indeede a cut, and the case to be lamented: This greefe is crown'd with Consolation, your old Smocke brings foorth a new Petticoate,

wohl, gemessen an einer welthistorischen Aufgabe, sie selbstverständlich für nichts gelten. Hört Cleopatra nur den leisesten Ton von der Sache, stirbt sie Euch auf der Stelle. Ich sah sie zwanzigmal aus weit geringerem Anlaß verbleichen: Ich glaube, der Tod ist ein Stecher, der eine Art Liebesakt an ihr begeht, darum hat sie sowas Geschwindes beim Sterben.

ANTONIUS Du ahnst nicht, wie schlau sie ist.

ENOBARBUS Ah nein, Sir, ihre Gefühle sind ganz und gar aus dem feinsten Stoff der reinen Liebe gemacht. Was da weht und wogt, das kann unsereins nicht bloß Seufzer und Tränen nennen; das sind gewaltigere Stürme und Unwetter, als wovon Kalender Meldung tun. Wenn das ihre Schlauheit zuwege bringt, dann ist sie als Regenmacher mindestens so gut wie Jupiter.

ANTONIUS Hätt ich sie nie gesehn!

ENOBARBUS O Sir, da wäre Euch ein Meisterwerk entgangen, mit dessen Anblick nicht gesegnet worden zu sein, ein ziemlich schlechtes Licht auf Eure Reise werfen würde.

ANTONIUS Fulvia ist tot.

ENOBARBUS Sir?

ANTONIUS Fulvia ist tot.

ENOBARBUS Fulvia?

ANTONIUS Tot.

ENOBARBUS Na also, Sir, bringt den Göttern ein Dankopfer. Wenn es den Himmelsherrschern gefällt, das Weib eines Mannes von ihm zu nehmen, verweisen sie den Mann an die Schneider auf Erden; denn tröstlicherweise gibt es, sind die alten Röcke durchgewetzt, solche Glieder der menschlichen Gesellschaft, die neue machen. Gäbe es keine Weiber außer Fulvia, dann allerdings hättet Ihr Euch geschnitten, und die Sache stünde beklagenswert: gegen-

aud indeed the teares liue in an Onion, that should water this sorrow.

Ant. The businesse she hath broached in the State,
Cannot endure my absence.

Eno. And the businesse you haue broach'd heere cannot be without you, especially that of *Cleopatra's*, which
wholly depends on your abode.

Ant. No more light Answeres:
Let our Officers
Haue notice what we purpose. I shall breake
The cause of our Expedience to the Queene,
And get her loue to part. For not alone
The death of Fuluia, with more vrgent touches
Do strongly speake to vs: but the Letters too
Of many our contriuing Friends in Rome,
Petition vs at home. *Sextus Pompeius*
Haue giuen the dare to *Cæsar*, and commands
The Empire of the Sea. Our slippery people,
Whose Loue is neuer link'd to the deseruer,
Till his deserts are past, begin to throw
Pompey the great, and all his Dignities
Vpon his Sonne, who high in Name and Power,
Higher then both in Blood and Life, stands vp
For the maine Souldier. Whose quality going on,
The sides o'th'world may danger. Much is breeding,
Which like the Coursers heire, hath yet but life,
And not a Serpents poyson. Say our pleasure,
To such whose places vnder vs, require
Our quicke remoue from hence.

Enob. I shall doo't.

wärtigen Gram jedoch krönt Trost, nämlich Euer Altwei-
berkittel schafft einen frischen Unterrock her, und die
Tränen müßten schon in einer Zwiebel hausen, die diese
Art Schmerz bewässern wollen.

ANTONIUS Das, was sie im Land politisch anfing,
Gelingt nicht ohne mich.

ENOBARBUS Und das, was Ihr hier politisch anfingt, gelingt
ohne Euch auch nicht, besonders das mit Cleopatra, welches ganz und gar von Eurem Hiersein abhängt.

ANTONIUS Schluß mit den Scherzen. Laß die Offiziere
Wissen, was wir planen. Ich erkläre
Der Königin die Gründe unsres Umschwungs
Und mache sie geneigt. Denn nicht allein
Der Fulvia Tod erfordert unsre Heimkehr.
Auch viele Briefe uns verbundner Freunde
Rufen uns zurück. Sextus Pompejus
Droht dem jungen Caesar und beherrscht
Bereits das Mittelmeer. Das schwanke Volk
Das den, der es verdient, erst dann hochhält,
Wenn sein Verdienst verraucht ist, häuft zunehmend
Das ganze Ansehn des Pompejus Magnus
Auf dessen Sohn, der, groß von Rang und Namen,
Größer noch an Mut und Kraft, sich aufwirft
Zum ersten Mann in Waffen, was, wenn's durchgeht,
Die Weltordnung ins Wanken bringen kann.
Viel keimt, was wie ein Roßhaar Leben hat,
Doch keinen Giftzahn noch. Den Unsern sagst du,
Wir wünschen nichts, als schnell hier abzurücken.

ENOBARBUS Das mach ich doch.

Enter Cleopatra, Charmian, Alexas, and Iras.

Cleo. Where is he?

Char. I did not see him since.

Cleo. See where he is,
    Whose with him, what he does:
    I did not send you. If you finde him sad,
    Say I am dauncing: if in Myrth, report
    That I am sodaine sicke. Quicke, and returne.

Char. Madam, me thinkes if you did loue him deerly,
    You do not hold the method, to enforce
    The like from him.

Cleo. What should I do, I do not?

Ch. In each thing giue him way, crosse him in nothing.

Cleo. Thou teachest like a foole: the way to lose him.

Char. Tempt him not so too farre. I wish forbeare,
    In time we hate that which we often feare.
           Enter Anthony.
    But heere comes *Anthony*.

Cleo. I am sicke, and sullen.

An. I am sorry to giue breathing to my purpose.

Cleo. Helpe me away deere *Charmian*, I shall fall,
    It cannot be thus long, the sides of Nature
    Will not sustaine it.

Ant. Now my deerest Queene.

Cleo. Pray you stand farther from mee.

Ant. What's the matter?

Dritte Szene

Cleopatra, Charmian, Alexas, Iras.

CLEOPATRA Wo ist er denn?
CHARMIAN   Ich sah ihn seither nicht.
CLEOPATRA Sieh, wo er steckt, wer bei ihm, was er macht:
    Ich hab dich nicht geschickt. Findst du ihn traurig,
    Sag, ich tanze; ist er munter, sagst du,
    Ich sei jäh erkrankt. Schnell, und komm wieder.

CHARMIAN Madam, mir scheint, Ihr liebt ihn zwar von Herzen,
    Doch kennt Ihr das Verfahren nicht, von ihm
    Das Gleiche zu erzwingen.
CLEOPATRA   Was kann ich
    Noch tun und tus nicht?
CHARMIAN   Gebt in allem nach,
    Und widersprecht in nichts.
CLEOPATRA   Absurder Rat:
    Das ist der sichre Weg, ihn zu verlieren.
CHARMIAN Reizt ihn nicht so, ich bitt Euch, seid bedacht:
    Wir hassen schnell, was zu oft Angst uns macht.
                 Antonius.
CHARMIAN Antonius kommt.
CLEOPATRA   Ich bin verstimmt und krank.
ANTONIUS Es tut mir leid, es auszusprechen, aber –
CLEOPATRA Charmian, hilf mir hinweg, ich falle.
    Es dauert nicht mehr lang, ich bin zu schwach,
    Das zu ertragen.
ANTONIUS   Teure Königin –
CLEOPATRA Ich bitte dich, komm mir nicht nah.
ANTONIUS   Warum nicht?

Cleo. I know by that same eye ther's some good news.
 What sayes the married woman you may goe?
 Would she had neuer giuen you leaue to come.
 Let her not say 'tis I that keepe you heere,
 I haue no power vpon you: Hers you are.
Ant. The Gods best know.
Cleo. Oh neuer was there Queene
 So mightily betrayed: yet at the first
 I saw the Treasons planted.
Ant. Cleopatra.
Cleo. Why should I thinke you can be mine, & true,
 (Though you in swearing shake the Throaned Gods)
 Who haue beene false to *Fuluia*?
 Riotous madnesse,
 To be entangled with those mouth-made vowes,
 Which breake themselues in swearing.
Ant. Most sweet Queene.
Cleo. Nay pray you seeke no colour for your going,
 But bid farewell, and goe:
 When you sued staying,
 Then was the time for words: No going then,
 Eternity was in our Lippes, and Eyes,
 Blisse in our browes bent: none our parts so poore,
 But was a race of Heauen. They are so still,
 Or thou the greatest Souldier of the world,
 Art turn'd the greatest Lyar.
Ant. How now Lady?
Cleo. I would I had thy inches, thou should'st know
 There were a heart in Egypt.
Ant. Heare me Queene:
 The strong necessity of Time, commands
 Our Seruicles a-while: but my full heart

CLEOPATRA Dein Blick allein verrät die gute Nachricht.
Was sagt die Angetraute? Darfst du kommen?
Hätte sie dir doch nie erlaubt zu gehn!
Laß sie nicht sprechen, ich seis, die dich hielte.
Ich bin ganz machtlos; du gehörst nur ihr.
ANTONIUS Die Götter wissen –
CLEOPATRA   Keine Königin
Ward je so grausamlich getäuscht! Dabei
Sah ich von Anfang an Betrug am Werk.
ANTONIUS Cleopatra –
CLEOPATRA   Wie kann ich glauben, du
Bist mein und treu (obgleich er, wenn er schwört,
Den Sitz der Götter wanken macht), der du doch
Fulvia täuschtest? Zügelloser Wahn,
Verstrickt zu sein in mundgewirkte Eide,
Die, kaum geschworen, brechen!
ANTONIUS   Liebste, Teure –
CLEOPATRA Versuch nicht, deine Flucht noch schönzufärben,
Sag mir Lebwohl und geh: für lange Worte
War Zeit, als du drum batest, hier zu bleiben;
Nichts da von Abschied; Ewigkeiten wohnten
Uns auf den Lippen, in den Blicken uns.
Auf unsern Brauen Seligkeit; und alles
An uns war göttlich. Ganz so ist es noch,
Es sei denn, aus der Erde größtem Krieger
Ward nun ihr größter Lügner.
ANTONIUS   Wie nun, Lady?
CLEOPATRA Wär ich so lang wie Ihr, ich ließ Euch spüren,
Selbst in Ägypten schlägt ein Herz.
ANTONIUS   Hoheit,
Vernehmt: das strenge Regiment der Zeiten
Erfordert unsern Dienst. Mein Herz jedoch

Remaines in vse with you. Our Italy,
Shines o're with ciuill Swords; *Sextus Pompeius*
Makes his approaches to the Port of Rome,
Equality of two Domesticke powers,
Breed scrupulous faction: The hated growne to strength
Are newly growne to Loue: The condemn'd *Pompey*,
Rich in his Fathers Honor, creepes apace
Into the hearts of such, as haue not thriued
Vpon the present state, whose Numbers threaten,
And quietnesse growne sicke of rest, would purge
By any desperate change: My more particular,
And that which most with you should safe my going,
Is *Fuluias* death.

Cleo. Though age from folly could not giue me freedom
    It does from childishnesse. Can *Fuluia* dye?
Ant. She's dead my Queene.
    Looke heere, and at thy Soueraigne leysure read
    The Garboyles she awak'd: at the last, best,
    See when, and where shee died.
Cleo. O most false Loue!
    Where be the Sacred Violles thou should'st fill
    With sorrowfull water? Now I see, I see,
    In *Fuluias* death, how mine receiu'd shall be.
Ant. Quarrell no more, but bee prepar'd to know
    The purposes I beare: which are, or cease,
    As you shall giue th'aduice. By the fire
    That quickens Nylus slime, I go from hence
    Thy Souldier, Seruant, making Peace or Warre,
    As thou affects.
Cleo. Cut my Lace, *Charmian* come,

Verbleibt bei Euch. Durch ganz Italien blitzt
Das Schwert des Bürgerkriegs; Sextus Pompejus
Naht sich von See her Rom, gleich starke Kräfte
Im Innern sorgen für Verwirrung, niemand
Weiß mehr, wer die Macht hat: die Beliebtheit
Der einst Verhaßten wächst mit ihrer Stärke:
Pompejus, der Verbannte, überglänzt
Von seines Vaters Ruhm, kriecht in die Herzen
Derer, die ihn zwar nicht mögen, aber
Ihren Schnitt bisher nicht machen konnten,
Und es werden mehr. Die Raffgier, krank
Vom langen Warten, sucht ihr Heil zuletzt
In wildverwegnem Umsturz. Letzter Grund
Der Reise, um Euch völlig zu beruhigen,
Ist Fulvias Tod.
CLEOPATRA Schützt mich mein Alter auch vor Torheit nicht,
So bin ich doch kein Kind. Kann Fulvia sterben?
ANTONIUS Sie ist gestorben, meine Königin.
Lies das, und nimm in einer Mußestunde
Zur Kenntnis, was sie trieb: zuletzt das Beste
Wann sie starb und wo.
CLEOPATRA   O Liebestrug!
Wo sind die Tränengläser, die dein Schmerz
Mit Wasser füllt? Ich sehe, was ich sah,
Wie Fulvias Tod geht einst dir meiner nah.
ANTONIUS Laß doch das Streiten, höre lieber an,
Was meine Pläne sind; sie stehn und fallen
Wie du es rätst. Beim Feuer, das im Nilschlamm
Leben zeugt, ich breche von hier auf
Als dein Soldat, der Krieg und Frieden macht,
Wie's dir gefällt.
CLEOPATRA   Komm, Charmian, schnür mich auf,

But let it be, I am quickly ill, and well,
So *Anthony* loues.

Ant. My precious Queene forbeare,
And giue true euidence to his Loue, which stands
An honourable Triall.

Cleo. So *Fuluia* told me.
I prythee turne aside, and weepe for her,
Then bid adiew to me, and say the teares
Belong to Egypt. Good now, play one Scene
Of excellent dissembling, and let it looke
Like perfect Honor.

Ant. You'l heat my blood no more?

Cleo. You can do better yet: but this is meetly.

Ant. Now by Sword.

Cleo. And Target. Still he mends.
But this is not the best. Looke prythee *Charmian*,
How this Herculean Roman do's become
The carriage of his chafe.

Ant. Ile leaue you Lady.

Cleo. Courteous Lord, one word:
Sir, you and I must part, but that's not it:
Sir, you and I haue lou'd, but there's not it:
That you know well, something it is I would:
Oh, my Obliuion is a very *Anthony*,
And I am all forgotten.

Ant. But that your Royalty
Holds Idlenesse your subiect, I should take you
For Idlenesse it selfe.

Cleo. 'Tis sweating Labour,
To beare such Idlenesse so neere the heart
As *Cleopatra* this. But Sir, forgiue me,
Since my becommings kill me, when they do not

Nein, laß, es geht mit mir so auf und nieder
Wie mit Antonius' Liebe.

ANTONIUS   Teure Fürstin,
Gebt still und wahres Zeugnis seiner Liebe,
Die jeder Prüfung standhält.

CLEOPATRA   Siehe Fulvia.
Ich bitt dich, geh beiseite und bewein sie,
Dann sage mir Adieu und sprich: die Tränen
Sind für Ägypten. Los, spiel eine Szene
Gekonnter Heuchelei und laß sie wirken
Wie echter Anstand.

ANTONIUS   Schluß : ich werde böse.

CLEOPATRA Das war ganz leidlich: doch du kannst es besser.

ANTONIUS Bei meinem Schwert –

CLEOPATRA   Und Schild. Er steigert sich.
Sein Bestes war's noch nicht. Sieh, Charmian,
Wie dieser Herkules von einem Römer
Den Eselskarren seines Zorns abgibt.

ANTONIUS Ich gehe, Lady.

CLEOPATRA   Lieber Herr, ein Wort:
Sir, Sie und ich, wir trennen uns, nein, falsch:
Sir, Sie und ich, wir liebten uns, nein, auch falsch;
Das wissen Sie, was war's doch, was ich wollte? –
Oh, mein Erinnern gleicht Antonius
Und vergißt mich.

ANTONIUS   Wäre Eitelkeit
Nicht Eure Untertanin, Hoheit, ich
Hielt Euch für die Eitelkeit höchstselbst.

CLEOPATRA Schwerstarbeit ist es, solche Eitelkeit
So nah am Herzen tragen müssen wie
Cleopatra die ihre. Aber, Sir,
Wenn Euch mein Tun nicht wohlgefällt, habt Nachsicht,

Eye well to you. Your Honor calles you hence,
Therefore be deafe to my vnpittied Folly,
And all the Gods go with you. Vpon your Sword
Sit Lawrell victory, and smooth successe
Be strew'd before your feete.
Ant. Let vs go.
Come: Our separation so abides and flies,
That thou reciding heere, goes yet with mee;
And I hence fleeting, heere remaine with thee.
Away. *Exeunt.*

Enter Octauius reading a Letter, Lepidus,
and their Traine.

Cæs. You may see *Lepidus*, and henceforth know,
It is not *Cæsars* Naturall vice, to hate
One great Competitor. From Alexandria
This is the newes: He fishes, drinkes, and wastes
The Lampes of night in reuell: Is not more manlike
Then *Cleopatra*: nor the Queene of *Ptolomy*
More Womanly then he. Hardly gaue audience
Or vouchsafe to thinke he had Partners. You
Shall finde there a man, who is th' abstracts of all faults,
That all men follow.

Lep. I must not thinke
There are, euils enow to darken all his goodnesse:
His faults in him, seeme as the Spots of Heauen,
More fierie by nights Blacknesse; Hereditarie,

Mich, müßt Ihr wissen, bringt es um. Euch ruft
Die Ehre. Drum seid taub für meinen Wahn.
Die Götter mögen Euch geleiten! Lorbeer
Des Siegs umwinde Euer Schwert, und sanft
Sei Euch Erfolg vor Euren Fuß gestreut.
ANTONIUS Wir gehn. Die Trennung weicht, solang sie weilt,
Denn du, hier auf dem Thron, gehst doch mit mir;
Und ich, wenngleich auf See, bin hier bei dir.
Hinweg. *Ab.*

Vierte Szene

Octavius, Lepidus, Gefolge.

CAESAR Ihr seht nun, Lepidus, und wißt hinkünftig,
Es ist nicht Caesars angeborne Tücke,
Wenn wir den großen Mitbeherrscher hassen.
Gemeldet wird aus Alexandria,
Er fischt, er säuft, vergeudet nächtlich feiernd
Das Öl der Lampen; ist nicht mehr Mann als
Cleopatra, noch ist die Königin
Der Ptolemäer weiblicher als er.
Audienzen gab er kaum und seine Partner
Sind Luft für ihn. Er ist der Inbegriff
Aller Laster, denen alle Männer
Nur allzu gern gehorchen.
LEPIDUS   Doch ich finde,
Dies Schlechte schwärzt nicht all sein Gutes an:
Die Laster sind bei ihm wie Himmelsfunken,
Weil Nacht herrscht, darum flammen sie; mehr Erbe

Rather then purchaste: what he cannot change,
Then what he chooses.
Cæs. You are too indulgent. Let's graunt it is not
Amisse to tumble on the bed of *Ptolomy*,
To giue a Kingdome for a Mirth, to sit
And keepe the turne of Tipling with a Slaue,
To reele the streets at noone, and stand the Buffet
With knaues that smels of sweate: Say this becoms him
(As his composure must be rare indeed,
Whom these things cannot blemish) yet must *Anthony*
No way excuse his foyles, when we do beare
So great waight in his lightnesse. If he fill'd
His vacancie with his Voluptuousnesse,
Full surfets, and the drinesse of his bones,
Call on him for't. But to confound such time,
That drummes him from his sport, and speakes as lowd
As his owne State, and ours, 'tis to be chid:
As we rate Boyes, who being mature in knowledge,
Pawne their experience to their present pleasure,
And so rebell to iudgement.

Enter a Messenger.

Lep. Heere's more newes.
Mes. Thy biddings haue beene done, & euerie houre
Most Noble *Cæsar*, shalt thou haue report
How 'tis abroad. *Pompey* is strong at Sea,
And it appeares, he is belou'd of those
That only haue feard *Cæsar*: to the Ports
The discontents repaire, and mens reports
Giue him much wrong'd.
Cæs. I should haue knowne no lesse,
It hath bin taught vs from the primall state

Als Erwerb; mehr was ihm aufgedrängt wird
Als seine freie Wahl.

CAESAR Ihr seid zu duldsam. Sollte es auch angehn,
Sich in der Ptolemäer Bett zu wälzen,
Ein Königreich für einen Witz zu zahlen,
Beim Pöbel sich die Gurgel abzusaufen,
Bereits am hellen Mittag schräg zu stehn
Und mit verschwitzten Kerlen in den Ring
Zu klettern: selbst falls ihm das guttut – und
Den möcht ich sehn, den sowas nicht kaputt macht –,
So muß es ihn doch kümmern, welche Last
Sein Leichtsinn uns aufbürdet. Wär's ein Urlaub,
Den ihm Genußsucht auszufüllen hilft,
Nun schön, der Ekel, die geschwollne Leber
Ging uns nichts an. Doch die Zeit zu vertun,
Die weg vom Tanz ihn trommelt, die mit keiner
Leisern Stimme ruft als der des Reiches,
Unsres Vaterlands, – das muß man tadeln:
So wie man Knaben schilt, die, wissend was
Sie tun, es dennoch tun, und reifer Einsicht
Nicht gehorchen wollen.

Bote 1.

LEPIDUS   Noch mehr Neues.

BOTE 1 Dein Auftrag ist erfüllt, einmal die Stunde,
Edler Caesar, wirst du unterrichtet,
Wie's auswärts steht. Pompejus herrscht zur See.
Und wie es scheint, gewinnt er jene Herzen,
Die Furcht vor Caesar haben: in den Häfen
Sammeln Unzufriedne sich, sie murr'n,
Man tät ihm Unrecht.

CAESAR   Ich hätt's wissen müssen;
Von allem Anfang an lehrt die Geschichte,

That he which is was wisht, vntill he were:
And the ebb'd man,
Ne're lou'd, till ne're worth loue,
Comes fear'd, by being lack'd. This common bodie,
Like to a Vagabond Flagge vpon the Streame,
Goes too, and backe, lacking the varrying tyde
To rot it selfe with motion.

Mes. *Cæsar* I bring thee word,
    Menacrates and *Menas* famous Pyrates
    Makes the Sea serue them, which they eare and wound
    With keeles of euery kinde. Many hot inrodes
    They make in Italy, the Borders Maritime
    Lacke blood to thinke on't, and flush youth reuolt,
    No Vessell can peepe forth: but 'tis as soone
    Taken as seene: for *Pompeyes* name strikes more
    Then could his Warre resisted.

Cæsar. *Anthony*,
    Leaue thy lasciuious Vassailes. When thou once
    Was beaten from *Medena*, where thou slew'st
    Hirsius, and *Pausa* Consuls, at thy heele
    Did Famine follow, whom thou fought'st against,
    (Though daintily brought vp) with patience more
    Then Sauages could suffer. Thou did'st drinke
    The stale of Horses, and the gilded Puddle
    Which Beasts would cough at. Thy pallat then did daine
    The roughest Berry, on the rudest Hedge.

    Yea, like the Stagge, when Snow the Pasture sheets,
    The barkes of Trees thou brows'd. On the Alpes,
    It is reported thou did'st eate strange flesh,

Daß, wer was ist, erwünscht war, bis er's wurde;
Und der Gesunkne, bis dahin gehaßt,
Gewinnt, weil er nun fehlt. Der große Haufe,
Wie Seetang auf der Flut, schwimmt her, schwimmt hin
Wie ihn die Tide fortspült oder antreibt,
Und so bewegt, verfault er.

Bote 2.

BOTE 2   Nachricht, Caesar:
Menecrates und Menas, große Räuber
Zur See, die sie sich dienstbar machen, pflügen
Und schneiden sie mit Kielen aller Art.
Italiens Küsten werden heimgesucht
Und erbleichen schon bei dem Gedanken:
Die mutigere Jugend revoltiert,
Zeigt sich ein Segel, wird es gleich gekapert;
Nur des Pompejus Name stiftet mehr
Unheil als sein Heer an.

CAESAR   Jetzt, Antonius,
Laß deine vollen Becher. Einst, als du
Aus Modena geschlagen abzogst, nach
Dem Schlachtfest an den Konsuln Hirtius
Und Pansa, heftete der Hunger sich
Dir an die Fersen, den du, obgleich doch
Verwöhnt von Kind auf, mit mehr Fassung littest
Als jeder Wilde. Du trankst Pferdepisse
Und braunes Wasser, das kein Tier uns soff,
Dein Gaumen wies die stacheligste Beere
Vom struppigsten Gesträuch nicht ab, ja, wie
Der Hirsch, wenn Schnee das gute Gras bedeckt,
Nagtest du die Rinde von den Bäumen.
In den Alpen, wird berichtet, aßest du

Which some did dye to looke on: And all this
(It wounds thine Honor that I speake it now)
Was borne so like a Soldiour, that thy cheeke
So much as lank'd not.

Lep. 'Tis pitty of him.
Cæs. Let his shames quickely
    Driue him to Rome, 'tis time we twaine
    Did shew our selues i'th' Field, and to that end
    Assemble me immediate counsell, *Pompey*
    Thriues in our Idlenesse.
Lep. To morrow *Cæsar*,
    I shall be furnisht to informe you rightly
    Both what by Sea and Land I can be able
    To front this present time.
Cæs. Til which encounter, it is my busines too. Farwell.

Lep. Farwell my Lord, what you shal know mean time
    Of stirres abroad, I shall beseech you Sir
    To let me be partaker.
Cæsar. Doubt not sir, I knew it for my Bond.   *Exeunt*

Enter Cleopatra, Charmian, Iras, & Mardian.

Cleo. Charmian.
Char. Madam.
Cleo. Ha, ha, giue me to drinke *Mandragora*.

Char. Why Madam?

So grünes Fleisch, daß mancher bloß vom Anblick
Tot umfiel: und all dies – es trübt die Ehre
Dir, daß ich daran erinnern muß hier –
Trugst du so heldenmäßig, daß die Wange
Sich dir nicht höhlte.

LEPIDUS   Es ist schad um ihn.

CAESAR Mag die Scham in Richtung Rom ihn treiben,
  's wird Zeit, daß er und ich im Feld uns zeigen;
  Dazu ist Rat zu halten, denn Pompejus
  Gedeiht durch unser Nichtstun.

LEPIDUS   Morgen, Caesar,
  Werd ich imstande sein, dir zu berichten,
  Was ich zur See aufbringe, was zu Land,
  Der Zeit die Stirn zu bieten.

CAESAR   Bis dahin
  Wird dies auch mein Geschäft sein. Lebe wohl.

LEPIDUS Lebt wohl, Mylord; wenn Ihr sonst was erfahrt,
  Was draußen los ist, Sir, ich bitte Euch,
  Mir's mitzuteilen.

CAESAR   Keine Sorge, Sir,
  Ich kenne meine Pflicht.

Fünfte Szene

Cleopatra, Charmian, Iras, Mardian.

CLEOPATRA Charmian!

CHARMIAN   Madam?

CLEOPATRA *gähnt*   Reich mir ein Glas
  Mandragora.

CHARMIAN   Madam, warum?

Cleo. That I might sleepe out this great gap of time:
  My *Anthony* is away.

Char. You thinke of him too much.
Cleo. O 'tis Treason.
Char. Madam, I trust not so.
Cleo. Thou, Eunuch *Mardian*?
Mar. What's your Highnesse pleasure?
Cleo. Not now to heare thee sing. I take no pleasure
  In ought an Eunuch ha's: Tis well for thee,
  That being vnseminar'd, thy freer thoughts
  May not flye forth of Egypt. Hast thou Affections?
Mar. Yes gracious Madam.
Cleo. Indeed?
Mar. Not in deed Madam, for I can do nothing
  But what in deede is honest to be done:
  Yet haue I fierce Affections, and thinke
  What Venus did with Mars.
Cleo. Oh *Charmion*:
  Where think'st thou he is now? Stands he, or sits he?
  Or does he walke? Or is he on his Horse?
  Oh happy horse to beare the weight of *Anthony*!
  Do brauely Horse, for wot'st thou whom thou moou'st,
  The demy *Atlas* of this Earth, the Arme
  And Burganet of men. Hee's speaking now,
  Or murmuring, where's my Serpent of old Nyle,
  (For so he cals me:) Now I feede my selfe
  With most delicious poyson. Thinke on me
  That am with Phœbus amorous pinches blacke,
  And wrinkled deepe in time. Broad-fronted *Cæsar*,
  When thou was't heere aboue the ground, I was
  A morsell for a Monarke: and great *Pompey*

CLEOPATRA   Daß ich
  Die lange, leere Zeit verschlafen kann,
  Die ohne ihn.
CHARMIAN   Ihr denkt zu viel an ihn.
CLEOPATRA O, Hochverrat!
CHARMIAN   Madam, ich glaube kaum.
CLEOPATRA Du, mein Eunuch, Mardian!
Mardian   Was wünschen Hoheit?
CLEOPATRA Jetzt nicht zu hören, wie du singst. Ich wünsche,
  Was kein Eunuch mir gibt: doch du kannst froh sein,
  Daß, so entsamt, du frei bist von Gedanken,
  Die aus Ägypten fliegen. Fühlst du Liebe?
MARDIAN Ja, Madam.
CLEOPATRA Tatsächlich?
MARDIAN Tatsächlich nicht, Madam, denn in der Sache
  Kann ich nur tun, was man mit Anstand tut:
  Doch fühl ich heiße Liebe, und ich denke
  An das, was Venus tat mit Mars.
CLEOPATRA   O Charmian!
  Wo, denkst du, ist er jetzt? Steht oder sitzt er?
  Oder geht er? Reitet er sein Pferd?
  Glückliches Pferd, Antonius' Last zu tragen!
  Trab zu, mein Pferd, denn weißt du, wen du trägst?
  Den Atlas einer Hälfte dieser Welt,
  Den starken Arm, die Nackenwehr der Menschheit.
  Ich hör ihn reden, oder wie er murmelt
  ›Wo steckt mein Nilwurm?‹ Denn so nennt er mich.
  Jetzt schwelge ich im köstlichsten der Gifte.
  Denk an mich, die Phoebus mit verliebten
  Stichen schwärzte, mich, in die die Zeit
  So tiefe Gräben zog. Breitstirn'ger Caesar,
  Als du noch unsre Erde tratst, galt ich

Would stand and make his eyes grow in my brow,
There would he anchor his Aspect, and dye
With looking on his life.

Enter Alexas from Cæsar.
Alex. Soueraigne of Egypt, haile.
Cleo. How much vnlike art thou *Marke Anthony*?
    Yet comming from him, that great Med'cine hath
    With his Tinct gilded thee.
    How goes it with my braue *Marke Anthonie*?
Alex. Last thing he did (deere Quene)
    He kist the last of many doubled kisses
    This Orient Pearle. His speech stickes in my heart.

Cleo. Mine eare must plucke it thence.
Alex. Good Friend, quoth he:
    Say the firme Roman to great Egypt sends
    This treasure of an Oyster: at whose foote
    To mend the petty present, I will peece
    Her opulent Throne, with Kingdomes. All the East,
    (Say thou) shall call her Mistris. So he nodded,
    And soberly did mount an Arme-gaunt Steede,
    Who neigh'd so hye, that what I would haue spoke,
    Was beastly dumbe by him.

Cleo. What was he sad, or merry?
Alex. Like to the time o'th' yeare, between ye extremes
    Of hot and cold, he was nor sad nor merrie.
Cleo. Oh well diuided disposition: Note him,
    Note him good *Charmian*, 'tis the man; but note him.
    He was not sad, for he would shine on those

Dem Weltbeherrscher als ein Leckerbissen:
Pompejus Magnus stand und ließ die Blicke
Stumm auf meiner Braue ruhn, sein Dasein
Warf da Anker, so, als wolle er
In Ansehn seines Lebens sterben.

ALEXAS   Heil Euch,
Herrscherin Ägyptens!

CLEOPATRA Wie ganz unähnlich bist du Marc Anton!
Doch da du von ihm kommst, erscheinst du mir
Als hätt der Stein der Weisen dich vergoldet.
Wie geht es meinem tapfren Marc Anton?

ALEXAS Das letzte, was er tat, war, teure Herrin,
Die Perle hier zu küssen – 's war der letzte
Von vielen zwiefach hingehauchten Küssen –
Er sprach dabei, mein Herz bewahrt sein Wort.

CLEOPATRA Von da pflückt es mein Ohr.

ALEXAS   ›Mein Freund‹, sprach er,
›Sag ihr, der treue Römer schenkt Ägypten
Dies Kleinod einer Auster; auf dem Fuße,
Die arme Gabe reich zu machen, will ich
Ägyptens Thron mit Königreichen zieren.
Der ganze Osten soll sie Herrin nennen,
Das sage ihr.‹ Er nickt mir zu und schwingt sich
Stilvoll auf ein kriegsgezäumtes Pferd,
Des helles Wiehern mich, der ich nun anhob,
Verstummen ließ.

CLEOPATRA   War er mehr froh als traurig?

ALEXAS Er glich der Zeit des Jahres, die nicht Frost
Noch Hitze kennt, war weder froh noch traurig.

CLEOPATRA O wohlverteilte Stimmung! Merkst du's, Charmian?
Merkst du es? Das ist er; merkst du es?
Er ist nicht traurig, denn dann machen's ihm,

That make their lookes by his. He was not merrie,
Which seem'd to tell them, his remembrance lay
In Egypt with his ioy, but betweene both.
Oh heauenly mingle! Bee'st thou sad, or merrie,
The violence of either thee becomes,
So do's it no mans else. Met'st thou my Posts?
Alex. I Madam, twenty seuerall Messengers.
 Why do you send so thicke?

Cleo. Who's borne that day, when I forget to send
 to *Anthonie*, shall dye a Begger. Inke and paper *Char-*
 mian. Welcome my good *Alexas.* Did I *Charmian,* e-
 uer loue *Cæsar* so?

Char. Oh that braue *Cæsar!*
Cleo. Be choak'd with such another Emphasis,
 Say the braue *Anthony.*
Char. The valiant *Cæsar.*
Cleo. By *Isis,* I will giue thee bloody teeth,
 If thou with *Cæsar* Paragonagaine:
 My man of men.
Char. By your most gracious pardon,
 I sing but after you.
Cleo. My Sallad dayes,
 When I was greene in iudgement, cold in blood,
 To say, as I saide then. But come, away,
 Get me Inke and Paper,
 he shall haue euery day a seuerall greeting, or Ile vnpeo-
 ple Egypt.   *Exeunt*

Die zu ihm aufschaun, nach; er ist nicht froh,
Was ihnen sagt, sein Herz und seine Freude
Bleibt in Ägypten; er ist zwischen beidem.
Oh, himmlische Vermischung! Denn du kannst
So froh sein und so traurig wie kein andrer.
Trafst du meine Briefträger?

ALEXAS   Ja, Madam,
An die zwanzig Boten: wozu schreibt Ihr
So hageldicht?

CLEOPATRA   Wer an dem Tag zur Welt kommt,
Da ich vergaß, Antonius zu schreiben,
Der stirbt als Bettler. Charmian, Tinte und Papier.
Willkommen, mein Alexas. Habe ich
Caesar je so geliebt?

CHARMIAN   O edler Caesar!

CLEOPATRA Erstick an der Emphase, sag wie ich:
O edler Marc Anton.

CHARMIAN   O kühner Caesar!

CLEOPATRA Bei Isis, du, ich schlag dir in die Zähne,
Wenn du noch einmal Caesar mir vergleichst
Mit meinem Mann der Männer.

CHARMIAN   Um Vergebung,
Ich singe nur Euch nach.

CLEOPATRA   Salatzeit das,
Grün mein Verstand, mein Blut noch kalt, damals,
Als ich das ausrief. Aber kommt hinweg,
Gebt mir Tinte und Papier,
Er soll tagtäglich einen Gruß erhalten,
Und müßte ich mein Land entvölkern.   *Ab.*

Enter Pompey, Menecrates, and Menas, in
warlike manner.

Pom. If the great Gods be iust, they shall assist
   The deeds of iustest men.
Mene. Know worthy *Pompey*, that what they do de-
   lay, they not deny.
Pom. Whiles we are sutors to their Throne, decayes
   the thing we sue for.
Mene. We ignorant of our selues,
   Begge often our owne harmes, which the wise Powres
   Deny vs for our good: so finde we profit
   By loosing of our Prayers.
Pom. I shall do well:
   The people loue me, and the Sea is mine;
   My powers are Cressent, and my Auguring hope
   Sayes it will come to'th'full. *Marke Anthony*
   In Egypt sits at dinner, and will make
   No warres without doores. *Cæsar* gets money where
   He looses hearts: *Lepidus* flatters both,
   Of both is flatter'd: but he neither loues,
   Nor either cares for him.

Mene. *Cæsar* and *Lepidus* are in the field,
   A mighty strength they carry.
Pom. Where haue you this? 'Tis false.
Mene. From *Siluius*, Sir.
Pom He dreames: I know they are in Rome together
   Looking for *Anthony*: but all the charmes of Loue,

ZWEITER AKT
Erste Szene

Pompejus, Menecrates, Menas.

POMPEJUS Wenn sie gerecht sind, unsre großen Götter,
Müssen sie gerechten Männern helfen.
MENECRATES Wißt, tapferer Pompjeus, wenn sie was
Verzögern, heißt das nicht, daß sies verweigern.
POMPEJUS Wir knien an ihrem Thron und währenddessen
Verfällt, worum wir knien.
MENECRATES   Wir Ahnungslosen
Erbitten uns oft eignes Unheil, das die Weisheit
Höhrer Mächte gnädig uns verweigert.
So profitieren wir, wenn unser Bitten fehlschlägt.
POMPEJUS Ich werde siegreich sein: mich liebt das Volk,
Das Meer ist mein; mein Glück nimmt stetig zu,
Und meine nimmermüde Hoffnung sagt mir,
Bald ist es voll. Marcus Antonius tafelt
In Ägypten und für keinen Krieg
Steht der vom Stuhl auf. Caesar sammelt Geld,
Wo er die Herzen einbüßt. Lepidus
Umgurrt sie alle beide und die beiden
Umgurren ihn: doch weder schätzt er sie,
Noch halten sie von ihm viel.
MENAS   Caesar rückte
Mit ihm ins Feld, samt einem Riesenheer.
POMPEJUS Wie wißt Ihr das? Ihr irrt.
MENAS   Von Silvius, Sir.
POMPEJUS Er träumt: ich weiß, sie sind in Rom und halten
Nach Antonius Ausschau: doch es möge

Salt *Cleopatra* soften thy wand lip,
Let Witchcraft ioyne with Beauty, Lust with both,
Tye vp the Libertine in a field of Feasts,
Keepe his Braine fuming. Epicurean Cookes,
Sharpen with cloylesse sawce his Appetite,
That sleepe and feeding may prorogue his Honour,
Euen till a Lethied dulnesse—

Enter Varrius.

How now *Varrius?*

Var. This is most certaine, that I shall deliuer:
Marke Anthony is euery houre in Rome
Expected. Since he went from Egypt, 'tis
A space for farther Trauaile.

Pom. I could haue giuen lesse matter
A better eare. *Menas*, I did not thinke
This amorous Surfetter would haue donn'd his Helme
For such a petty Warre: His Souldiership
Is twice the other twaine: But let vs reare
The higher our Opinion, that our stirring
Can from the lap of Egypts Widdow, plucke
The neere Lust-wearied *Anthony.*

Mene. I cannot hope,
Cæsar and *Anthony* shall well greet together;
His Wife that's dead, did trespasses to *Cæsar*,
His Brother war'd vpon him, although I thinke
Not mou'd by *Anthony.*

Pom. I know not *Menas*,
How lesser Enmities may giue way to greater,
Were't not that we stand vp against them all:
'Twer pregnant they should square between themselues,

Liebeszauber dir die Lippen würzen,
Geile Cleopatra! Misch Hexenkunst
Mit Schönheit, Lust mit beidem, den Genießer
Halte fest in einem Strom von Festen,
Sorg in seinem Hirn für Nebel: Köche
Epikurs mit Brühen, die nicht sätt'gen,
Schärft stets aufs neue seinen Appetit,
Bis Schlaf und Fraß die Ehre ihm ermatten,
Bis hin zu Lethes Dumpfheit –

Varrius.

POMPEJUS   Varrius!

VARRIUS Fakt ist, was ich melde: Marc Anton
   Wird jeden Augenblick in Rom erwartet;
   Die Nachricht aus Ägypten traf so spät ein,
   Daß er gut noch näher rücken konnte.

POMPEJUS Für kleinre Botschaft hätt ich größre Ohren.
   Menas, das dacht ich nicht, daß der verliebte
   Lustmolch sich für einen solchen Kleinkrieg
   Den Helm aufstülpt. Als Feldherr überragt er
   Doppelt die zwei andern. Doch das soll uns
   Nur mehr ermutigen, daß unser Feldzug
   Selbst den vergnügungssüchtigen Antonius
   Aus der Ägypt'rin Schoß gepflückt.

MENAS   Grün sind sich
   Caesar und Antonius wohl kaum.
   Vor ihrem Tod griff sein Weib Caesar an,
   So auch sein Bruder, wozu allerdings
   Antonius nichts beitrug.

POMPEJUS   Fraglich ist,
   Wie fix der kleine Haß dem größern Platz macht.
   Ging unser Aufstand jetzt nicht gegen alle,
   Gerieten sie ganz sicher aneinander,

For they haue entertained cause enough
To draw their swords: but how the feare of vs
May Ciment their diuisions, and binde vp
The petty difference, we yet not know:
Bee't as our Gods will haue't; it onely stands
Our liues vpon, to vse our strongest hands
Come *Menas*.   *Exeunt.*

Enter Enobarbus and Lepidus.

Lep. Good *Enobarbus*, 'tis a worthy deed,
     And shall become you well, to intreat your Captaine
     To soft and gentle speech.
Enob. I shall intreat him
     To answer like himselfe: if *Cæsar* moue him,
     Let *Anthony* looke ouer *Cæsars* head,
     And speake as lowd as Mars. By Iupiter,
     Were I the wearer of *Anthonio's* Beard,
     I would not shaue't to day.
Lep. 'Tis not a time for priuate stomacking.

Eno. Euery time serues for the matter that is then
     borne in't.
Lep. But small to greater matters must giue way.
Eno. Not if the small come first.
Lep. Your speech is passion: but pray you stirre
     No Embers vp. Heere comes the Noble *Anthony*.

            Enter Anthony and Ventidius.
Eno. And yonder *Cæsar*.

Denn Anlaß haben sie mehr als genug,
Das Schwert zu ziehn: doch ob die Furcht vor uns
Die Risse noch vermauern und den Zank
Im Zaume halten kann, das wird sich zeigen.
Die Götter mögen's lenken! Wir hier wagen,
Im Feld auf Tod und Leben uns zu schlagen.
Komm, Menas. *Ab.*

Zweite Szene

Enobarbus. Lepidus.

LEPIDUS Mein Enobarbus, es wär wohl getan
    Und dir bekömmlich, deinen General
    Zu sanfter Rede zu bewegen.
ENOBARBUS   Er
    Soll reden wie er selbst: reizt Caesar ihn
    Dann sieht Antonius ihm übern Kopf
    Und schreit so laut wie Mars. Bei Jupiter,
    Wüchs mir der Bart wie dem Antonius,
    Rasieren fiel heut aus.
LEPIDUS   Jetzt ist nicht Zeit,
    Sich kleinlich zu verzanken.
ENOBARBUS   Jede Zeit
    Ist gut genug für das, was sie hervorbringt.
LEPIDUS Doch gehn die großen Dinge vor den kleinen.
ENOBARBUS Nicht, wenn die kleinen vorgehn.
LEPIDUS   Ihr verrennt Euch:
    Ich bitt Euch, blast nicht in die Glut. Da kommt
    Der edle Marc Anton.
            Antonius, Ventidius.
ENOBARBUS   Und dort kommt Caesar.

Enter Cæsar, Mecenas, and Agrippa.

Ant. If we compose well heere, to Parthia:
　　Hearke *Ventidius.*

Cæsar. I do not know *Mecenas,* aske *Agrippa.*

Lep. Noble Friends:
　　That which combin'd vs was most great, and let not
　　A leaner action rend vs. What's amisse,
　　May it be gently heard. When we debate
　　Our triuiall difference loud, we do commit
　　Murther in healing wounds. Then Noble Partners,
　　The rather for I earnestly beseech,
　　Touch you the sowrest points with sweetest tearmes,
　　Nor curstnesse grow to'th'matter.

Ant. 'Tis spoken well:
　　Were we before our Armies, and to fight,
　　I should do thus.　　　　　　　　　　　*Flourish.*

Cæs. Welcome to Rome.

Ant. Thanke you.

Cæs. Sit.

Ant, Sit sir.

Cæs. Nay then.

Ant. I learne, you take things ill, which are not so:
　　Or being, concerne you not.

Cæs. I must be laught at, if or for nothing, or a little, I
　　Should say my selfe offended, and with you
　　Chiefely i'th'world. More laught at, that I should
　　Once name you derogately: when to sound your name
　　It not concern'd me.

Ant. My being in Egypt *Caesar,* what was't to you?

Caesar, Maecenas, Agrippa.

ANTONIUS Sind wir uns einig, auf nach Parthien:
Ventidius, hörst du zu?

CAESAR   Ich weiß es nicht,
Maecenas, frag Agrippa.

LEPIDUS   Werte Freunde,
Was uns vereinte, war so groß, nun darf
Nicht Kleinkram uns zersplittern. Das, was unschön,
Hört es mit Ruhe an. Wenn wir hier laut
Banale Differenzen debattieren,
So sind wir Mörder, wo wir Arzt sein müssen.
Auf, Partner, und je mehr ich ernstlich bitte,
Sprecht desto süßer bei den sauren Fragen,
Und laßt den Ärger draußen.

ANTONIUS   Gut gesagt.
Ich würde dies auch dann tun, wenn wir alle
Vor unsern Heeren stünden.

CAESAR   Seid in Rom
Willkommen.

ANTONIUS   Danke.

CAESAR   Setzt Euch.

ANTONIUS   Ihr, Sir.

CAESAR   Nein,
Dann nicht.

ANTONIUS   Ihr nehmt gern krumm, was grad ist, seh ich:
Oder, wenn's denn krumm ist, Euch nichts angeht.

CAESAR Auslachen müßte man mich, wäre ich
Durch nichts, durch wenig mehr als nichts gekränkt,
Und das von Euch: noch lächerlicher wär es,
Verächtlich Euren Namen auszusprechen,
Der mich nichts anging.

ANTONIUS   Mein Ägyptenurlaub,

Cæs. No more then my reciding heere at Rome
Might be to you in Egypt: yet if you there
Did practise on my State, your being in Egypt
Might be my question.

Ant. How intend you, practis'd?
Cæs. You may be pleas'd to catch at mine intent,
By what did heere befall me. Your Wife and Brother
Made warres vpon me, and their contestation
Was Theame for you, you were the word of warre.

Ant. You do mistake your busines, my Brother neuer
Did vrge me in his Act: I did inquire it,
And haue my Learning from some true reports
That drew their swords with you, did he not rather
Discredit my authority with yours,
And make the warres alike against my stomacke,
Hauing alike your cause. Of this, my Letters
Before did satisfie you. If you'l patch a quarrell,
As matter whole you haue to make it with,
It must not be with this.
Cæs. You praise your selfe, by laying defects of iudge-
ment to me: but you patcht vp your excuses.
Anth. Not so, not so:
I know you could not lacke, I am certaine on't,
Very necessity of this thought, that I
Your Partner in the cause 'gainst which he fought,
Could not with gracefull eyes attend those Warres
Which fronted mine owne peace. As for my wife,
I would you had her spirit, in such another,
The third oth'world is yours, which with a Snaffle,

Wie kam er Euch vor?

CAESAR　　　　　　　Nicht anders, als
　　Mein Romverbleib Euch in Ägypten vorkam:
　　Doch für den Fall, Ihr hättet Euch von da aus
　　Um mich bemüht, so gäbe Euer Urlaub
　　In Ägypten Grund zu Fragen.

ANTONIUS　　　　　　　Wie ›bemüht‹?

CAESAR Es möge Euch gefallen, dieses ›Wie‹
　　Aus dem zu lesen, was mir hier geschah.
　　Krieg haben Eure Gattin und Eu'r Bruder
　　Gegen mich geführt, für ihren Aufruhr
　　Wart Ihr der Grund, ›Antonius!‹ war der Schlachtruf.

ANTONIUS Ihr ziehts falsch auf, mein Bruder brachte mich
　　Kein Mal ins Spiel. Ich forschte nach und weiß,
　　Was ich hier sage, aus Berichten derer,
　　Die das Schwert auf Eurer Seite zogen.
　　Setzte er nicht vielmehr mich zugleich
　　Mit Euch herab? Und führte gegen mich
　　Als Euren Busenfreund den gleichen Krieg
　　Wie gegen Euch? Meine Briefe haben
　　Euch damals überzeugt. Sucht nicht den Riß
　　In einem unzerschnitt'nen Tuch zu flicken.

CAESAR Ihr glaubt, es hebt Euch, wenn Ihr mich verkleinert.
　　Doch flickt Ihr Euch nur Ausreden zusammen.

ANTONIUS Hört auf, hört auf; ich weiß, Euch konnte es
　　Nicht entgehn, daß nach der Logik ich,
　　Eu'r Partner in der Sache, die er angriff,
　　Unmöglich Kriegen beistehn konnte, die mir
　　An meinen Frieden gingen. Und zu Fulvia
　　Sag ich nur, ich wünschte, von der Sorte
　　Gäb es noch mehr; ein Drittel dieser Welt
　　Ist dein, steck ihm 'nen Zaum ins Maul, dann lenkst du's

You may pace easie, but not such a wife.
Enobar. Would we had all such wiues, that the men
might go to Warres with the women.

Anth. So much vncurbable, her Garboiles (*Cæsar*)
Made out of her impatience: which not wanted
Shrodenesse of policie to: I greeuing grant,
Did you too much disquiet, for that you must,
But say I could not helpe it.
Cæsar. I wrote to you, when rioting in Alexandria you
Did pocket vp my Letters: and with taunts
Did gibe my Misiue out of audience.

Ant. Sir, he fell vpon me, ere admitted, then:
Three Kings I had newly feasted, and did want
Of what I was i'th'morning: but next day
I told him of my selfe, which was as much
As to haue askt him pardon. Let this Fellow
Be nothing of our strife: if we contend
Out of our question wipe him.

Cæsar. You haue broken the Article of your oath,
which you shall neuer haue tongue to charge me with.

Lep. Soft *Cæsar.*
Ant. No *Lepidus*, let him speake,
The Honour is Sacred which he talks on now,
Supposing that I lackt it: but on *Cæsar*,
The Article of my oath.
Cæsar. To lend me Armes, and aide when I requir'd
them, the which you both denied.

Mit Leichtigkeit, doch niemals solch ein Weib.

ENOBARBUS Ach, hätten wir doch alle solche Weiber, auf
daß die Männer nur noch Krieg gegen ihre Frauen führen müßten!

ANTONIUS Nicht stillzustellen, wie sie war, hat Euch
Caesar, Ihr Gerangel, dem's an Politik
Nicht mangelte, ich geb's bedauernd zu,
Schwer zugesetzt: doch einsehn müßt selbst Ihr,
Daß ich's nicht ändern konnte.

CAESAR   Meine Briefe
Habt Ihr, berauscht in Alexandria,
Ungelesen weggesteckt und höhnisch
Den Botschafter aus der Audienz gejagt.

ANTONIUS Sir, er überfiel mich, ungemeldet:
Ein Gastmahl für drei Könige zugleich
Lag hinter mir, und ich war nicht mehr der,
Der ich am Morgen war. Das habe ich
Ihm tags drauf erklärt, was so viel war,
Als würd ich mich bei ihm entschuldigen.
Der Trottel ist nicht wert, daß wir uns streiten:
Streich ihn von der Liste.

CAESAR   Wagt Ihr es,
Hier zu behaupten, es sei meine Schuld,
Daß Ihr in einem wesentlichen Punkt
Den Eid gebrochen habt?

LEPIDUS   Nur sachte, Caesar!

ANTONIUS Nein, laß ihn reden, Lepidus;
Die Ehre, die er anführt, weil er glaubt,
Ich hätte sie verletzt, ist heilig. Weiter,
Caesar, nenn den Punkt des Eides.

CAESAR Mit Waffen mir und Mannschaft auszuhelfen
Wenn ichs verlange, beides habt Ihr mir

Anth. Neglected rather:
　　And then when poysoned houres had bound me vp
　　From mine owne knowledge, as neerely as I may,
　　Ile play the penitent to you. But mine honesty,
　　Shall not make poore my greatnesse, nor my power
　　Worke without it. Truth is, that *Fuluia*,
　　To haue me out of Egypt, made Warres heere,
　　For which my selfe, the ignorant motiue, do
　　So farre aske pardon, as befits mine Honour
　　To stoope in such a case.

Lep. 'Tis Noble spoken.
Mece. If it might please you, to enforce no further
　　The griefes betweene ye: to forget them quite,
　　Were to remember: that the present neede,
　　Speakes to attone you.
Lep. Worthily spoken *Mecenas.*
Enobar. Or if you borrow one anothers Loue for the
　　instant, you may when you heare no more words of
　　Pompey returne it againe: you shall haue time to wrangle
　　in, when you haue nothing else to do.
Anth. Thou art a Souldier, onely speake no more.
Enob. That trueth should be silent, I had almost for-
　　got.
Anth. You wrong this presence, therefore speake no
　　more.
Enob. Go too then: your Considerate stone.
Cæsar. I do not much dislike the matter, but
　　The manner of his speech: for't cannot be,
　　We shall remaine in friendship, our conditions

Verweigert.

ANTONIUS   Mehr verschlampt; zu einer Zeit
Da mir, betäubt von schlimm gewürzten Stunden,
Nicht mehr ganz klar war, was ich tat, was ließ;
So gut ich kann, spiel ich den Reuigen
Vor Euch. Doch meine Offenherzigkeit
Schrumpft mir nicht die Statur, noch wäre
Ich mächtig ohne sie. Die Wahrheit ist,
Daß Fulvia, um aus Ägypten mich
Abzuziehn, dich hier bekriegte. Wofür
Ich, ihr schimmerloser Anlaß, soweit
Um Vergebung bitte, als es meine Ehre
In diesem Fall erlaubt.

LEPIDUS   Herrlich gesprochen.

MAECENAS Wenn es Euch doch gefiele, Eure Wunden
Nicht zu vertiefen: sie vergessen, hieße
Sich erinnern, daß die Gegenwart
Zur Einheit mahnt.

LEPIDUS   Maecenas, das war würdig.

ENOBARBUS Oder Ihr pumpt einander Freundschaft, befri-
stet, und wenn mit Pompejus Schluß ist, zahlt ihr sie
zurück: ihr habt Zeit genug für Hakeleien, wenn sonst
nichts zu tun ist.

ANTONIUS Du bist nur ein Soldat und hältst den Mund.

ENOBARBUS Die Wahrheit muß schweigen, ich vergaß es
beinah.

ANTONIUS Ihr stört den hohen Kreis, darum seid still.

ENOBARDUS Nur zu: ich bin ein Stein, gedankenschwer.

CAESAR Was mir mißfällt, ist wie er sprach und nicht
Wovon; denn ganz unmöglich können wir
Freunde bleiben, während unser Wesen

So diffring in their acts. Yet if I knew,
What Hoope should hold vs staunch from edge to edge
Ath'world: I would persue it.

Agri. Giue me leaue *Cæsar.*
Cæsar. Speake *Agrippa.*
Agri. Thou hast a Sister by the Mothers side, admir'd
   Octauia: Great *Mark Anthony* is now a widdower.

Cæsar. Say not, say *Agrippa*; if *Cleopater* heard you, your
   proofe were well deserued of rashnesse.

Anth. I am not marryed *Cæsar:* let me heere *Agrippa*
   further speake.
Agri. To hold you in perpetuall amitie,
   To make you Brothers, and to knit your hearts
   With an vn-slipping knot, take *Anthony,*
   Octauia to his wife: whose beauty claimes
   No worse a husband then the best of men: whose
   Vertue, and whose generall graces, speake
   That which none else can vtter. By this marriage,
   All little Ielousies which now seeme great,
   And all great feares, which now import their dangers,
   Would then be nothing. Truth's would be tales,
   Where now halfe tales be truth's: her loue to both,
   Would each to other, and all loues to both
   Draw after her. Pardon what I haue spoke,
   For 'tis a studied not a present thought,
   By duty ruminated.

Anth. Will *Cæsar* speake?

In unserm Tun so auseinanderstrebt.
Doch wüßte ich den Ring, der uns vom einen
Ende dieser Welt bis zu dem andern
Zusammenschlösse, ich ergriffe ihn.

AGRIPPA Wenn Ihr gestattet, Caesar.

CAESAR   Sprich, Agrippa.

AGRIPPA Ihr habt eine Schwester, mutterseitig,
Die rühmliche Octavia. Mark Anton,
Der große, ist nun Witwer.

CAESAR   Das sag nicht,
Agrippa: wenn Cleopatra dich hörte,
Sie könnte dich mit Recht als vorschnell tadeln.

ANTONIUS Ich bin nicht verheiratet: laß mich
Agrippas weitere Meinung hören, Caesar.

AGRIPPA Um Freundesliebe ewig Euch zu sichern,
Zu Brüdern Euch zu machen, Eure Herzen
Untrennbar zu verknüpfen, nimmt Antonius
Octavia zur Frau; denn keinen schlechtern
Gemahl verdient die Schönheit als den besten;
Für welchen seine Tugend lauter wirbt,
Als irgend jemand sonst. Durch diese Heirat
Wird kleine Mißgunst, die jetzt groß erscheint,
Und große Furcht, die jetzt Gefahren schafft,
Zu nichts: die Wahrheit wird zum Märchen, da,
Wo halbe Märchen jetzt als Wahrheit gehn:
Octavias Liebe zu den beiden zieht
Die Liebe beider zueinander und
Die Liebe aller zu den beiden nach sich.
Verzeiht mir, was ich sprach, denn der Gedanke
Ist lang erwogen, ausschließlich die Pflicht
Ließ mich ihn denken.

ANTONIUS   Was sagt Caesar?

Cæsar. Not till he heares how *Anthony* is toucht,
   With what is spoke already.

Anth. What power is in *Agrippa*,
   If I would say *Agrippa*, be it so,
   To make this good?
Cæsar. The power of *Cæsar*,
   And his power, vnto *Octauia*.
Anth. May I neuer
   (To this good purpose, that so fairely shewes)
   Dreame of impediment: let me haue thy hand
   Further this act of Grace: and from this houre,
   The heart of Brothers gouerne in our Loues,
   And sway our great Designes.
Cæsar. There's my hand:
   A Sister I bequeath you, whom no Brother
   Did euer loue so deerely. Let her liue
   To ioyne our kingdomes, and our hearts, and neuer
   Flie off our Loues againe.
Lepi. Happily, Amen.
Ant. I did not think to draw my Sword 'gainst *Pompey*,
   For he hath laid strange courtesies, and great
   Of late vpon me. I must thanke him onely,
   Least my remembrance, suffer ill report:
   At heele of that, defie him.
Lepi. Time cals vpon's,
   Of vs must *Pompey* presently be sought,
   Or else he seekes out vs.
Anth. Where lies he?
Cæsar. About the Mount-Mesena.
Anth. What is his strength by land?
Cæsar. Great, and encreasing:

CAESAR   Nichts,
  Eh er nicht hört, wie das, was schon gesagt ist,
  Bei Antonius ankommt.
ANTONIUS   Welchen Einfluß
  Hat Agrippa in der Sache, sollte
  Ich ›So sei es‹ sagen?
CAESAR   Caesars Einfluß
  Und dessen Einfluß auf Octavia.
ANTONIUS Mir fiele nicht im Traum ein, mich dem hohen
  Zweck, der mir so reizend naht, zu sperren!
  Gib mir die Hand auf diesen würdigen
  Beschluß: von dieser Stunde an regiert
  Uns im Herzen brüderliche Liebe
  Und wiegt die großen Pläne!
CAESAR   Meine Hand:
  Eine Schwester laß ich dir, kein Bruder
  Liebte je die seine so. Sie lebe,
  Zu einen unsre Reiche, unsre Herzen,
  Und niemals soll die Liebe enden.
LEPIDUS   Amen.
ANTONIUS Das dacht ich nicht, daß ich das Schwert ziehn
  Gegen den Pompejus, denn zuletzt   [müsse
  Erwies er groß mir Ehren, zweifelhafte.
  Erst muß ich ihm danken, soll mein Ruf
  Nicht Schaden nehmen. Und dann weg mit ihm.
LEPIDUS Pompejus braucht jetzt schnell von uns Besuch,
  Denn sonst besucht er uns.

ANTONIUS   Wo lagert er?
CAESAR Am Kap Misenum.
ANTONIUS   Und in welcher Stärke?
CAESAR Zu Land erheblich, und sie wächst; zur See

But by Sea he is an absolute Master.

Anth. So is the Fame,
Would we had spoke together. Hast we for it.
Yet ere we put our selues in Armes, dispatch we
The businesse we haue talkt of.

Cæsar. With most gladnesse,
And do inuite you to my Sisters view,
Whether straight Ile lead you.

Anth. Let vs *Lepidus* not lacke your companie.

Lep. Noble *Anthony*, not sickenesse should detaine
me.

Flourish. Exit omnes.

Manet Enobarbus, Agrippa, Mecenas.

Mec. Welcome from Ægypt Sir.

Eno. Halfe the heart of *Cæsar*, worthy *Mecenas.* My
honourable Friend *Agrippa.*

Agri. Good *Enobarbus.*

Mece. We haue cause to be glad, that matters are so
well disgested: you staid well by't in Egypt.

Enob. I Sir, we did sleepe day out of countenaunce:
and made the night light with drinking.

Mece. Eight Wilde-Boares rosted whole at a break-
fast: and but twelue persons there. Is this true?

Eno. This was but as a Flye by an Eagle: we had much
more monstrous matter of Feast, which worthily deserued noting.

Mecenas. She's a most triumphant Lady, if report be
square to her.

Enob. When she first met *Marke Anthony*, she purst
vp his heart vpon the Riuer of Sidnis.

Ist er der absolute Meister.
ANTONIUS   Sagt man.
Wir hätten reden müssen miteinander!
Laßt uns eilen, doch vor wir uns rüsten,
Besprochenes erledigen.
CAESAR   Sehr gern.
Noch heute sollt Ihr meine Schwester sehn,
Ich selber führ Euch hin.
ANTONIUS   Ihr, Lepidus,
Dürft da nicht fehlen.
LEPIDUS   Edler Marc Anton,
Selbst Krankheit hielte mich nicht ab.

    Caesar, Antonius, Lepidus, Ventidius ab.

MAECENAS Willkommen aus Ägypten, Sir.
ENOBARBUS Halb Caesars Herz, mein würdiger Maecenas!
Mein ehrenwerter Freund Agrippa!
AGRIPPA Braver Enobarbus!
MAECENAS Wir haben allen Grund, froh zu sein, daß die
Dinge sich so lösen. Ihr habts euch in Ägypten gut gehn
lassen, wie?
ENOBARBUS Ay, Sir, wir haben den Tag aus der Ruhe ge-
schlafen und die Nacht durch Trinken erhellt.
MAECENAS Acht ganze Wildschweine gebraten zum Früh-
stück, und für nur zwölf Personen; ist das wahr?
ENOBARBUS Das war nur ein Spatz, verglichen mit dem
Adler der meisterlichen, machtvollen Monstrositäten
unserer Feste, die aller Achtung wert sind.
MAECENAS Die Lady soll ja ganz unwiderstehlich sein, nach
allem, was man hört.
ENOBARBUS Als Antonius sie zum ersten Mal traf, stopfte
sie sein Herz in ihr Täschchen; so geschehn auf den

Agri. There she appear'd indeed: or my reporter de-
uis'd well for her.

Eno. I will tell you,
    The Barge she sat in, like a burnisht Throne
    Burnt on the water: the Poope was beaten Gold,
    Purple the Sailes: and so perfumed that
    The Windes were Loue-sicke.
    With them the Owers were Siluer,
    Which to the tune of Flutes kept stroke, and made
    The water which they beate, to follow faster;
    As amorous of their strokes. For her owne person,
    It beggerd all discription, she did lye
    In her Pauillion, cloth of Gold, of Tissue,
    O're-picturing that Venus, where we see
    The fancie out-worke Nature. On each side her,
    Stood pretty Dimpled Boyes, like smiling Cupids,
    With diuers coulour'd Fannes whose winde did seeme,
    To gloue the delicate cheekes which they did coole,
    And what they vndid did.

Agrip. Oh rare for *Anthony*.

Eno. Her Gentlewomen, like the Nereides,
    So many Mer-maides tended her i'th'eyes,
    And made their bends adornings. At the Helme.
    A seeming Mer-maide steeres: The Silken Tackle,
    Swell with the touches of those Flower-soft hands,
    That yarely frame the office. From the Barge
    A strange inuisible perfume hits the sense
    Of the adiacent Wharfes. The Citty cast
    Her people out vpon her: and *Anthony*
    Enthron'd i'th'Market-place, did sit alone,

Wellen des Cydnus.

AGRIPPA Da kreuzte sie tatsächlich auf; oder meine Spione haben geflunkert.

ENOBARBUS Ich erzähls euch.

Die Barke, die sie trug, ein Thron aus Feuer,
Flammte im Strom: getriebnes Gold der Spiegel;
Die Segel purpurn und so voller Duft,
Daß liebeskrank die Winde ihnen folgten;
Die Ruder waren silbern, mit dem Klang
Von Flöten hielten sie den Takt und ließen
Das Wasser, das sie schlugen, schneller strömen,
Als wäre es verliebt in ihren Schlag.
Nun zu ihr selbst: es spottet der Beschreibung,
Wie sie da lag, in eines Goldstoffs Schatten,
Ein Überbildnis der gemalten Venus,
An der wir sehn, wie Kunst Natur besiegt.
Ihr zur Seite allerliebste Knaben,
Mit holden Grübchen und Cupidos Lächeln
Bunte Fächer schwenkend, deren Luftzug
Die zarten Wangen glühn ließ, die er kühlte,
Und, was er abtat, tat.

AGRIPPA   O, und Antonius!

ENOBARBUS Und ihre Frauen, gleich des Meergotts Töchtern,
War'n um sie her, in ihren Blicken lesend,
Und jeder Schritt war Anbetung. Das Steuer
Hielt eine Meerjungfrau: das seidne Tauwerk
Schwoll unterm Griff der blumenweichen Hand,
Die kundig ihr Geschäft versah. Die Barke
Verströmte seltsam unsichtbaren Duft
Rings auf den Strand. Die Stadt ergoß ihr Volk
Dorthin, das Schauspiel anzusehn; Antonius,
Hochthronend auf dem Markt, saß ganz allein

Whisling to'th'ayre: which but for vacancie,
Had gone to gaze on *Cleopater* too,
And made a gap in Nature.
Agri. Rare Egiptian.
Eno. Vpon her landing, *Anthony* sent to her,
Inuited her to Supper: she replyed,
It should be better, he became her guest:
Which she entreated, our Courteous *Anthony*,
Whom nere the word of no woman hard speake,
Being barber'd ten times o're, goes to the Feast;
And for his ordinary, paies his heart,
For what his eyes eate onely.

Agri. Royall Wench:
She made great *Cæsar* lay his Sword to bed,
He ploughed her, and she cropt.
Eno. I saw her once
Hop forty Paces through the publicke streete,
And hauing lost her breath, she spoke, and panted,
That she did make defect, perfection,
And breathlesse powre breath forth.
Mece. Now *Anthony*, must leaue her vtterly.
Eno. Neuer he will not:
Age cannot wither her, nor custome stale
Her infinite variety: other women cloy
The appetites they feede, but she makes hungry,
Where most she satisfies. For vildest things
Become themselues in her, that the holy Priests
Blesse her, when she is Riggish.
Mece If Beauty, Wisedome, Modesty, can settle
The heart of *Anthony*: *Octauia* is

Und pfiff der Luft, die, könnt was leer von ihr sein
Auch loszog, nach Cleopatra zu gaffen,
Und der Natur ein Loch gerissen hätte.
AGRIPPA Oh, seltene Ägypt'rin!
ENOBARBUS   Kaum an Land,
  Sandte Antonius zu ihr und lud sie
  Zum Abendessen ein: sie ließ erwidern,
  Es wäre besser, ihn zu Gast zu haben,
  Und bat um den Besuch: Antonius,
  Den, höflich wie er ist, noch keine Frau .
  Jemals das Wörtchen ›Nein‹ hat sprechen hören,
  Zehnmal blitzblank barbiert, geht er zum Fest
  Und zahlt mit seinem Herzen für das Mahl,
  Das nur sein Auge aß.
MAECENAS   Die Königshure!
AGRIPPA Sie ließ des großen Caesar Schwert zu Bett gehn;
  Er pflügte sie, und sie trug Frucht.
ENOBARBUS   Ich sah sie
  Einst vierzig Meter durch die Straßen hüpfen,
  Und, außer Atem, sprach sie, und die Brust
  Hob sich in ihrem Mangel so vollkommen,
  Daß sie uns atemlos den Atem raubte.
MAECENAS Nun muß Antonius sie partout verlassen.
ENOBARBUS Niemals; das wird er nicht:
  Kein Altern schadet ihr, Gewohnheit strandet
  An ihrem immer neuen Wechselwesen:
  Wo andre Frauen sätt'gen, macht sie hungrig.
  Auch das Gemeinste wird in ihr verwandelt,
  Bis selbst die Priester ihre Wollust segnen.

MAECENAS Wenn Liebreiz, Jugend, Sittsamkeit Antonius
  Noch halten können, ist Octavia

A blessed Lottery to him.

Agrip. Let vs go. Good *Enobarbus*, make your selfe
my guest, whilst you abide heere.

Eno. Humbly Sir I thanke you. *Exeunt*

Enter Anthony, Cæsar, Octauia betweene them.

Anth. The world, and my great office, will
Sometimes deuide me from your bosome.
Octa. All which time, before the Gods my knee shall
bowe my prayers to them for you.

Anth. Goodnight Sir. My *Octauia*
Read not my blemishes in the worlds report:
I haue not kept my square, but that to come
Shall all be done byth'Rule: good night deere Lady:
Octa. Good night Sir.
Cæsar. Goodnight. *Exit.*
Enter Soothsaier.
Anth. Now sirrah: you do wish your selfe in Egypt?
Sooth. Would I had neuer come from thence, nor you
thither.
Ant. If you can, your reason?
Sooth. I see it in my motion: haue it not in my tongue,
But yet hie you to Egypt againe.

Antho. Say to me, whose Fortunes shall rise higher
Cæsars or mine?
Soot. *Cæsars.* Therefore (oh *Anthony*) stay not by his side

Für ihn ein Segen.

AGRIPPA   Kommt, wir wollen gehn.
  Ihr, guter Enobarbus, seid mein Gast,
  Solang Ihr hier verweilt.

ENOBARBUS   Ergebnen Dank, Sir.

Dritte Szene

Antonius, Octavia, Caesar.

ANTONIUS Die Welt, mein großes Amt, wird hin und wieder
  Von deiner Brust mich trennen.

OCTAVIA   All die Zeit
  Beugt sich mein Knie den Göttern zum Gebet
  An sie für dich.

ANTONIUS   Sir, gute Nacht. Octavia,
  Lies meine Schande nicht im Buch der Welt:
  Ich hielt nicht Maß, in Zukunft spiele ich,
  Wie es die Regel will. Gut Nacht, Geliebte.

OCTAVIA Gute Nacht, Sir.

Wahrsager.

ANTONIUS Nun, mein Bester? Fehlt dir dein Ägypten?

WAHRSAGER Hätt ich es nie verlassen, noch du selbst
  Es aufgesucht.

ANTONIUS   Dein Grund?

WAHRSAGER   Er liegt mir
  Auf der Seele, auf der Zunge nicht:
  Und doch: geh nach Ägypten wieder.

ANTONIUS   Sag mir,
  Wird mein Glück höher steigen oder Caesars?

WAHRSAGER Caesars.

Thy Dæmon that thy spirit which keepes thee, is
Noble, Couragious, high vnmatchable,
Where *Cæsars* is not. But neere him, thy Angell
Becomes a feare: as being o're-powr'd, therefore
Make space enough betweene you.

Anth. Speake this no more.
Sooth. To none but thee no more but: when to thee,
If thou dost play with him at any game,
Thou art sure to loose: And of that Naturall lucke,
He beats thee 'gainst the oddes. Thy Luster thickens,
When he shines by: I say againe, thy spirit
Is all affraid to gouerne thee neere him:
But he alway 'tis Noble.
Anth. Get thee gone:
Say to *Ventigius* I would speake with him.   *Exit.*
He shall to Parthia, be it Art or hap,
He hath spoken true. The very Dice obey him,
And in our sports my better cunning faints,
Vnder his chance, if we draw lots he speeds,
His Cocks do winne the Battaile, still of mine,
When it is all to naught: and his Quailes euer
Beate mine (in hoopt) at odd's. I will to Egypte:
And though I make this marriage for my peace,
I'th'East my pleasure lies. Oh come *Ventigius*.

Enter Ventigius.
You must to Parthia, your Commissions ready:
Follow me, and reciue't.   *Exeunt*

Darum, Antonius, geh von seiner Seite:
Dein Dämon, er, der Geist, der dich erhält,
Ist edel, tapfer, groß und unbesieglich,
Wo Caesars Dämon fern. Doch nah ihm geht
Dein Engel kraftlos, wie in Angst, zu Boden.
Drum schaff du Raum von dir zu ihm.
ANTONIUS   Schweig still.
WAHRSAGER Zu allen außer dir; nach dir zu jedem.
Ganz gleich, was für ein Spiel du mit ihm spielst,
Du unterliegst; sein Glück schlägt dich noch dann,
Wenn du schon Sieger scheinst. Dein Glanz verblaßt
Vor seinem Licht: ich wiederhols, dein Geist
Hat Furcht, in seiner Nähe zu regieren;
Doch ohne ihn erhebt er sich.
ANTONIUS   Verschwinde.
Sag dem Ventidius, ich will ihn sprechen.
Er soll nach Parthien. Ob Kunst, ob Zufall,
Er sprach, was wahr ist. Ihm gehorchen selbst
Die Würfel, meine Könnerschaft versagt
Bei unsern Wetten, ziehen wir das Los,
Gewinnt er, meinen Hahn schlägt seiner
Auch dann, wenn's Hundert steht zu Null, und aus
Dem Kreis wirft seine Wachtel meine. Ich
Will nach Ägypten. Schloß ich diese Ehe
Auch mir zum Frieden, liegt, was mich belebt,
Im Osten.
                        Ventidius.
        O, Ventidius, komm. Du mußt
Nach Parthien. Dein Marschbefehl ist fertig;
Folge mir und nimm ihn in Empfang.

Enter Lepidus, Mecenas and Agrippa.

Lepidus. Trouble your selues no further: pray you
    hasten your Generals after.
Agr. Sir, *Marke Anthony*, will e'ne but kisse *Octauia*,
    and weele follow.

Lepi. Till I shall see you in your Souldiers dresse,
    Which will become you both: Farewell.
Mece. We shall: as I conceiue the iourney, be at
    Mount before you *Lepidus*.

Lepi. Your way is shorter, my purposes do draw me
    much about, you'le win two dayes vpon me.

Both. Sir good successe.
Lepi. Farewell.   *Exeunt.*

Enter Cleopater, Charmian, Iras, and Alexas.

Cleo. Giue me some Musicke: Musicke, moody foode
    of vs that trade in Loue.
Omnes. The Musicke, hoa.
        Enter Mardian the Eunuch.
Cleo. Let it alone, let's to Billards: come *Charmian*.
Char. My arme is sore, best play with *Mardian*.
Cleopa. As well a woman with an Eunuch plaide, as
    with a woman. Come you'le play with me Sir?

Vierte Szene

Lepidus, Maecenas, Agrippa.

LEPIDUS Bemüht euch länger nicht: ich bitt euch, folgt
In Eile euren Generälen.
AGRIPPA   Sir,
Antonius küßt Octavia nur eben,
Schon folgen wir.
LEPIDUS   Bis ihr gerüstet seid,
Was euch gut stehn wird, lebt nun wohl.
MAECENAS   Wir sind,
Wie ich die Reise sehe, an dem Kap
Vor Euch, mein Lepidus.
LEPIDUS   Ihr habt
Den kürzern Weg, viel zu bestellen hab ich,
Zwei Tage gebe ich euch vor.
AGRIPPA, MAECENAS   Viel Glück, Sir.
LEPIDUS Lebt wohl.   *Alle ab.*

Fünfte Szene

Cleopatra, Charmian, Iras, Alexas, Mardian.

CLEOPATRA Macht mir Musik; Musik, die dunkle Nahrung
Für uns, die Liebe leben.
DIENER   He, Musik!

CLEOPATRA Genug, laß uns die Kugeln spielen, Charmian.
CHARMIAN Mein Arm tut weh, spielt lieber mit Mardian.
CLEOPATRA Mit dem Eunuchen spielt sich's für ein Weib
So gut wie mit 'nem Weib. Wie steht es, Sir,

Mardi. As well as I can Madam.

Cleo. And when good will is shewed,
    Though't come to short
    The Actor may pleade pardon. Ile none now,
    Giue me mine Angle, weele to'th'Riuer there
    My Musicke playing farre off. I will betray
    Tawny fine fishes, my bended hooke shall pierce
    Their slimy iawes: and as I draw them vp,
    Ile thinke them euery one an *Anthony*,
    And say, ah ha; y'are caught.

Char. 'Twas merry when you wager'd on your Ang-
    ling, when your diuer did hang a salt fish on his hooke
    which he with feruencie drew vp.

Cleo. That time? Oh times:
    I laught him out of patience: and that night
    I laught him into patience, and next morne,
    Ere the ninth houre, I drunke him to his bed:
    Then put my Tires and Mantles on him, whilst
    I wore his Sword Phillippan. Oh from Italie,

            Enter a Messenger.
    Ramme thou thy fruitefull tidings in mine eares,
    That long time haue bin barren.

Mes. Madam, Madam.

Cleo. *Anthonyo's* dead.
    If thou say so Villaine, thou kil'st thy Mistris:
    But well and free, if thou so yeild him.
    There is Gold, and heere
    My blewest vaines to kisse: a hand that Kings

Spielt Ihr mit mir?

ALEXAS   Madam, so gut ich kann.

CLEOPATRA Wo guter Wille herrscht, selbst ein zu kurzer,
Verzeiht man gern dem Spieler. Ich verzichte.
Gebt mir die Angel, und wir gehn zum Fluß.
Von fern machst du Musik. Betrügen will ich
Braungeflosste Fische, will mit krummen
Haken mich in ihre schleim'gen Kiefer
Bohren; und wenn ich sie einhol, will ich
In jedem einen Marc Anton erkennen
Und sprechen, ›So, dich fing ich‹.

CHARMIAN   Es war lustig,
Als bei dem Angelwettkampf Euer Taucher
Ihm einen Stockfisch auf den Haken hing,
Den er mit Eifer hochzog.

CLEOPATRA   Damals, ja? O Zeiten!
Ich lachte ihn aus seiner Ruhe; nachts dann
Lachte ich ihn in die Ruh zurück,
Noch vor neun Uhr trank ich ihn in die Kissen;
Tat meine Mäntel ihm und Spangen an,
Derweil ich selbst sein Schwert trug, das den Brutus
Besiegte bei Philippi.

Ein Bote.

CLEOPATRA   Von Italien!
Du regne Worte fruchtbar mir ins Ohr,
Das schon zur Wüste wurde.

BOTE   Madam, Madam –

CLEOPATRA Antonius tot! – Wenn du das aussprichst, Schurke,
Erdolchst du deine Herrin: läßt du ihn
Gesund und frei erblühen, hier ist Gold
Und hier die blauste Vene dir zum Kuß,
Auf einer Hand, die Königslippen spürte

Haue lipt, and trembled kissing.

Mes. First Madam, he is well.

Cleo. Why there's more Gold.
But sirrah marke, we vse
To say, the dead are well: bring it to that,
The Gold I giue thee, will I melt and powr
Downe thy ill vttering throate.

Mes. Good Madam heare me.

Cleo. Well, go too I will:
But there's no goodnesse in thy face if *Anthony*
Be free and healthfull; so tart a fauour
To trumpet such good tidings. If not well,
Thou shouldst come like a Furie crown'd with Snakes,
Not like a formall man.

Mes. Wilt please you heare me?

Cleo. I haue a mind to strike thee ere thou speak'st:
Yet if thou say *Anthony* liues, 'tis well,
Or friends with *Cæsar*, or not Captiue to him,
Ile set thee in a shower of Gold, and haile
Rich Pearles vpon thee.

Mes. Madam, he's well.

Cleo. Well said.

Mes. And Friends with *Caesar*.

Cleo. Th'art an honest man.

Mes. *Caesar*, and he, are greater Friends then euer.

Cleo. Make thee a Fortune from me.

Mes. But yet Madam.

Cleo. I do not like but yet, it does alay
The good precedence, fie vpon but yet,
But yet is as a Iaylor to bring foorth
Some monstrous Malefactor. Prythee Friend,

Und wie sie zitterten, die da geküßt.
BOTE Madam, zunächst, es geht ihm gut.
CLEOPATRA   Nun denn,
  Hier ist mehr Gold. Doch, Mann, wir sagen gern,
  Den Toten geht es gut: drehst du es so,
  Dann schmelze ich das Gold, das ich dir gab,
  Und gieß es dir in deinen Unglücksrachen.
BOTE Gute Herrin, hört mich.
CLEOPATRA   Schön, das will ich;
  Doch les ich dir nichts Gutes vom Gesicht,
  Antonius ist frei, er ist gesund, –
  Wenn das die gute Nachricht ist, warum
  Posaunt so saure Miene sie hinaus?
  Geht es ihm schlecht, dann komm als Furie,
  Bekränzt mit Schlangen, nicht in Mannsgestalt.
BOTE Oh, wollt mich bitte hören!
CLEOPATRA Ich hätte Lust, dich, eh du sprichst, zu prügeln:
  Sagst du jedoch, Antonius lebt, ist wohl,
  Ist Caesars Freund, nicht sein Gefangener,
  So stell ich dich in einen goldnen Regen
  Und hagle reiche Perlen auf dich nieder.
BOTE Madam, er ist gesund.
CLEOPATRA   Ein gutes Wort.
BOTE Und Caesars Freund.
CLEOPATRA   Du bist ein braver Kerl.
BOTE Caesar und er war'n nie so gute Freunde.
CLEOPATRA So mach dein Glück durch mich.
BOTE   Madam, und doch –
CLEOPATRA Ich mag nicht dies ›und doch‹, es trübt den klaren
  Beginn, ich spucke auf ›und doch‹, ›und doch‹
  Zerrt wie ein Kerkermeister irgendeinen
  Monströsen Missetäter an das Licht.

Powre out the packe of matter to mine eare,
The good and bad together: he's friends with *Cæsar*,
In state of health thou saist, and thou saist, free.

Mes. Free Madam, no: I made no such report,
He's bound vnto *Octauia*.

Cleo. For what good turne?
Mes. For the best turne i'th'bed.
Cleo. I am pale *Charmian*.

Mes. Madam, he's married to *Octauia*.

Cleo. The most infectious Pestilence vpon thee.

                              Strikes him downe.
Mes. Good Madam patience.
Cleo. What say you?   *Strikes him.*
    Hence horrible Villaine, or Ile spurne thine eyes
    Like balls before me: Ile vnhaire thy head,
                         She hales him vp and downe.
    Thou shalt be whipt with Wyer, and stew'd in brine,
    Smarting in lingring pickle.
Mes. Gratious Madam,
    I that do bring the newes, made not the match.
Cleo. Say 'tis not so, a Prouince I will giue thee,
    And make thy Fortunes proud: the blow thou had'st
    Shall make thy peace, for mouing me to rage,
    And I will boot thee with what guift beside
    Thy modestie can begge.
Mes. He's married Madam.
Cleo. Rogue, thou hast liu'd too long.   *Draw a knife.*

Ich bitt dich, Freund, schütt mir den ganzen Packen
Mit eins vor's Ohr, das Gute wie das Schlechte:
Er ist gut Freund mit Caesar, ist gesund,
Sagst du, und, sagst du, frei.

BOTE   Frei, Madam, nein;
Das war nicht mein Bericht. Er ist Octavia
Verbunden.

CLEOPATRA   Und in welcher guten Sache?

BOTE Der besten, der im Bett.

CLEOPATRA   Ich werde blaß.
Charmian.

BOTE   Madam, er ist mit Octavia
Vermählt.

CLEOPATRA Die fressendste der Pestilenzen
Dir!

BOTE   Madam, Geduld.

CLEOPATRA   Was sagst du? Hierher,
Entsetzlicher! Sonst tret ich deine Augen
Wie Bälle vor mir her, enthaare dich,

Du wirst mit Draht gepeitscht, in Salz gekocht,
In saurer Brühe totgeätzt.

BOTE   Ich, Madam,
Der Euch die Nachricht bringt, bin nicht der Macher.

CLEOPATRA Sag, es ist nicht, ich geb dir 'ne Provinz
Und mach dich groß: der Hieb, den du bekamst,
Soll dir's vergelten, mich erzürnt zu haben,
Und was sich deine Scham noch wünschen kann,
Soll dir gehörn.

BOTE   Madam, er ist vermählt.

CLEOPATRA Hund, du hast zu lang gelebt.

Mes. Nay then Ile runne:
  What meane you Madam, I haue made no fault.   *Exit.*
Char. Good Madam keepe your selfe within your selfe,
  The man is innocent.
Cleo. Some Innocents scape not the thunderbolt:
  Melt Egypt into Nyle: and kindly creatures
  Turne all to Serpents. Call the slaue againe,
  Though I am mad, I will not byte him :Call?
Char. He is afeard to come.
Cleo. I will not hurt him,
  These hands do lacke Nobility, that they strike
  A meaner then my selfe: since I my selfe
  Haue giuen my selfe the cause. Come hither Sir.
            Enter the Messenger againe.
  Though it be honest, it is neuer good
  To bring bad newes: giue to a gratious Message
  An host of tongues, but let ill tydings tell
  Themselues, when they be felt.
Mes. I haue done my duty.
Cleo. Is he married?
  I cannot hate thee worser then I do,
  If thou againe say yes.
Mes. He's married Madam.
Cleo. The Gods confound thee,
  Dost thou hold there still?
Mes. Should I lye Madame?
Cleo. Oh, I would thou didst:
  So halfe my Egypt were submerg'd and made
  A Cesterne for scal'd Snakes. Go get thee hence,
  Had'st thou *Narcissus* in thy face to me,
  Thou would'st appeere most vgly: He is married?

BOTE   Ich laufe.
  Was wollt Ihr, Madam? Ich hab nichts getan.
CHARMIAN Madam, kommt zu Euch selbst zurück, der Mann
  Ist schuldlos.
CLEOPATRA Auch den, der schuldlos ist, erschlägt der Blitz:
  Schmilz in den Nil, Ägypten! Ihr Geschöpfe,
  Wandelt euch zu Nattern! Ruft den Kerl her,
  So toll ich bin, ich beiße nicht: so ruft ihn!
CHARMIAN Er fürchtet sich.
CLEOPATRA   Ich tu ihm nichts zuleid.
  Der Hand hier mangelt Größe, daß sie den schlägt,
  Der mir untersteht, wo doch der Grund
  Ich selbst bin. Komm ruhig näher, Sir.

  Die schlechte Nachricht bringen, ist zwar brav,
  Doch selten lohnend: einer Freudenbotschaft
  Leiht hundert Zungen, doch das üble Neue
  Mag sich selbst verbreiten, wenn es Zeit ist.
BOTE Ich tat nur meine Pflicht.
CLEOPATRA   Er ist vermählt?
  Mehr kann ich dich nicht hassen, als ich's tue,
  Sagst du noch weiter ›Ja‹.
BOTE   Er ist vermählt.
CLEOPATRA Der Götter Fluch auf dich, du bleibst dabei?

BOTE Soll ich denn lügen?
CLEOPATRA   O, ich wollt du tätst es,
  Und ginge mir auch halb Ägypten unter
  Und würd zu einem Sumpf voll schupp'ger Schlangen.
  Mach, daß du verschwindest, wärst du auch
  Wie Narcissus anzusehn, mir bist du
  Ganz und gar widerlich. Er ist vermählt?

Mes. I craue your Highnesse pardon.

Cleo. He is married?

Mes. Take no offence, that I would not offend you,
  To punnish me for what you make me do
  Seemes much vnequall, he's married to *Octauia*.

Cleo. Oh that his fault should make a knaue of thee,
  That art not what th'art sure of. Get thee hence,
  The Marchandize which thou hast brought from Rome
  Are all too deere for me:
  Lye they vpon thy hand, and be vndone by em.

Char. Good your Highnesse patience.

Cleo. In praysing *Anthony*, I haue disprais'd *Cæsar*.

Char. Many times Madam.

Cleo. I am paid for't now: lead me from hence,
  I faint, oh *Iras*, *Charmian*: 'tis no matter.
  Go to the Fellow, good *Alexas* bid him
  Report the feature of *Octauia*: her yeares,
  Her inclination, let him not leaue out
  The colour of her haire. Bring me word quickly,
  Let him for euer go, let him not *Charmian*,
  Though he be painted one way like a Gorgon,
  The other wayes a Mars. Bid you *Alexas*
  Bring me word, how tall she is: pitty me *Charmian*,
  But do not speake to me. Lead me to my Chamber.

  Exeunt.

Flourish. Enter Pompey, at one doore with Drum and Trum-
pet: at another Cæsar, Lepidus, Anthony, Enobarbus, Me-
cenas, Agrippa, Menas with Souldiers Marching.

BOTE Ich bitte Euch, verzeiht.

CLEOPATRA   Er ist vermählt?

BOTE Seht nicht in mir das Ärgernis, ich bins nicht:
Und straft an mir, was Ihr mich tun laßt, nicht,
's wär ungerecht: er ist Octavia vermählt.

CLEOPATRA O sein Verbrechen zeichne dich zum Schurken,
Dich, der du, was du glaubst zu sein, nicht bist.
Pack dich mit deiner Ware da aus Rom,
Sie ist mir viel zu teuer: bleibe sie
Dir unverkäuflich und vernichte dich!   *Bote ab.*

CHARMIAN Fürstin, faßt Euch.

CLEOPATRA Was ich Antonius schenkte, stahl ich Caesar.

CHARMIAN Sehr häufig, Madam.

CLEOPATRA Ich bin belohnt. Führt mich hinweg; ich falle,
O Iras, Charmian! Es ist gleich.
Der Bursche, geh ihm nach, Alexas, frag ihn
Nach der Gestalt Octavias, ihrem Alter,
Ihrem Wesen, sorg dafür, daß er
Die Farbe ihres Haars nicht ausläßt; eil dich.
Ihn gehn zu lassen, ihn zu halten – Charmian,
Blickt mich in ihm das Bild der Gorgo an,
So doch auch das des Mars. Bitte Alexas,
Auch ihre Größe zu erfragen. Charmian,
Hab Mitleid, sage nichts. Führt mich hinweg.

Sechste Szene

Pompejus. Caesar, Lepidus, Antonius, Enobarbus, Maecenas,
Agrippa, Menas.

Pom. Your Hostages I haue, so haue you mine:
  And we shall talke before we fight.
Cæsar. Most meete that first we come to words,
  And therefore haue we
  Our written purposes before vs sent,
  Which if thou hast considered, let vs know,
  If'twill tye vp thy discontented Sword,
  And carry backe to Cicelie much tall youth,
  That else must perish heere.
Pom. To you all three,
  The Senators alone of this great world,
  Chiefe Factors for the Gods. I do not know,
  Wherefore my Father should reuengers want,
  Hauing a Sonne and Friends, since *Iulius Cæsar*,
  Who at Phillippi the good *Brutus* ghosted,
  There saw you labouring for him. What was't
  That mou'd pale *Cassius* to conspire? And what
  Made all-honor'd, honest, Romaine *Brutus*,
  With the arm'd rest, Courtiers of beautious freedome,
  To drench the Capitoll, but that they would
  Haue one man but a man, and that is it
  Hath made me rigge my Nauie. At whose burthen,
  The anger'd Ocean fomes, with which I meant
  To scourge th'ingratitude, that despightfull Rome
  Cast on my Noble Father.

Cæsar. Take your time.
Ant. Thou can'st not feare vs *Pompey* with thy sailes.
  Weele speake with thee at Sea. At land thou know'st
  How much we do o're-count thee.

POMPEJUS Eure Geiseln hab ich, Ihr habt meine;
  Und eh wir kämpfen, reden wir.
CAESAR   Sehr gut,
  Daß wir erst Worte wechseln, deshalb sandten
  Wir schriftlich unsre Vorschläge voraus,
  Von denen wir gern wüßten, ob sie Euer
  Erbostes Schwert zur Ruhe bringen können
  Und nach Sizilien heim die Jugend führen,
  Die sonst hier fallen muß.
POMPEJUS   An Euch, ihr drei
  Einzigen Senatoren dieser Welt,
  Statthalter der Götter: Warum soll
  Mein Vater ohne Rächer bleiben, wo
  Er doch einen Sohn und Freunde hat,
  Und Julius Caesar, der den tapfren Brutus
  Als Geist heimsuchte bei Philippi, Euch
  An der Arbeit für sich sah. Was wars denn?
  Was trieb den bleichen Cassius zur Verschwörung?
  Was war es, das den allverehrten, festen
  Römer Brutus und die andern alle,
  Die sich bewaffnet für die Freiheit schlugen,
  Bewog, mit Blut das Capitol zu tränken,
  Wenn nicht der Wille, keinen Mann je über
  Einem andern Mann zu sehn? Und darum
  Lief meine Flotte aus: wutschnaubend
  Trägt der Ozean die Last, mit der ich
  Den Undank geißle, den das schnöde Rom
  Auf meinen Vater warf.
CAESAR   Laßt Euch doch Zeit.
ANTONIUS Mit deinen Segeln kannst du uns nicht schrecken,
  Pompejus. Wart es ab, wir sprechen uns
  Zur See, zu Land, das weißt du, haben wir

Pom. At Land indeed
　　Thou dost orecount me of my Fatherrs house:
　　But since the Cuckoo buildes not for himselfe,
　　Remaine in't as thou maist.
Lepi. Be pleas'd to tell vs,
　　(For this is from the present how you take)
　　The offers we haue sent you.
Cæsar. There's the point.
Ant. Which do not be entreated too,
　　But waigh what it is worth imbrac'd
Cæsar. And what may follow to try a larger Fortune.

Pom. You haue made me offer
　　Of Cicelie, Sardinia: and I must
　　Rid all the Sea of Pirats. Then, to send
　　Measures of Wheate to Rome: this greed vpon,
　　To part with vnhackt edges, and beare backe
　　Our Targes vndinted.
Omnes. That's our offer.
Pom. Know then I came before you heere,
　　A man prepar'd
　　To take this offer. But *Marke Anthony*,
　　Put me to some impatience: though I loose
　　The praise of it by telling. You must know
　　When *Cæsar* and your Brother were at blowes,
　　Your Mother came to Cicelie, and did finde
　　Her welcome Friendly.
Ant. I haue heard it *Pompey*,
　　And am well studied for a liberall thanks,
　　Which I do owe you.
Pom. Let me haue your hand:

Dir was voraus.

POMPEJUS   Allerdings habt Ihr zu Land
    Mir was voraus durch meines Vaters Haus:
    Doch weil der Kuckuck für sich selbst nicht baut,
    Bleibt drin, solang Ihr wollt.

LEPIDUS   Sagt uns doch bitte –
    Denn dies führt weg vom Ziel – was haltet Ihr
    Von unserm Angebot?

CAESAR   Das ist der Punkt.

ANTONIUS Fühl dich nicht gebeten, wäg nur ab,
    Was du gewinnst.

CAESAR   Und was geschehen kann,
    Wenn Ihr's aufs Spiel setzt.

POMPEJUS   Euer Angebot
    Umfaßt Sizilien und Sardinien;
    Und von Piraten soll die See ich säubern.
    Für Rom mit Weizenlieferungen sorgen;
    Dies zugestanden, gehn wir auseinander
    Mit glattem Schwert und unzerhacktem Schild.

CAESAR/ANTONIUS/LEPIDUS Das ist das Angebot.

POMPEJUS   Dann sollt Ihr wissen,
    Ich bin vor Euch getreten als ein Mann,
    Bereit, es anzunehmen. Nur Antonius
    Hat mich provoziert. Büß ich auch Ruhm ein,
    Wenn ich es selbst erzähle, müßt Ihr wissen,
    Daß, als sich Caesar und Eu'r Bruder schlugen,
    Eure Mutter, nach Sizilien vertrieben,
    Dort sehr willkommen war.

ANTONIUS   Das hörte ich,
    Pompejus, und es ist mir sehr bewußt,
    Was ich Euch schulde.

POMPEJUS   Gebt mir Eure Hand:

I did not thinke Sir, to haue met you heere,
Ant. The beds i'th'East are soft, and thanks to you,
That cal'd me timelier then my purpose hither:
For I haue gained by't.
Cæsar. Since I saw you last, ther's a change vpon you.

Pom. Well, I know not,
What counts harsh Fotune cast's vpon my face,
But in my bosome shall she neuer come,
To make my heart her vassaile.
Lep. Well met heere.
Pom. I hope so *Lepidus*, thus we are agreed:
I craue our composition may be written
And seal'd betweene vs,
Cæsar. That's the next to do.
Pom. Weele feast each other, ere we part, and lett's
Draw lots who shall begin.
Ant. That will I *Pompey*.
Pompey. No *Anthony* take the lot: but first or last,
your fine Egyptian cookerie shall haue the fame, I haue
heard that *Iulius Cæsar*, grew fat with feasting there.

Anth. You haue heard much.
Pom. I haue faire meaning Sir.
Ant. And faire words to them.
Pom. Then so much haue I heard,
And I haue heard *Appolodorus* carried———
Eno. No more that: he did so.
Pom. What I pray you?
Eno. A certaine Queene to *Cæsar* in a Matris.
Pom. I know thee now, how far'st thou Souldier?

Ich dachte nicht, Euch hier zu treffen, Sir.

ANTONIUS Es liegt sich weich im Osten, und Euch dank ich's,
    Daß Ihr mich herrieft, früher als ich's plante;
    Denn ich gewann dabei.

CAESAR   Ihr habt Euch sehr
    Verändert seit dem letzten Mal.

POMPEJUS   Mag sein,
    Daß mir Fortuna das Gesicht gekerbt,
    Doch meine Brust verwehr ich ihr, mein Herz
    Wird nie ihr Sklave.

LEPIDUS   Schön, Euch hier zu sehn.

POMPEJUS Das hoff ich, Lepidus, wir sind uns einig:
    Nun laßt die Verträge schreiben, bitte,
    Und wir siegeln sie.

CAESAR   Das soll sogleich geschehn.

POMPEJUS Wir wollen uns bewirten, eh wir scheiden,
    Und losen, wer beginnt.

ANTONIUS   Ich bin der erste.

POMPEJUS Nein, Antonius, Ihr zieht ein Los:
    Doch ob Ihr erster werdet oder letzter,
    Ägyptens Küche wird das Rennen machen.
    Ich hab gehört, selbst Julius Caesar sei
    Dort fett geworden.

ANTONIUS   Du hörst wohl so manches.

POMPEJUS Das war nicht bös gemeint.

ANTONIUS   Und nett gesagt.

POMPEJUS Also, das hab ich gehört, und ferner
    Hörte ich, Apollodorus trug –

ENOBARBUS Nichts mehr davon: er tat es.

POMPEJUS   Was denn, bitte?

ENOBARBUS 'ne Königin zu Caesar in 'nem Teppich.

POMPEJUS Nun weiß ich wieder, wer du bist: wie gehts,

Eno. Well, and well am like to do, for I perceiue
    Foure Feasts are toward.
Pom. Let me shake thy hand,
    I neuer hated thee: I haue seene thee fight,
    When I haue enuied thy behauiour.

Enob. Sir, I neuer lou'd you much, but I ha'prais'd ye,
    When you haue well deseru'd ten times as much,
    As I haue said you did.

Pom. Inioy thy plainnesse,
    It nothing ill becomes thee:
    Aboord my Gally, I inuite you all.
    Will you leade Lords?
All. Shew's the way, sir.
Pom. Come.   *Exeunt.*   *Manet Enob. & Menas*

Men. Thy Father *Pompey* would ne're haue made this
    Treaty. You, and I haue knowne sir.
Enob. At Sea, I thinke.
Men. We haue Sir.
Enob. You haue done well by water.
Men. And you by Land.
Enob. I will praise any man that will praise me, thogh
    it cannot be denied what I haue done by Land.
Men. Nor what I haue done by water.
Enob. Yes some-thing you can deny for your owne
    safety: you haue bin a great Theefe by Sea.
Men. And you by Land.
Enob. There I deny my Land seruice: but giue mee
    your hand *Menas*, if our eyes had authority, heere they

Soldat?

ENOBARBUS Mir? Gut, und gut gehn soll mirs weiter,
Denn Feste sind in Sicht, vier Stück.

POMPEJUS   Die Hand
Laß mich dir schütteln, Haß empfand ich nie
Für dich: ich hab dich kämpfen sehn
Und dir den Mut geneidet.

ENOBARBUS   Sir, geliebt
Hab ich Euch nicht besonders, nur gepriesen,
Wobei Euch zehnmal mehr zukommt, als ich
Behauptet habe.

POMPEJUS   Eure Offenheit
Schadet Euch mitnichten.
Kommt auf mein Schiff, ich bin's, der alle einlädt
Lords, geht Ihr vor?

CAESAR/ANTONIUS/LEPIDUS Zeigt uns den Weg.

POMPEJUS   Dann kommt.

        Alle ab bis auf Enobarbus und Menas.

MENAS Dein Vater, Pompejus, hätte keinen solchen Ver-
trag geschlossen. Ihr und ich, wir kennen uns, Sir.

ENOBARBUS Von See her, denke ich.

MENAS Kennen wir uns, Sir.

ENOBARBUS Ihr habt Euch gut geschlagen zu Wasser.

MENAS Und Ihr zu Lande.

ENOBARBUS Wer immer mich lobt, den lob ich zurück, ist
mein Verdienst zu Land auch nicht zu leugnen.

MENAS Noch meins zu Wasser.

ENOBARBUS Doch, das dürft Ihr um Eurer Wohlfahrt willen leugnen: Ihr wart ein großer Dieb zur See.

Menas Und Ihr zu Lande.

Enobarbus Schon leugne ich meine Landtaten. Aber gebt
mir die Hand, Menas: wären unsre Augen Büttel, hier

might take two Theeues kissing.

Men. All mens faces are true, whatsomere their hands
are.

Enob. But there is neuer a fayre Woman, ha's a true
Face.

Men. No slander, they steale hearts.

Enob. We came hither to fight with you.

Men. For my part, I am sorry it is turn'd to a Drinking. *Pompey* doth this day laugh away his Fortune.

Enob. If he do, sure he cannot weep't backe againe.

Men. Y'haue said Sir, we look'd not for *Marke Anthony* heere, pray you, is he married to *Cleopatra*?

Enob. *Cæsars* Sister is call'd *Octauia.*

Men. True Sir, she was the wife of *Caius Marcellus.*

Enob. But she is now the wife of *Marcus Anthonius.*

Men. Pray'ye sir.

Enob. 'Tis true.

Men. Then is *Cæsar* and he, for euer knit together.

Enob. If I were bound to Diuine of this vnity, I wold
not Prophesie so.

Men. I thinke the policy of that purpose, made more
in the Marriage, then the loue of the parties.

Enob. I thinke so too. But you shall finde the band
that seemes to tye their friendship together, will bee the
very strangler of their Amity: *Octauia* is of a holy, cold,
and still conuersation.

Men. Who would not haue his wife so?

Eno. Not he that himselfe is not so: which is *Marke
Anthony*: he will to his Egyptian dish againe: then shall

könnten sie zwei Diebe beim Küssen erwischen.

MENAS Alle Mannsgesichter sind ehrlich, unabhängig von was ihre Hände sind.

ENOBARBUS Aber ein schönes Weibsgesicht, ein ehrliches, gibt's nicht.

MENAS Nichts für ungut, sie stehlen Herzen.

ENOBARBUS Wir kamen, uns mit Euch zu hauen.

MENAS Mir für mein Teil tut's leid, daß daraus ein Besäufnis wurde. Pompejus lacht sein Glück weg heute Nacht.

ENOBARBUS Zurückweinen wird er's nicht können, wenn.

MENAS Ihr sagt es, Sir. Auf Marc Anton waren wir nicht gefaßt hier: sagt mir, hat er Cleopatra geheiratet?

ENOBARBUS Caesars Schwester heißt Octavia.

MENAS Das schon, Sir, sie war von Caius Marcellus die Frau.

ENOBARBUS Doch nun ist sie die Frau von Marcus Antonius.

MENAS Wie bitte, Sir?

ENOBARBUS Wie ich sage.

MENAS Dann sind Caesar und er vertäut auf ewig.

ENOBARBUS Sollte ich von dieser Union was orakeln, ich würde so nicht prophezeien.

MENAS Ich denke mir, da war mehr Politik bei dieser Heirat im Spiel als Liebe der Partner.

ENOBARBUS Ich denke desgleichen. Aber Ihr werdet es erleben, das Tau, welches ihr Bündnis zusammenhalten soll, wird sein Würgestrick. Octavia ist eine von der frommen, kalten, stillen Sorte.

MENAS Wer wünschte sich seine Frau nicht so?

ENOBARBUS Der nicht, der selber nicht so ist: das ist Marc Anton. Er wird zurück an seinen ägyptischen Fleisch-

the sighes of *Octauia* blow the fire vp in *Caesar*, and (as I
said before) that which is the strength of their Amity,
shall proue the immediate Author of their variance. *Anthony* will vse his affection where it is. Hee married but
his occasion heere.

Men. And thus it may be. Come Sir, will you aboord?
    I haue a health for you.
Enob. I shall take it sir: we haue vs'd our Throats in
    Egypt.
Men. Come, let's away.   *Exeunt.*

Musicke playes.
Enter two or three Seruants with a Banket.

1 Heere they'l be man: some o'th'their Plants are ill
  rooted already, the least winde i'th'world wil blow them
  downe.
2 *Lepidus* is high Coulord.
1 They haue made him drinke Almes drinke.
2 As they pinch one another by the disposition, hee
  cries out, no more; reconciles them to his entreatie, and
  himselfe to'th'drinke.
1 But it raises the greater warre betweene him & his
  discretion.
2 Why this it is to haue a name in great mens Fel-
  lowship: I had as liue haue a Reede that will doe me no
  seruice, as a Partizan I could not heaue.

1 To be call'd into a huge Sphere, and not to be seene

topf wollen: dann blasen Octavias Seufzer Caesars Flammen an, und (wie ich soeben ausführen durfte), das, was den Halt ihres Bündnisses ausmacht, erweist sich prompt als der Urheber ihrer Entzweiung. Antonius wird sich kratzen, wo's ihn juckt. Hier hat er nur seinen Vorteil gefreit.

MENAS So kanns kommen. Los, Sir, wollt Ihr an Bord? Ich hab da was für Eure Gesundheit.

ENOBARBUS Ich will es schlucken, Sir. Unsre Kehlen sind in Übung seit Ägypten.

MENAS Kommt, gehn wir. *Beide ab*

Siebte Szene

Diener 1, Diener 2.

DIENER 1 Sie komm' gleich, Mann. Einige von denen ihre Standbeine sind ganz hübsch ausgewurzelt, die allerkleinste Brise bläst sie um.

DIENER 2 Lepidus hat 'ne Spitzenfarbe.

DIENER 1 Den hamse zum Friedenstrinker gemacht. Kaum fang' sie an, sich zu sticheln, schreit er ›Friiieden!‹, guckt scharf in die Runde und tief ins Glas.

DIENER 2 Desto doller bekriegt er seinen Brägen.

DIENER 1 So is das, wenn du in die feine Gesellschaft gerätst: entweder du hockst da mitm Strohhalm, wo zu nischt nutze is, oder mit 'ner Hellebarde, die du gar nich hochkriegst.

Diener 2 In höhere Sphären gerufen sein, und dann nich

to moue in't, are the holes where eyes should bee, which
pittifully disaster the cheekes.

A Sennet sounded.

Enter Caesar, Anthony, Pompey, Lepidus, Agrippa, Mecenas,
Enobarbus, Menes, with other Captaines.

Ant. Thus do they Sir: they take the flow o'th'Nyle
By certaine scales i'th' Pyramid: they know
By'th'height, the lownesse, or the meane: If dearth
Or Foizon follow. The higher Nilus swels,
The more it promises: as it ebbes, the Seedsman
Vpon the slime and Ooze scatters his graine,
And shortly comes to Haruest.

Lep. Y'haue strange Serpents there?

Anth. I *Lepidus.*

Lep. Your Serpent of Egypt, is bred now of your mud
by the operation of your Sun: so is your Crocodile.

Ant. They are so.

Pom. Sit, and some Wine: A health to *Lepidus.*

Lep. I am not so well as I should be:
But Ile ne're out.

Enob. Not till you haue slept: I feare me you'l bee in
till then.

Lep. Nay certainly, I haue heard the *Ptolomies* Pyra-
misis are very goodly things: without contradiction I
haue heard that.

Menas. Pompey, a word.

Pomp. Say in mine eare, what is't.

Men. Forsake thy seate I do beseech thee Captaine,
And heare me speake a word.

wissen, was läuft, das is wie Löcher haben, wo Augen
hingehörn, und die Backen sehn scheußlich aus dadurch.

*Caesar, Antonius, Pompejus, Lepidus, Agrippa, Maecenas, Eno-
barbus, Menas.*

ANTONIUS Sie machens so, Sir: wie der Nil steht, messen
Sie mittels Skalen an den Pyramiden;
Hoch, tief und normal zeigt ihnen an,
Ob Teurung folgt, ob Überfluß. Je höher
Der Nil schwillt, desto mehr verheißt er. Ebbt es,
Dann streut der Sämann seine Körner aus
Auf Schlick und Schlamm und erntet schnell und viel.
LEPIDUS Da hat's seltsame Giftwürmer, wie?
ANTONIUS Lepidus, auch das.
LEPIDUS Eurer Ägypftwurm wird somit gebrütet aus eurem
Modder infolge der Operation eurer Sonne: so auch euer
Krokodil.
ANTONIUS So auch dieses.
POMPEJUS Hinsetzen – mehr Wein! Auf Lepidus' Gesund-
heit!
LEPIDUS Ich bin nicht mehr ganz so präsent, wie ich sollte:
aber ich bin dabei.
ENOBARBUS Bis du schnarchst: ich fürchte, von da an bist du
draußen vor.
LEPIDUS Nein, jetzt im Ernst, ich hörte, diese ptolemäßigen
Pyramisen wärn dolle Dinger; kein Widerspruch, das
hörte ich.
MENAS Pompejus, auf ein Wort.
POMPEJUS   Sags mir ins Ohr,
Was gibt's?
MENAS   Komm hoch, ich bitt dich, Kapitän,
Und laß mich dir was sagen.

Pom.   Forbeare me till anon.   *Whispers in's Eare.*
   This Wine for *Lepidus*.

Lep.   Whar manner o'thing is your Crocodile?

Ant.   It is shap'd sir like it selfe, and it is as broad as it
   hath bredth; It is iust so high as it is, and mooues with it
   owne organs. It liues by that which nourisheth it, and
   the Elements once out of it, it Transmigrates.

Lep.   What colour is it of?

Ant.   Of it owne colour too.

Lep.   'Tis a strange Serpent.

Ant.   'Tis so, and the teares of it are wet.

Cæs.   Will this description satisfie him?

Ant.   With the Health that *Pompey* giues him, else he
   is a very Epicure.

Pomp.   Go hang sir, hang: tell me of that? Away:
   Do as I bid you. Where's this Cup I call'd for?

Men.   If for the sake of Merit thou wilt heare mee,
   Rise from thy stoole.

Pom.   I thinke th'art mad: the matter?

Men.   I haue euer held my cap off to thy Fortunes.

Pom.   Thou hast seru'd me with much faith: what's
   else to say? Be iolly Lords.

Anth.   These Quicke-sands *Lepidus*,
   Keepe off, them for you sinke.

Men.   Wilt thou be Lord of all the world?

Pom.   What saist thou?

Men.   Wilt thou be Lord of the whole world?
   That's twice.

Pom.   How should that be?

Men.   But entertaine it, and though thou thinke me
   poore, I am the man will giue thee all the world.

POMPEJUS   Doch nicht jetzt.
   Der Wein für Lepidus!
LEPIDUS Euer Krokodil, was ist das für ein Dingsbums?
ANTONIUS Es ist gestaltet, Sir, wie es selbst, und so breit wie
   seine Breite: es ist so hoch, wie es ist und steht auf
   eignen Beinen. Es lebt von was es am Leben hält, und
   zerfällt es in die Elemente, wird es ein neues Wesen.
LEPIDUS Von welcher Farbe ist es?
ANTONIUS Von seiner eignen.
LEPIDUS 's ist ein seltsamer Wurm.
ANTONIUS Richtig, und seine Tränen sind feucht.
CAESAR Ob die Beschreibung ihn zufrieden stellt?
ANTONIUS Bei der vielen Gesundheit, die Pompejus ihm
   zutrinkt – andernfalls wäre er ein abnormer Epikuräer.
POMPEJUS Geht, hängt Euch, Sir! Was für ein Zeug! Haut ab!
   Tut mir die Liebe. Wo ist denn mein Becher?
MENAS Ich hab es mir verdient, daß du mich anhörst,
   Also komm hoch.
POMPEJUS   Ich glaub, du spinnst. Was soll das?
MENAS Vor deinem Glück zog ich noch stets die Mütze.
POMPEJUS Du hast mir treu gedient: was noch liegt an?
   Seid heiter, Lords.
ANTONIUS   He, Lepidus, bleibt weg
   Von dieser Pfütze, oder Ihr ersauft.
MENAS Willst du der Herr der Welt sein?
POMPEJUS   Was sagst du?
MENAS Dann noch einmal: willst du der Herr der Welt sein?

POMPEJUS Wie soll das gehn?
MENAS   Du brauchst es nur zu wollen,
   Und ich, den du für blöd hältst, bin der Mann,
   Der dir die Welt verschafft.

Pom. Hast thou drunke well.

Men. No *Pompey*, I haue kept me from the cup,
    Thou art if thou dar'st be, the earthly Ioue:
    What ere the Ocean pales, or skie inclippes,
    Is thine, if thou wilt ha't.

Pom. Shew me which way?

Men. These three World-sharers, these Competitors
    Are in thy vessell. Let me cut the Cable,
    And when we are put off, fall to their throates:
    All there is thine.

Pom. Ah, this thou shouldst haue done,
    And not haue spoke on't. In me 'tis villanie,
    In thee,'t had bin good seruice: thou must know,
    'Tis not my profit that does lead mine Honour:
    Mine Honour it, Repent that ere thy tongue,
    Hath so betraide thine acte. Being done vnknowne,
    I should haue found it afterwards well done,
    But must condemne it now: desist, and drinke.

Men. For this, Ile neuer follow
    Thy paul'd Fortunes more,
    Who seekes and will not take, when once 'tis offer'd,
    Shall neuer finde it more.

Pom. This health to *Lepidus*.

Ant. Beare him ashore,
    Ile pledge it for him *Pompey*.

Eno. Heere's to thee *Menas*.

Men. *Enobarbus*, welcome.

Pom. Fill till the cup be hid.

Eno. There's a strong Fellow *Menas*.

Men. Why?

Eno. A beares the third part of the world man: seest

POMPEJUS   Bist du besoffen?
MENAS Nee, Pompejus, ich trank keinen Tropfen.
    Du bist, wagst du's, Jupiter auf Erden:
    Das Meerumschlossne, Himmelüberwölbte
    Ist, willst du's haben, dein.
POMPEJUS   Zeig mir den Weg.
MENAS Die drei Weltteilhaber, die Rivalen,
    Sind auf deinem Kahn. Laß mich die Taue kappen,
    Wir segeln ab, ich pack sie an der Gurgel:
    Alles ist dein.
POMPEJUS   Ah, das hättst du tun
    Und nicht erst sagen solln! Von mir wär das
    Verrat, von dir ein guter Dienst. Kapierst du,
    Mir gängelt nicht mein Vorteil meine Ehre,
    Nee, meine Ehre ihn. Beschwer bei deiner
    Zunge dich, daß sie die Faust dir austrickst.
    Heimlich getan, hätt ich es hinterher
    Für gut getan befunden, aber so rum
    Muß ich's verdammen, Schluß. Besauf dich.
MENAS   Dafür
    Folg ich nicht länger deinem morschen Glück.
    Wer nach was sucht und packt's nicht, wenn sich's bietet,
    Der findet's nicht nochmal.
POMPEJUS   Prost, Lepidus!
ANTONIUS Schafft ihn an Land, ich steh für ihn, Pompejus.

ENOBARBUS Menas, auf dich!
MENAS   Willkommen, Enobarbus!
POMPEJUS Füllt die Tassen bis sie platzen.
ENOBARBUS Der Kerl hat Körner, Menas.
MENAS Wie?
ENOBARBUS Er schleppt den Dritteil dieser Welt, Mann;

not?

Men. The third part, then he is drunk: would it were
all, that it might go on wheeles.

Eno. Drinke thou: encrease the Reeles.

Men Come.

Pom. This is not yet an Alexandrian Feast.

Ant. It ripen's towards it: strike the Vessells hoa.
Heere's to *Cæsar.*

Cæsar. I could well forbear't, it's monstrous labour
when I wash my braine, and it grow fouler.

Ant. Be a Child o'th'time.

Cæsar. Possesse it, Ile make answer: but I had rather
fast from all, foure dayes, then drinke so much in one.

Enob. Ha my braue Emperour, shall we daunce now
the Egyptian Backenals, and celebrate our drinke?

Pom. Let's ha't good Souldier.

Ant. Come, let's all take hands,
Till that the conquering Wine hath steep't our sense,
In soft and delicate Lethe.

Eno. All take hands:
Make battery to our eares with the loud Musicke,
The while, Ile place you, then the Boy shall sing.
The holding euery man shall beate as loud,
As his strong sides can volly.

    Musicke Playes. Enobarbus places them hand in hand.
              The Song.
    Come thou Monarch of the Vine,
    Plumpie Bacchus, with pinke eyne:
    In thy Fattes our Cares be drown'd,
    With thy Grapes our haires be Crown'd.

siehst du?

MENAS Der Dritteil ist besoffen, ich wollt, sie wär es
Ganz und käm ins Trudeln.

ENOBARBUS Da hilft nur sich bedudeln.

MENAS Komm.

POMPEJUS Ein Fest wie in Ägypten ist das nicht.

ANTONIUS Es macht sich: schlagt die Pauken, ihr da!
Auf Caesar!

CAESAR   Ich kann drauf verzichten.
Ein Schwachsinn, mir das Hirn mit Wein zu waschen
Und es kriegt Stellen.

ANTONIUS   Sei ein Kind der Stunde.

CAESAR Meistre sie, sag ich und faste lieber
Vier Tage, als an einem so zu trinken.

ENOBARBUS Mein tapfrer Imperator, tanzen wir
Ägyptisch, unser Bacchanal, zur Feier
Unsres Umtrunks?

POMPEJUS   So soll's sein, Soldat.

ANTONIUS Kommt und faßt euch alle an der Hand,
Bis uns der Kaiser Wein die Sinne sämtlich
In schwarzer Lethe auflöst.

ENOBARBUS   Nehmt die Hände!
Bestürmt das Ohr mit schmetternder Musik:
Ich stell euch auf, dann soll der Knabe singen.
In den Refrain fall'n alle ein, so laut,
Als es ihr Brustkorb hergibt.

DAS LIED

Bacchus, komm, du Fürst des Weines,
Kein Äuglein funkelt rot wie deines!
Allein dein Faß heilt den, der krankt,
Weinlaub sei ums Haupt gerankt:

Cup vs till the world go round,
Cup vs till the world go round.

Cæsar. What would you more?
  Pompey goodnight. Good Brother
  Let me request you of our grauer businesse
  Frownes at this leuitie. Gentle Lords let's part,
  You see we haue burnt our cheekes. Strong *Enobarbe*
  Is weaker then the Wine, and mine owne tongue
  Spleet's what it speakes: the wilde disguise hath almost
  Antickt vs all. What needs more words? goodnight.
  Good *Anthony* your hand.
Pom. Ile try you on the shore.
Anth. And shall Sir, giues your hand.
Pom. Oh *Anthony*, you haue my Father house.
  But what, we are Friends?
  Come downe into the Boate.
Eno. Take heed you fall not *Menas*: Ile not on shore,

  No to my Cabin: these Drummes,
  These Trumpets, Flutes: what
  Let Neptune heare, we bid aloud farewell
  To these great Fellowes. Sound and be hang'd,sound out.
      Sound a Flourish with Drummes.
Enor. Hoo saies a there's my Cap.
Men. Hoa, Noble Captaine, come.   *Exeunt.*

Tränk uns, bis die Erde wankt,
Tränk uns, bis die Erde wankt!
CAESAR Was wollt ihr noch? Pompejus, gute Nacht.
Lieber Bruder, sehn wir auf den Abgang,
Die Staatsgeschäfte zürnen unserm Leichtsinn.
Ihr Herrn, wir gehn, ihr seht, uns glühn die Wangen.
Der Wein ist stärker als selbst Enobarbus,
Und meine Zunge spaltet was sie spricht:
Die wilde Ausschweifung macht aus uns allen
Popanze. Kein Wort mehr. Gute Nacht.
Antonius, Bester, Eure Hand.
POMPEJUS   Ich fahr euch.
ANTONIUS Das müßt Ihr, Sir; gebt mir die Hand.
POMPEJUS   Antonius,
Ihr habt mein Vaterhaus. Egal, wir sind jetzt
Freunde, oder? Steigt ins Boot.
ENOBARBUS   Und fallt nicht.
Menas, ich will nicht an Land.
MENAS   Zu mir
In die Kajüte. Was, die Trommeln und
Trompeten, Flöten! Schlaft ihr! Laßt Neptun
Das Ständchen hören, das wir diesen Größen
Zum Abschied bringen. Tönt und hängt euch, tönt!

ENOBARBUS Hoo! Sessa! Da meine Mütze!
MENAS Hoo! Hochedler Hauptmann, kommt.
                          Beide ab.

Enter Ventidius as it were in triumph, the dead body of Paco-
rus borne before him.

Ven. Now darting Parthya art thou stroke, and now
 Pleas'd Fortune does of *Marcus Crassus* death
 Make me reuenger. Beare the Kings Sonnes body,
 Before our Army, thy *Pacorus Orades*,
 Paies this for *Marcus Crassus*.

Romaine. Noble *Ventidius*,
 Whil'st yet with Parthian blood thy Sword is warme,
 The Fugitiue Parthians follow. Spurre through Media,
 Mesapotamia, and the shelters, whether
 The routed flie. So thy grand Captaine *Anthony*
 Shall set thee on triumphant Chariots, and
 Put Garlands on thy head.

Ven. Oh *Sillius, Sillius*,
 I haue done enough. A lower place note well
 May make too great an act. For learne this *Sillius*,
 Better to leaue vndone, then by our deed
 Acquire too high a Fame, when him we serues away.
 Cæsar and *Anthony*, haue euer wonne
 More in their officer, then person. *Sossius*
 One of my place in Syria, his Lieutenant,
 For quicke accumulation of renowne,
 Which he atchiu'd by'th'minute, lost his fauour.
 Who does i'th'Warres more then his Captaine can,
 Becomes his Captaines Captaine: and Ambition

DRITTER AKT
Erste Szene

Ventidius, Silius, der Leichnam des Pacorus.

VENTIDIUS So, freches Parthien, du bist bestraft,
Und mich erhob das Kriegsglück zu dem Rächer
Von Marcus Crassus' Tod. Dem Heer voran
Tragt mir den Leichnam dieses Königssohns.
Orodes, dein Pacorus zahlt Rom so
Den Mord an Crassus.
SILIUS   Noch ist dir das Schwert,
Edler Ventidius, vom Blut der Parther
Heiß: verfolg die, die entkamen. Falle
In Medien ein, in das Zweistromland, jeden
Winkel, in den die Geschlagnen krochen.
Dann hebt Antonius, dein Feldherr, dich
Auf einen Siegeswagen und bekränzt
Dein Haupt mit Lorbeer.
VENTIDIUS   Silius, Silius!
Ich tat genug. Ein untrer Rang, das merk dir,
Kann leicht zuviel aufstelln. Das mußt du lernen,
Silius, besser nichts tun, als durch Taten
Zu steilen Ruhm einheimsen, wenn die Chefs
Nicht da sind. Caesar wie Antonius
Gewannen mehr durch ihre Offiziere,
Als in Person: zu fix erwarb sich Sossius,
Der vor mir sein Leutnant war in Syrien,
Berühmtheit und verspielte seine Gunst.
Wer auf dem Schlachtfeld mehr macht als sein Feldherr,
Wird Feldherr seines Feldherrn: und die Ruhmsucht,

(The Souldiers vertue) rather makes choise of losse
Then gaine, which darkens him.
I could do more to do *Anthonius* good,
But 'twould offend him. And in his offence,
Should my performance perish.

Rom. Thou hast *Ventidius* that, without the which a
Souldier and his Sword graunts scarce distinction: thou
wilt write to *Anthony*.
Ven. Ile humbly signifie what in his name,
That magicall word of Warre we haue effected,
How with his Banners, and his well paid ranks,
The nere-yet beaten Horse of Parthia,
We haue iaded out o'th'Field.
Rom. Where is he now?
Ven. He purposeth to Athens, whither with what hast
The waight we must conuay with's, will permit:
We shall appeare before him. On there, passe along.

Exeunt.

Enter Agrippa at one doore, Enobarbus at another.

Agri. What are the Brothers parted?
Eno. They haue dispatcht with *Pompey*, he is gone,
The other three are Sealing. *Octauia* weepes
To part from Rome: *Cæsar* is sad, and *Lepidus*
Since *Pompey's* feast, as *Menas* saies, is troubled
With the Greene-Sicknesse.

Agri. 'Tis a Noble *Lepidus*.

Die Tugend des Soldaten, läßt sich lieber
Mal was entgehn, als alles mitzunehmen
Und dann im Aus zu stehn. Noch mehr Gutes
Könnt ich Antonius tun, nur würd ihn das
Kränken, und in seiner Kränkung ginge
Mein Verdienst mir flöten.

SILIUS   Du, Ventidius,
Hast das, was, wenn es fehlt, den Kriegsmann
Ununterscheidbar macht von seinem Schwert.

VENTIDIUS Ich melde still, was wir in seinem Namen,
Der magischen Parole, ausgerichtet;
Wie sein Banner, seine gut bezahlte Mannschaft,
Die nie geschlagne Reiterei der Parther
Aus dem Rennen warf.

SILIUS   Wo ist er jetzt?

VENTIDIUS Auf dem Wege nach Athen, wo wir,
So rasch, wie unsre Kriegsbeute es zuläßt,
Vor ihm erscheinen sollen. Vorwärts, marsch!

Zweite Szene

Agrippa, Enobarbus.

AGRIPPA Wie, die Bruderherzen sind getrennt?

ENOBARBUS Mit Pompejus sind sie fertig, er ist weg,
Beim Siegeln sind die drei. Octavia weint,
Weil sie fort aus Rom muß, das umdüstert
Caesar, und der liebe Lepidus
Ist seit dem Pompejus-Fest, sagt Menas,
Seekrank.

AGRIPPA   's ist ein edler Lepidus.

Eno. A very fine one: oh, how he loues *Cæsar*.

Agri. Nay but how deerely he adores *Mark Anthony*.

Eno. *Cæsar*? why he's the Iupiter of men.

Ant. What's *Anthony*, the God of Iupiter?

Eno. Spake you of *Cæsar*? How, the non-pareill?

Agri. Oh *Anthony*, oh thou Arabian Bird!

Eno. Would you praise *Cæsar*, say *Caesar* go no further.

Agr. Indeed he plied them both with excellent praises.

Eno. But he loues *Cæsar* best, yet he loues *Anthony*:
Hoo, Hearts, Tongues, Figure,
Scribes, Bards, Poets, cannot
Thinke speake, cast, write, sing, number: hoo,
His loue to *Anthony*. But as for *Cæsar*,
Kneele downe, kneele downe, and wonder.

Agri. Both he loues.

Eno. They are his Shards, and he their Beetle, so:

This is to horse: Adieu, Noble *Agrippa*.

Agri. Good Fortune worthy Souldier, and farewell.

    Enter Cæsar, Anthony, Lepidus, and Octauia.

Antho. No further Sir.

Cæsar. You take from me a great part of my selfe:
Vse me well in't. Sister, proue such a wife
As my thoughts make thee, and as my farthest Band
Shall passe on thy approofe: most Noble *Anthony*,
Let not the peece of Vertue which is set
Betwixt vs, as the Cyment of our loue
To keepe it builded, be the Ramme to batter
The Fortresse of it: for better might we
Haue lou'd without this meane, if on bothparts
This be not cherisht.

Ant. Make me not offended, in your distrust.

ENOBARBUS Ein ganz besondrer: o, wie liebt er Caesar!

AGRIPPA Nein, wie tief verehrt er Marc Anton!

ENOBARBUS Caesar! Als den Jupiter der Menschheit!

AGRIPPA Wer ist Antonius? Jupiters Abgott.

ENOBARBUS Ihr sprecht von Caesar, wie? Dem Unerreichten?

AGRIPPA Antonius, o du Phönix aus Arabien!

ENOBARBUS Zu Caesars Ruhm sprecht ›Caesar‹, weiter nichts.

AGRIPPA Tatsächlich preist er beide, als gäbs Preise.

ENOBARBUS Das Caesarlob liegt vorn, dichtauf lobt er
    Antonius: Hoo! Nicht Herzen, Zungen, Zahlen,
    Schreiber, Sänger, Dichter können reimen,
    Singen, schreiben, rechnen, sagen, fühlen,
    Hoo! wie er Antonius ehrt. Doch gehts um Caesar,
    Kniet nieder und bewundert.

AGRIPPA   Er schätzt beide.

ENOBARBUS Sie sind ihm Flügeldecken, er ihr Käfer.

                    Signal.

    So: aufgesessen. Wiedersehn, Agrippa.

AGRIPPA Glück dir, wackrer Krieger, und leb wohl.

        Caesar, Antonius, Lepidus, Octavia.

ANTONIUS Nicht weiter, Sir.

CAESAR Ihr nehmt von mir ein Großteil meiner selbst;
    Ehrt mich in ihm. Du, Schwester, sei die Frau,
    Als die mein Herz dich sieht, ich setze viel
    Darauf, daß du es bist. Edler Antonius,
    Laßt nicht die Tugend, zwischen uns gebettet
    Als Mörtel in dem Bauwerk unsrer Liebe,
    Zum Rammbock werden, der die Festung sprengt;
    Denn besser schlossen anders wir das Bündnis,
    Wird seine Mittlerin nicht beidseitig geachtet.

ANTONIUS Dein Mißtraun kränkt mich.

Cæsar. I haue said.

Ant. You shall not finde,
Though you be therein curious, the lest cause
For what you seeme to feare, so the Gods keepe you,
And make the hearts of Romaines serue your ends:
We will heere part.

Cæsar. Farewell my deerest Sister, fare thee well,
The Elements be kind to thee, and make
Thy spirits all of comfort: fare thee well.

Octa. My Noble Brother.

Anth. The Aprill's in her eyes, it is Loues spring,
And these the showers to bring it on: be cheerfull.

Octa. Sir, looke well to my Husbands house: and —

Cæsar. What *Octauia*?

Octa. Ile tell you in your eare.

Ant. Her tongue will not obey her heart, nor can
Her heart informe her tougue.
The Swannes downe feather
That stands vpon the Swell at the full of Tide:
And neither way inclines.

Eno. Will *Cæsar* weepe?

Agr. He ha's a cloud in's face.

Eno. He were the worse for that were he a Horse, so is
he being a man.

Agri. Why *Enobarbus*:
When *Anthony* found *Iulius Cæsar* dead,
He cried almost to roaring: And he wept,
When at Phillippi he found *Brutus* slaine.

Eno. That year indeed, he was trobled with a rheume,

CAESAR Alles ist gesagt.

ANTONIUS Du wirst für das, was du zu fürchten scheinst,
Wie streng dus auch besiehst, nicht den geringsten
Anlaß finden: So, die Götter mögen
Dich erhalten und die Herzen Roms
In deinem Sinne lenken! Wir jedoch,
Wir scheiden hier.

CAESAR Leb wohl, geliebte Schwester, lebe wohl,
Die Elemente mögen deiner Reise
Gewogen sein und dir die Sinne stärken!
Leb nun wohl.

OCTAVIA Leb wohl, mein lieber Bruder!

ANTONIUS In ihren Augen wirds April, der Frühling
Der Liebe naht mit diesen Schauern. Lächle.

OCTAVIA Sir, seht nach meines Mannes Haus; und –

CAESAR Was denn,
Octavia?

OCTAVIA Ich sag es Euch ins Ohr.

ANTONIUS Die Zunge will dem Herzen nicht gehorchen,
Noch kann das Herz ihr sagen, was es wünscht –
Wie eine Schwanenfeder auf der Meerflut,
Wenn sie am höchsten steht, reglos verharrt
Und nirgendhin treibt.

ENOBARBUS Caesar, weint er etwa?

AGRIPPA Er zeigt eine Blässe –

ENOBARBUS Bei 'nem Pferd
Ging's an, doch bei 'nem Mann –

AGRIPPA Wie, Enobarbus?
Antonius, als er Julius Caesar tot sah,
Schrie auf, und schluchzte wild, als bei Philippi
Er Brutus glücklich in den Tod gehetzt.

ENOBARBUS Da plagte ihn 'ne Bindehautentzündung;

What willingly he did confound, he wail'd,
Beleeu't till I weepe too.

Cæsar. No sweet *Octauia,*
You shall heare from me still: the time shall not
Out-go my thinking on you.

Ant. Come Sir, come,
Ile wrastle with you in my strength of loue,
Looke heere I haue you, thus I let you go,
And giue you to the Gods.

Cæsar. Adieu, be happy.

Lep. Let all the number of the Starres giue light
To thy faire way.

Cæsar. Farewell, farewell.   *Kisses Octauia.*
Ant. Farewell.   *Trumpets sound.*   *Exeunt.*

Enter Cleopatra, Charmian, Iras, and Alexas.

Cleo. Where is the Fellow?
Alex. Halfe afeard to come.
Cleo. Go too, go too: Come hither Sir.
          Enter the Messenger as before.
Alex. Good Maiestie: *Herod* of Iury dare not looke
vpon you, but when you are well pleas'd.

Cleo. That *Herods* head, Ile haue: but how? When
Anthony is gone, through whom I might commaund it:
Come thou neere.
Mes. Most gratious Maiestie.

120

Glaubt mir, das mit Vorsatz Ruinierte
Beträufte er, bis ich mitheulte.
CAESAR   Nein,
  Süßeste Octavia, du hörst
  Auch künftig von mir; nicht die Zeit schreibt vor,
  Wie ich an dich denke.
ANTONIUS   Komm, Sir, komm;
  Ich ringe mit dir, was die Liebe angeht,
  Sieh, ich habe dich und lasse dich
  Und gebe dich den Göttern.
CAESAR   Adieu;
  Seid glücklich!
LEPIDUS   Mögen alle Sternlein dir
  Den Weg erhellen.
CAESAR   Lebt nun wohl!
ANTONIUS   Lebt wohl. *Alle ab.*

Dritte Szene

Cleopatra, Charmian, Iras, Alexas, der Bote.

CLEOPATRA Wo ist der Mensch?
ALEXAS   Noch hat er Angst zu kommen.
CLEOPATRA Nur zu, nur zu. Kommt näher, Sir.

ALEXAS   Eu'r Hoheit,
  König Herodes schlüge einen Bogen
  Um Euch in dieser Laune.
CLEOPATRA   Seinen Kopf,
  Ich hätt ihn gern, doch wenn Antonius fehlt,
  Wem sag ich, bring mir den? Du kommst jetzt näher.
BOTE Gnädigste Majestät!

Cleo. Did'st thou behold *Octauia*?

Mes. I dread Queene.
Cleo. Where?
Mes. Madam in Rome, I lookt her in the face: and
saw her led betweene her Brother, and *Marke Anthony*.

Cleo. Is she as tall as me?
Mes. She is not Madam.
Cleo. Didst heare her speake?
Is she shrill tongu'd or low?
Mes. Madam, I heard her speake, she is low voic'd.
Cleo. That's not so good: he cannot like her long.
Char. Like her? Oh *Isis*: 'tis impossible.
Cleo. I thinke so *Charmian*: dull of tongue, & dwarfish
What Maiestie is in her gate, remember
If ere thou look'st on Maiestie.
Mes. She creepes: her motion, & her station are as one.
She shewes a body, rather then a life,
A Statue, then a Breather.

Cleo. Is this certaine?
Mes. Or I haue no obseruance.
Cha. Three in Egypt cannot make better note.

Cleo. He's very knowing, I do perceiu't,
There's nothing in her yet.
The Fellow ha's good iudgement.
Char. Excellent.
Cleo. Guesse at her yeares, I prythee.
Mess. Madam, she was a widdow.

CLEOPATRA   Hast du Octavia
   Gesehn?
BOTE   Ja, hohe Herrin.
CLEOPATRA   Wo?
BOTE   In Rom;
   Ich sah sie, als sie zwischen ihrem Bruder
   Und Marc Anton an mir vorüberging.
CLEOPATRA Ist sie so groß wie ich?
BOTE   Das ist sie nicht.
CLEOPATRA Hörstest du sie sprechen? Spricht sie schrill
   Oder tief?
BOTE   Ich hört es, Madam. Tief.
CLEOPATRA Das klingt nicht gut: Dann mag er sie nicht lang.
CHARMIAN Sie mögen? Nein, bei Isis! Ganz unmöglich.
CLEOPATRA Ich denke auch: so zungenlahm und zwergenhaft!
   Liegt Majestät in ihrem Gang? Besinn dich,
   Wenn du je Majestät gesehn!
BOTE   Sie kriecht:
   Man weiß nie, geht sie oder steht sie still:
   Sie scheint mehr totenstarr als lebend, mehr
   Standbild als beseeltes Wesen.
CLEOPATRA   Stimmt das?
BOTE So wahr ich Augen habe.
CHARMIAN   Drei Ägypter
   Sehn nicht so scharf wie dieser eine hier.
CLEOPATRA Er ist sehr tüchtig, ich begreife langsam,
   An ihr ist nichts. Der junge Mensch hat ein
   Sehr sichres Urteil.
CHARMIAN   Wirklich exzellent.
CLEOPATRA Wie alt wird sie wohl sein?
BOTE   Sie war schon Witwe,
   Madam.

Cleo. Widdow? *Charmian*, hearke.

Mes. And I do thinke she's thirtie.

Cle. Bear'st thou her face in mind? is't long or round?

Mess. Round, euen to faultinesse.

Cleo. For the most part too, they are foolish that are
    so. Her haire what colour?

Mess. Browne Madam: and her forehead
    As low as she would wish it.

Cleo. There's Gold for thee,
    Thou must not take my former sharpenesse ill,
    I will employ thee backe againe: I finde thee
    Most fit for businesse. Go, make thee ready,
    Our Letters are prepar'd.

Char. A proper man.

Cleo. Indeed he is so: I repent me much
    That so I harried him. Why me think's by him,
    This Creature's no such thing.

Char. Nothing Madam.

Cleo. The man hath seene some Maiesty, and should
    know.

Char. Hath he seene Maiestie? *Isis* else defend: and
    seruing you so long.

Cleopa. I haue one thing more to aske him yet good
    Charmian: but 'tis no matter, thou shalt bring him to me
    where I will write; all may be well enough.

Char. I warrant you Madam.   *Exeunt.*

CLEOPATRA Witwe? Denk dir, Charmian.

BOTE Ich schätze sie auf dreißig.

CLEOPATRA Und ihr Gesicht? Mehr länglich oder rund?

BOTE Kreisrund.

CLEOPATRA   Das deutet meist auf Einfalt hin.
   Das Haar hat welche Farbe?

BOTE   Braun, die Stirn
   Kann niedriger nicht sein.

CLEOPATRA   Hier hast du Gold.
   Nimm mir den Ausbruch von vorhin nicht übel,
   Ich sende dich mit Aufträgen zurück;
   Du bist als Bote, scheint mir, sehr geeignet.
   Geh, mach dich bereit, unsere Briefe
   Sind abgefaßt.

CHARMIAN   Ein hübscher Mann.

CLEOPATRA Das ist er in der Tat: es reut mich tief, daß ich
   Ihn so mißhandelt habe. Ihm zufolge
   Kann das Geschöpf nicht viel bedeuten.

CHARMIAN   Gar nichts.

CLEOPATRA Der Mann kennt Majestät und muß es wissen.

CHARMIAN Der Mann kennt Majestät? Bewahr mich Isis!
   Wie denn auch nicht, so lang in Eurem Dienst.

CLEOPATRA Ich muß ihn eins noch fragen, liebe Charmian:
   Es ist nicht wichtig, führ ihn zu mir, wo
   Ich schreibe; noch steht alles nicht so schlecht.

CHARMIAN Da bin ich sicher, Madam.

Enter Anthony and Octauia.

Ant. Nay, nay *Octauia*, not onely that,
　　That were excusable, that and thousands more
　　Of semblable import, but he hath wag'd
　　New Warres 'gainst *Pompey*. Made his will, and read it,
　　To publicke eare, spoke scantly of me,
　　When perforce he could not
　　But pay me tearmes of Honour: cold and sickly
　　He vented then most narrow measure: lent me,
　　When the best hint was giuen him: he not look't,
　　Or did it from his teeth.
Octaui. Oh my good Lord,
　　Beleeue not all, or if you must beleeue,
　　Stomacke not all. A more vnhappie Lady,
　　If this deuision chance, ne're stood betweene
　　Praying for both parts:
　　The good Gods wil mocke me presently,
　　When I shall pray: Oh blesse my Lord, and Husband,
　　Vndo that prayer, by crying out as loud,
　　Oh blesse my Brother. Husband winne, winne Brother,
　　Prayes, and distroyes the prayer, no midway
　　'Twixt these extreames at all.

Ant. Gentle *Octauia*,
　　Let your best loue draw to that point which seeks
　　Best to preserue it: if I loose mine Honour,
　　I loose my selfe: better I were not yours
　　Then your so branchlesse. But as you requested,
　　Your selfe shall go between's, the meane time Lady,

Vierte Szene

Antonius, Octavia.

ANTONIUS Nein, nein, Octavia, nicht das allein –
Das wär entschuldbar, das und tausend weitre
Stiche dieser Art – nur hat er neu
Gegen den Pompejus Krieg geführt,
Sein Testament gemacht und laut verlesen,
Mich kaum erwähnt, und sieht er sich gezwungen,
Mich mit Respekt zu nennen, tut er's kalt
Und widerwillig; setzt mich, wo er kann, herab.
Was ich ihn wissen lasse, liest er nicht
Oder mißversteht's.
OCTAVIA   O teurer Herr,
Glaubt nur nicht alles, oder, müßt Ihr glauben,
Nehmt es nicht schwer. Noch nie stand eine Frau,
Wenn dieser Bruch geschieht, unsel'ger zwischen
Zwei Partein und betete für beide:
Die guten Götter werden meiner spotten,
Wenn ich sie bitte ›Segnet den Gemahl!‹
Und dies Gebet auslösch, indem ich schreie
›Segnet den Bruder mir!‹ Ob der Gemahl,
Ob mir der Bruder siegt, Gebet verheert
Gebet, und zwischen den Extremen
Führt kein Mittelweg hindurch.
ANTONIUS   Octavia,
Laß deine Liebe da, wo sie am höchsten
Geachtet wird, verweilen: ohne Ehre
Bin ich nicht ich und wäre besser dein nicht,
Als dein und so gestutzt. Du aber magst,
Ganz wie du es dir wünschst, dazwischen gehn,

Ile raise the preparation of a Warre
Shall staine your Brother, make your soonest hast,
So your desires are yours.
Oct. Thanks to my Lord,
The Ioue of power make me most weake, most weake,
You reconciler: Warres 'twixt you twaine would be,
As if the world should cleaue, and that slaine men
Should soader vp the Rift.

Anth. When it appeeres to you where this begins,
Turne your displeasure that way, for our faults
Can neuer be so equall, that your loue
Can equally moue with them. Prouide your going,
Choose your owne company, and command what cost
Your heart he's mind too.   *Exeunt.*

Enter Enobarbus, and Eros.

Eno. How now Friend *Eros*?
Eros. Ther's strange Newes come Sir.
Eno. What man?
Ero. *Cæsar* & *Lepidus* haue made warres vpon *Pompey*.

Eno. This is old, what is the successe?
Eros. *Cæsar* hauing made vse of him in the warres
'gainst *Pompey*: presently denied him riuality, would not
let him partake in the glory of the action, and not resting
here, accuses him of Letters he had formerly wrote to
Pompey. Vpon his owne appeale seizes him, so the poore
third is vp, till death enlarge his Confine.

Indes ich einen Krieg in Angriff nehme,
Der rostig machen wird des Bruders Glanz:
Eil dich, und du hast, was du gewollt.
OCTAVIA Dank Euch. Der mächtigste der Götter mache
Die Schwächste, mich, die Aller-, Allerschwächste,
Euch zur Versöhnerin! Krieg zwischen Euch,
Das wär, als ob die Welt sich spalten sollte,
Und erschlagne Männer dazu dienen,
Den Abgrund aufzufüllen.
ANTONIUS Wenn es dir dämmert, wo dies anfängt, wende
Dahin den Unmut auch, denn unsre Schuld,
Sie kann so gleich nicht sein, daß deine Liebe
Beiden gleich gehören kann. Geh du auf Reisen
Such dir Gesellschaft und sei so verschwendrisch,
Wie's dir beliebt.

Fünfte Szene

Enobarbus, Eros.

ENOBARBUS Wie geht es, Freund Eros?
EROS Es gibt seltsame Neuigkeiten, Sir.
ENOBARBUS Welche, Mann?
EROS Caesar und Lepidus haben den Pompejus bekriegt
und geschlagen.
ENOBARBUS Das ist alt. Was weiter?
EROS Obwohl Caesar den Lepidus zum Sieg über Pompejus
gebraucht hat, verweigert er ihm jetzt alle Rechte, will
den Ruhm des Feldzugs nicht mit ihm teilen und geht so
weit, ihn zu beschuldigen, er habe dem Pompejus Briefe
geschrieben; auf diese selbstgemachte Anklage hin läßt er
Lepidus festnehmen, und nun sitzt der arme Dritte, bis

Eno. Then would thou hadst a paire of chaps no more,
   and throw betweene them all the food thou hast, they'le
   grinde the other. Where's *Anthony*?
Eros. He's walking in the garden thus, and spurnes
   The rush that lies before him. Cries Foole *Lepidus*,
   And threats the throate of that his Officer,
   That murdred *Pompey*.
Eno. Our great Nauies rig'd.
Eros. For Italy and *Cæsar*, more *Domitius*,
   My Lord desires you presently: my Newes
   I might haue told heareafter.
Eno.'Twillbe naught, but let it be: bring me to *Anthony*.

Eros. Come Sir,   *Exeunt.*

Enter Agrippa, Mecenas, and Cæsar.

Cæs. Contemning Rome he ha's done all this, & more
   In Alexandria: heere's the manner of't:
   I'th'Market-place on a Tribunall siluer'd,
   Cleopatra and himselfe in Chaires of Gold
   Were publikely enthron'd: at the feet, sat
   Cæsarion whom they call my Fathers Sonne,
   And all the vnlawfull issue, that their Lust
   Since then hath made betweene them. Vnto her,
   He gaue the stablishment of Egypt, made her
   Of lower Syria, Cyprus, Lydia, absolute Queene.

der Tod ihn befreit.

ENOBARBUS Jetzt hast du, Welt, zwei Kinnbacken, nicht mehr,
Schieb alles Futter, das du hast, dazwischen,
Sie knirschen aufeinander. Und Antonius?

EROS Stapft herum im Garten – so, tritt Äste,
Schreit ›Lepidus, du Narr!‹ und droht, er werde
Den Offizier erwürgen, der Pompejus
Mordete.

ENOBARBUS Die Flotte setzt die Segel.

EROS Gegen Caesar und Italien. Hört, Domitius,
Der Herr verlangt Euch dringend: mein Geplapper
Hätt ich verschieben solln.

ENOBARBUS   Er wird nichts wollen,
Aber sei's drum. Bring mich zu Antonius.

EROS Kommt, Sir.

Sechste Szene

Caesar, Agrippa, Maecenas.

CAESAR Verachtung Roms spricht laut aus seinem Tun
In Alexandria: hört Näheres.
Ein silbernes Gerüst war auf dem Platz
Errichtet, auf zwei goldnen Stühlen thronten
Cleopatra und er vor allem Volk:
Zu ihren Füßen saß Caesarion,
Den sie den Sohn von meinem Vater nennen,
Und all die Brut, die ungesetzliche,
Die Wollust ihnen angeschafft. Und er
Gab ihr Ägyptens Unabhängigkeit
Zurück, er setzte über Zypern, Lydien
Sowie das untre Syrien sie als die

Mece. This in the publike eye?

Caesar. I'th'common shew place, where they exercise,
    His Sonnes hither proclaimed the King of Kings,
    Great Media, Parthia, and Armenia
    He gaue to *Alexander*. To *Ptolomy* he assign'd,
    Syria, Silicia, and Phœnetia: she
    In th'abiliments of the Goddesse *Isis*
    That day appeer'd, and oft before gaue audience,
    As 'tis reported so.
Mece. Let Rome be thus inform'd.

Agri. Who queazie with his insolence already,
    Will their good thoughts call from him.
Cæsar. The people knowes it,
    And haue now receiu'd his accusations.
Agri. Who does he accuse?
Cæsar. *Cæsar*, and that hauing in Cicilie
    Sextus Pompeius spoil'd, we had not rated him
    His part o'th'Isle. Then does he say, he lent me
    Some shipping vnrestor'd. Lastly, he frets
    That *Lepidus* of the Triumpherate, should be depos'd,
    And being that, we detaine all his Reuenue.

Agri. Sir, this should be answer'd.
Cæsar. 'Tis done already, and the Messenger gone:
    I haue told him *Lepidus* was growne too cruell,
    That he his high Authority abus'd,
    And did deserue his change: for what I haue conquer'd,
    I grant him part: but then in his Armenia,

Absolute Herrscherin.

MAECENAS   All das
Tat er ganz öffentlich, vor aller Augen?

CAESAR Auf dem Paradeplatz, wo sonst marschiert wird.
Zu Königen der Könige ernannte
Er seine Söhne; Alexander gab er
Groß-Medien, Parthien und Armenien; Syrien,
Cilicien und Phönizien überschrieb er
Dem Ptolemäus. Sie erschien dazu noch
Verkleidet wie die Göttin Isis, und das nicht
Zum ersten Mal, sagt der Bericht.

MAECENAS   Ganz Rom
Soll davon wissen.

AGRIPPA   Seiner Frechheit satt
Wird es ihm alle Sympathie entziehen.

CAESAR Die Menschen wissen es; und er hat ihnen
Anklagen zugesandt.

AGRIPPA   Wen klagt er an?

CAESAR Caesar, deshalb, weil wir auf Sizilien
Pompejus schlugen und ihm seinen Teil
Der Insel vorenthielten. Ferner sagt er,
Er habe Schiffe ausgeliehn, die wir ihm schulden.
Auch regt es ihn auf, daß Lepidus
Aus dem Triumvirat befördert wurde,
Und wir, als das geschehn war, sein Vermögen
Beschlagnahmten.

MAECENAS   Sir, dies will eine Antwort.

CAESAR Ist schon erteilt, der Bote unterwegs.
Ich schrieb, daß Lepidus zu grausam wurde
Und seine Macht mißbrauchte, darum hab er
Die Kaltstellung verdient: ich wolle, was ich
Hinzugewann, gern teilen, doch verlang ich

And other of his conquer'd Kingdoms, I demand the like

Mec. Hee'l neuer yeeld to that.
Cæs. Nor must not then be yeelded to in this.
    Enter Octauia with her Traine.
Octa. Haile *Cæsar*, and my L. haile most deere *Cæsar*.
Cæsar. That euer I should call thee Cast-away.
Octa. You haue not call'd me so, nor haue you cause.
Cæs. Why haue you stoln vpon vs thus? you come not
 Like *Cæsars* Sister, The wife of *Anthony*
 Should haue an Army for an Vsher, and
 The neighes of Horse to tell of her approach,
 Long ere she did appeare. The trees by'th'way
 Should haue borne men, and expectation fainted,
 Longing for what it had not. Nay, the dust
 Should haue ascended to the Roofe of Heauen,
 Rais'd by your populous Troopes: But you are come
 A Market-maid to Rome, and haue preuented
 The ostentation of our loue; which left vnshewne,
 Is often left vnlou'd: we should haue met you
 By Sea, and Land, supplying euery Stage
 With an augmented greeting.

Octa. Good my Lord,
 To come thus was I not constrain'd, but did it
 On my free-will. My Lord *Marke Anthony*,
 Hearing that you prepar'd for Warre, acquainted
 My greeued eare withall: whereon I begg'd
 His pardon for returne.

Cæs. Which soone he granted,
 Being an abstract 'tweene his Lust, and him.

In Armenien und seinen andern Reichen
Dies auch von ihm.

MAECENAS   Das räumt er niemals ein.

CAESAR So wird in diesem ihm nichts eingeräumt.

Octavia.

OCTAVIA Heil, Caesar, dir! Ihr Herrn! Heil, liebster Caesar!

CAESAR Daß ich dich je Verstoßne nennen müßte!

OCTAVIA Du nanntest mich nicht so, noch hast du Grund.

CAESAR Was stiehlst du dich so zu uns? Du kommst nicht
Wie Caesars Schwester: des Antonius' Weib,
Muß nicht ein Heer ihr Herold sein und Schnauben
Von Pferden uns verkünden, daß sie naht,
Lang eh sie selbst erscheint? Am Weg die Bäume
Müßten Menschen tragen, die, erwartend,
Was erst noch kommt, schon wie von Sinnen sind.
Zum Himmelsdach muß sich der Staub erheben,
Vom Stiefel deiner Truppen aufgewirbelt:
Doch du kommst wie ein Marktweib bloß nach Rom,
Vermeidend die Bezeugung unsrer Liebe,
Die, wenn sie nicht gezeigt wird, oft als gar nicht
Vorhanden gilt: wir hätten dich zur See,
Wie auch an Land begrüßen müssen mit
Sich steigernden Empfängen.

OCTAVIA   Lieber Herr,
So herzukommen war ich nicht gezwungen,
Ich tat's aus freiem Willen. Denn kaum hatte
Marc Anton vernommen, daß Ihr rüstet,
Da ließ er schon mein armes Ohr es wissen;
Worauf ich ihn um die Erlaubnis bat,
Zurückzukehren.

CAESAR   Die er gerne gab,
Weil, was von seiner Lust ihn trennt, verschwand.

Octa. Do not say so, my Lord.

Cæs. I haue eyes vpon him,
  And his affaires come to me on the wind: wher is he now?

Octa. My Lord, in Athens.

Cæsar. No my most wronged Sister, *Cleopatra*
  Hath nodded him to her. He hath giuen his Empire
  Vp to a Whore, who now are leuying
  The Kings o'th'earth for Warre. He hath assembled,
  Bochus the King of Lybia, *Archilaus*
  Of Cappadocia, *Philadelphos* King
  Of Paphlagonia: the Thracian King *Adullas*,
  King *Manchus* of Arabia, King of Pont,
  Herod of Iewry, *Mithridates* King
  Of Comageat, *Polemen* and *Amintas*,
  The Kings of Mede, and Licoania,
  With a more larger List of Scepters.

Octa. Aye me most wretched,
  That haue my heart parted betwixt two Friends,
  That does afflict each other.   (breaking forth

Cæs. Welcom hither: your Letters did with-holde our
  Till we perceiu'd both how you were wrong led,
  And we in negligent danger: cheere your heart,
  Be you not troubled with the time, which driues
  O're your content, these strong necessities,
  But let determin'd things to destinie
  Hold vnbewayl'd their way. Welcome to Rome,
  Nothing more deere to me: You are abus'd
  Beyond the marke of thought: and the high Gods
  To do you Iustice, makes his Ministers
  Of vs, and those that loue you. Best of comfort,

OCTAVIA Sprecht nicht so.

CAESAR   Ich hab ein Auge auf ihn,
Und was er treibt, der Wind erzählt es mir.
Wo, glaubst du, ist er?

OCTAVIA   In Athen, Mylord.

CAESAR Nein, sehr betrog'ne Schwester, denn es hat ihn
Cleopatra zu sich gewunken. Er,
Sein Reich hat er an diese Hure abgetreten,
Nun werben sie zum Kriege wider mich
Die Könige der Erde. Einberufen
Hat er Bocchus, Libyens König, Archelaus
Von Cappadozien, Philadelphos, König
Von Paphlagonien; Thraziens Adallas,
Malchus von Arabien, Herodes
Von Judäa, Mithridates, König
Von Comagene, Polemon von Medien,
Amyntas, König von Lycaonía
Und viele Szepter mehr.

OCTAVIA   Ach, ich Verworfne,
Deren Herz geteilt schlägt für zwei Freunde,
Die sich bekriegen müssen.

CAESAR   Sei willkommen:
Nur deine Briefe bremsten noch den Ausbruch,
Bis wir nicht nur, wie man dich hinterging,
Erkannten, sondern auch was wir gefährlich
Schleifen ließen. Heitere dich auf:
Laß nicht die Zeit in ihrem Lauf dich kränken,
Die, was du wünschst, notwendig überrollt,
Das Vorbeschloss'ne laß zu seinem Ziel
Du klaglos gehn. Willkommen hier in Rom,
Mir teurer als zuvor. Du wardst mißbraucht,
Ganz unerdenklich, und zu Helfern machen

And euer welcom to vs.

Agrip. Welcome Lady.
Mec. Welcome deere Madam,
    Each heart in Rome does loue and pitty you,
    Onely th'adulterous *Anthony*, most large
    In his abhominations, turnes you off,
    And giues his potent Regiment to a Trull
    That noyses it against vs.
Octa. Is it so sir?
Cæs. Most certaine: Sister welcome: pray you
    Be euer knowne to patience. My deer'st Sister.   *Exeunt*

Enter Cleopatra, and Enobarbus.

Cleo. I will be euen with thee, doubt it not.
Eno. But why, why, why?
Cleo. Thou hast forespoke my being in these warres,
    And say'st it is not fit.
Eno. Well: is it, is it.
Cleo. If not, denounc'd against vs, why should not
    we be there in person.
Enob. Well, I could reply: if wee should serue with
    Horse and Mares together, the Horse were meerly lost:
    the Mares would beare a Soldiour and his Horse.

Cleo. What is't you say?
Enob. Your presence needs must puzle *Anthony*,
    Take from his heart, take from his Braine, from's time,

Die großen Götter, das zu sühnen, uns
Und alle, die dich lieben. Fasse dich,
Und noch einmal willkommen.
AGRIPPA   Willkommen, Lady.
MAECENAS Ein jedes Herz in Rom liebt und beklagt Euch.
Nur Marc Anton stößt ehebrecherisch,
Ein Riese an Verkommenheit, Euch von sich,
Und überläßt sein Regiment 'ner Dirne,
Die gegen uns mobil macht.

OCTAVIA   Ist das wahr, Sir?
CAESAR Aber ja. Willkommen, Schwester: bitte,
Sei geduldig. Meine liebste Schwester!

Siebte Szene

Cleopatra, Enobarbus.

CLEOPATRA Ich rechne mit dir ab, verlaß dich drauf.
ENOBARBUS Warum denn nur, warum, warum?
CLEOPATRA Ging es nach dir, käm ich nicht mit zum Krieg,
Weils dir nicht passend scheint.
ENOBARBUS   Ja, ist's das, ist's das?
CLEOPATRA Uns auch ward Krieg erklärt, und selbst
Warum sich da nicht zeigen?   [wenn nicht,
ENOBARBUS   Ich würd sagen,
Ziehn Hengst und Stute in die Schlacht, so ist
Der Hengst umsonst; besteigt ihn auch der Reiter,
Steigt er mitsamt dem Reiter auf die Stute.
CLEOPATRA Was murmelst du?
ENOBARBUS   Daß Eure Gegenwart
Antonius verwirrt, ihm Herz und Hirn

What should not then be spar'd. He is already
Traduc'd for Leuity, and 'tis said in Rome,
That *Photinus* an Eunuch, and your Maides
Mannage this warre.

Cleo. Sinke Rome, and their tongues rot
That speake against vs. A Charge we beare i'th'Warre,
And as the president of my Kingdome will
Appeare there for a man. Speake not against it,
I will not stay behinde.

      Enter Anthony and Camidias.

Eno. Nay I haue done, here comes the Emperor.

Ant. Is it not strange *Camidius*,
That from Tarrentum, and Brandusium,
He could so quickly cut the Ionian Sea,
And take in Troine. You haue heard on't (Sweet?)

Cleo. Celerity is neuer more admir'd,
Then by the negligent.

Ant. A good rebuke,
Which might haue well becom'd the best of men
To taunt at slacknesse. *Camidius*, wee
Will fight with him by Sea.

Cleo. By Sea, what else?

Cam. Why will my Lord, do so?

Ant. For that he dares vs too't.

Enob. So hath my Lord, dar'd him to single fight.

Cam. I, and to wage this Battell at Pharsalia,
Where *Cæsar* fought with *Pompey*. But these offers
Which serue not for his vantage, he shakes off,
And so should you.

Enob. Your Shippes are not well mann'd,
Your Marriners are Muliters, Reapers, people

Und Zeit ihm stiehlt, wo er sie nötig braucht.
Er wird des Leichtsinns ohnehin bezichtigt,
Man raunt in Rom, Photinus, der Eunuch,
Und Eure Zofen führten diesen Krieg.

CLEOPATRA Versenkt doch Rom, dann fault die Zunge derer,
Die uns jetzt lästern! Ich bezahl den Krieg,
Und werd als Oberhaupt Ägyptens meinen
Mann stehn. Widersprich mir nicht, ich
Bleibe nicht zurück.

Antonius, Canidius

ENOBARDUS　　　　Gut, ich gebs auf.
Der Imperator kommt.

ANTONIUS　　　　Seltsam, Canidius,
Daß von Tarent er und Brundisium
So schnell das Ion'sche Meer durchschneiden konnte
Und Toryn nehmen. Hörtest dus, Geliebte?

CLEOPATRA Das rasche Tun bestaunt am meisten der,
Der gerne zaudert.

ANTONIUS　　　　Gut, der Rüffel, wert,
Ihn aus dem Mund des besten Manns zu hören,
Zu unsrer Trägheit Spott. Canidius, wir
Greifen ihn zur See an.

CLEOPATRA　　　　Zur See, wo sonst?

CANIDIUS Warum das, Mylord?

ANTONIUS　　　　Weil er das fordert.

ENOBARBUS So habt Ihr zum Zweikampf ihn gefordert.

CANIDIUS Ja, und bei Pharsalia zur Schlacht
Wo er Pompejus niederwarf. Doch er
Sah seinen Nachteil, lehnte beides ab:
Tut es ihm nach.

ENOBARBUS　　　　Die Schiffe sind nicht voll
Bemannt, den Dienst tun Eseltreiber, Landvolk,

Ingrost by swift Impresse. In *Cæsars* Fleete,
Are those, that often haue 'gainst *Pompey* fought,
Their shippes are yare, yours heauy: no disgrace
Shall fall you for refusing him at Sea,
Being prepar'd for Land.
Ant. By Sea, by Sea.
Eno. Most worthy Sir, you therein throw away
The absolute Soldiership you haue by Land,
Distract your Armie, which doth most consist
Of Warre-markt-footmen, leaue vnexecuted
Your owne renowned knowledge, quite forgoe
The way which promises assurance, and
Giue vp your selfe meerly to chance and hazard,
From firme Securitie.
Ant. Ile fight at Sea.
Cleo. I haue sixty Sailes, *Caesar* none better.

Ant. Our ouer-plus of shipping will we burne,
And with the rest full mann'd, from th'head of Action
Beate th'approaching *Cæsar*. But if we faile,

We then can doo't at Land.   *Enter a Messenger.*
Thy Businesse?
Mes. The Newes is true, my Lord, he is descried,
Cæsar ha's taken Toryne.

Ant, Can he be there in person? 'Tis impossible
Strange, that his power should be. *Camidius*,
Our nineteene Legions thou shalt hold by Land,
And our twelue thousand Horse. Wee'l to our Ship,
Away my *Thetis*.

Leute, schnell dazu gepreßt. In Caesars Flotte
Sind, die Pompejus schlugen, ihre Schiffe
Leicht, die Euren ungefüg; es fällt
Nicht Schande auf Euch, weigert Ihr, zu Lande
Stark, die Seeschlacht ihm.

ANTONIUS   Zur See, zur See.

ENOBARBUS Mein edler Feldherr, so verschenkt Ihr selbst
Die absolute Vorherrschaft an Land,
Verwirrt das Heer aus kriegserprobtem Fußvolk,
Schiebt Euer eignes reiches Wissen weg,
Verfehlt den Weg, der Sicherheit verspricht,
Und setzt auf puren Zufall und auf Kriegsglück,
Statt auf Strategie.

ANTONIUS   Ich greif zur See an.

CLEOPATRA Ich habe sechzig Segel, bessre hat
Auch Caesar nicht.

ANTONIUS   Die überzähl'gen Schiffe
Verbrennen wir, und mit den voll bemannten
Schlagen wir bei Aktium, sobald er
Aufkreuzt, Caesar. Geht das schief, dann schnappen
Wir ihn zu Land.   *Ein Bote.*
                    Was bringst du uns?

BOTE   Mylord,
Die Nachricht ist bestätigt, man hat ihn
Gesehen. Caesar selbst nahm Toryn ein.

ANTONIUS Kann er persönlich dort sein? 's ist unmöglich;
Daß seine Truppen da sind, ist schon viel.
Canidius, die neunzehn Legionen
Stellst du an Land auf, und desgleichen unsre
Zwölftausend Reiter. Wir selbst gehn an Bord,
Komm, meine Thetis.

Enter a Soldiour.

How now worthy Souldier?

Soul. Oh Noble Emperor, do not fight by Sea,
  Trust not to rotten plankes: Do you misdoubt
  This Sword, and these my Wounds; let th'Egyptians
  And the Phœnicians go a ducking: wee
  Haue vs'd to conquer standing on the earth,
  And fighting foot to foot.

Ant. Well, well, away.   *exit Ant. Cleo. & Enob.*

Soul. By *Hercules* I thinke I am i'th' right.

Cam. Souldier thou art: but his whole action growes
  Not in the power on't: so our Leaders leade,
  And we are Womens men.

Soul. You keepe by Land the Legions and the Horse
  whole, do you not?

Ven. Marcus Octauius, Marcus Iusteus,
  Publicola, and *Celius,* are for Sea:
  But we keepe whole by Land. This speede of *Cæsars*
  Carries beyond beleefe.

Soul. While he was yet in Rome,
  His power went out in such distractions,
  As beguilde all Spies.

Cam. Who's his Lieutenant, heare you?

Soul. They say, one *Towrus.*

Cam. Well, I know the man.

                    Enter a Messenger.

Mes. The Emperor cals *Camidius.*

Cam. With Newes the times with Labour,
  And throwes forth each minute, some.   *exeunt*

Ein Soldat.

ANTONIUS   Nun, mein tapfrer Krieger?

SOLDAT Mein edler General, kämpft nicht zur See,
  Vertraut nicht morschen Planken: zweifelt Ihr
  An diesem Schwert und meinen Narben? Laßt
  Ägypter Ente spielen und Phönizier:
  Wir stehn mit beiden Beinen auf der Erde
  Und fechten Fuß an Fuß.

ANTONIUS   Gut, gut, hinweg!

SOLDAT Bei Herkules, ich denk, ich habe Recht.

ENOBARBUS Du hast, Soldat: doch was geschieht, hat Gründe
  Anderswo: der Lenker wird gelenkt,
  Und wir sind Weiberknechte.

SOLDAT   Ihr befehligt
  Die Legionen und die Reiterei?

CANIDIUS Marcus Octavius, Marcus Justeius,
  Publicola und Caelius sind zur See:
  Ich warte ab zu Land. Es ist unglaublich,
  Wie schnell Caesar ist.

SOLDAT   Von Rom aus zog er
  Die Truppen so verteilt ab, daß er alle
  Späher täuschte.

CANIDIUS   Hörtest du, wer ihm
  Als Adjutant dient?

SOLDAT   Ein gewisser Taurus,
  Heißt es.

CANIDIUS   Allerdings, ich kenn den Mann.

Der Bote.

BOTE Der General verlangt Canidius.

CANIDIUS Mit Neuigkeiten trächtig ist die Zeit,
  Und Minute für Minute wirft sie.

Enter Cæsar with his Army, marching.

Cæs. Towrus?
Tow. My Lord.
Cæs. Strike not by Land,
    Keepe whole, prouoke not Battaile
    Till we haue done at Sea. Do not exceede
    The Prescript of this Scroule: Our fortune lyes
    Vpon this iumpe.   *exit.*

Enter Anthony, and Enobarbus.

Ant. Set we our Squadrons on yond side o'th'Hill,
    In eye of *Cæsars* battaile, from which place
    We may the number of the Ships behold,
    And so proceed accordingly.   *exit.*

*Camidius Marcheth with his Land Army one way ouer the
stage, and Towrus the Lieutenant of Cæsar the other way:
    After their going in, is heard the noise of a Sea-fight.
        Alarum. Enter Enobarbus and Scarus.*

Eno. Naught, naught, al naught, I can behold no longer:
    Thantoniad, the Egyptian Admirall,
    With all their sixty flye, and turne the Rudder:
    To see't, mine eyes are blasted.

Achte Szene

Caesar, Taurus.

CAESAR Taurus!
TAURUS Mylord?
CAESAR Stoßt nicht an Land vor, meidet das Gefecht,
Bis zum Sieg zur See, und haltet euch
An diese Order: unser aller Schicksal
Hängt davon ab.

Neunte Szene

Antonius, Enobarbus.

ANTONIUS Postier mir die Schwadronen hügelaufwärts,
In Sicht von Caesars Truppen, von wo aus
Wir die Zahl der Schiffe überblicken
Und entsprechend vorgehn können.

Zehnte Szene

Enobarbus

ENOBARBUS Nichts, aus, vorbei, ich kanns nicht mehr
Mitansehn: die Antoniad, Ägyptens
Flaggschiff, mit ihr alle sechzig, fliehn
Und drehn das Ruder: das zu sehn, brennt mir

Enter Scarrus.

Scar. Gods, & Goddesses, all the whol synod of them!

Eno. What's thy passion.

Scar. The greater Cantle of the world, is lost
　　With very ignorance, we haue kist away
　　Kingdomes, and Prouinces.

Eno. How appeares the Fight?

Scar. On our side, like the Token'd Pestilence,
　　Where death is sure. Yon ribaudred Nagge of Egypt,
　　(Whom Leprosie o're-take) i'th'midst o'th'fight,
　　When vantage like a payre of Twinnes appear'd
　　Both as the same, or rather ours the elder;
　　(The Breeze vpon her) like a Cow in Iune,
　　Hoists Sailes, and flyes.

Eno. That I beheld:
　　Mine eyes did sicken at the sight, and could not
　　Indure a further view.

Scar. She once being looft,
　　The Noble ruine of her Magicke, *Anthony*,
　　Claps on his Sea-wing, and (like a doting Mallard)
　　Leauing the Fight in heighth, flyes after her:
　　I neuer saw an Action of such shame;
　　Experience, Man-hood, Honor, ne're before,
　　Did violate so it selfe.

Enob. Alacke, alacke.

Enter Camidius.

Cam. Our Fortune on the Sea is out of breath,
　　And sinkes most lamentably. Had our Generall

Die Augen weg.

SCARUS   Ihr Göttinnen und Götter,
Und der ganze Rat!
ENOBARBUS   Was bringt dich auf?
SCARUS Das größte Stück der Welt ist weg, verloren
Durch pure Dummheit, fortgeküßt sind uns
Die Königreiche und Provinzen.
EROS   Wie
Steht die Schlacht?
SCARUS   Für uns so tödlich wie
Die Pest. Ägyptens Afterkönigin –
Hol sie der Aussatz! – mitten in der Schlacht,
Der Vorteil war wie Zwillinge sich gleich
Auf beiden Seiten, unsrer fast der ältre,
Als hätt 'ne Bremse sie gestochen, zieht die Kuh
Die Segel auf und flieht.
ENOBARBUS   Das sah ich: krank
Wurden mir die Augen von dem Anblick
Und wollten nicht mehr hinsehn.
SCARUS   Sie liegt kaum
Am Wind, da spreizt auch schon die edle
Ruine ihres Zaubers, Marc Anton,
Gleich einem brünst'gen Enterich die Schwingen
Und flattert auf dem Höhepunkt der Schlacht
Ihr nach: ich weiß von keiner Tat, die so
Beschämt. Noch nie hat sich Erfahrung, Ehre,
Männlichkeit so selbst verstümmelt.
ENOBARBUS   Weh uns!

Canidius.

CANIDIUS Zur See geht unserm Glück der Atem aus,
Es sinkt höchst jämmerlich. Wär unser General

Bin what he knew himselfe, it had gone well:
Oh his ha's giuen example for our flight,
Most grossely by his owne.

Enob. I, are you thereabouts? Why then goodnight
indeede.

Cam. Toward Peloponnesus are they fled.

Scar. 'Tis easie toot,
And there I will attend what further comes.

Camid. To *Cæsar* will I render
My Legions and my Horse, sixe Kings alreadie
Shew me the way of yeelding.

Eno. Ile yet follow
The wounded chance of *Anthony*, though my reason
Sits in the winde against me.

Enter Anthony with Attendants.

Ant. Hearke, the Land bids me tread no more vpon't,
It is asham'd to beare me. Friends, come hither,
I am so lated in the world, that I
Haue lost my way for euer. I haue a shippe,
Laden with Gold, take that, diuide it: flye,
And make your peace with *Cæsar*.

Omnes. Fly? Not wee.

Ant. I haue fled my selfe, and haue instructed cowards
To runne, and shew their shoulders. Friends be gone,
I haue my selfe resolu'd vpon a course,
Which has no neede of you. Be gone,
My Treasure's in the Harbour. Take it: Oh,

Noch der er war, es hätte gut gehn können:
O, das Signal für unser aller Flucht kam
Höchst schmählich von ihm selbst!
ENOBARBUS Ach, geht es da entlang? Na dann gut Nacht.

CANIDIUS Zur Peloponnesus sind sie geflohn.
SCARUS Das ist nicht weit, und da will ich erwarten,
   Wie's weitergeht.
CANIDIUS   Ich übergebe Caesar
   Die Reiterei und meine Legionen,
   Sechs Könige schon lehrten mich die Kunst
   Der Unterwerfung.
ENOBARBUS   Und ich folge doch noch
   Antonius' wundem Glück, dreht auch der Wind
   Mir die Vernunft auf Gegenkurs.

Elfte Szene

Antonius, Gefolge.

ANTONIUS Horcht, mir verwehrt die Erde, sie zu treten,
   Sie schämt sich, mich zu tragen. Freunde, kommt:
   So sehr verspätet bin ich in der Welt
   Daß sich mein Weg auf ewig mir verlor.
   Mir blieb ein Schiff voll Gold, das nehmt und teilt;
   Flieht und macht mit Caesar euren Frieden.
ALLE Fliehen, wir? Niemals.
ANTONIUS   Ich floh ja selbst
   Und instruierte Memmen, wegzurennen
   Und ihren Rücken zeigen. Freunde, geht,
   Ich hab zu einer Laufbahn mich entschlossen,
   Die eurer nicht bedarf. So geht, im Hafen

I follow'd that I blush to looke vpon,
My very haires do mutiny: for the white
Reproue the browne for rashnesse, and they them
For feare, and doting. Friends be gone, you shall
Haue Letters from me to some Friends, that will
Sweepe your way for you. Pray you looke not sad,
Nor make replyes of loathnesse, take the hint
Which my dispaire proclaimes. Let them be left
Which leaues it selfe, to the Sea-side straight way;
I will possesse you of that ship and Treasure.
Leaue me, I pray a little: pray you now,
Nay do so: for indeede I haue lost command,
Therefore I pray you, Ile see you by and by.   *Sits downe*

Enter Cleopatra led by Charmian and Eros.
Eros. Nay gentle Madam, to him, comfort him.
Iras. Do most deere Queene.
Char. Do, why, what else?
Cleo. Let me sit downe: Oh *Iuno.*
Ant. No, no, no, no, no.
Eros. See you heere, Sir?
Ant. Oh fie, fie, fie.
Char. Madam.
Iras. Madam, oh good Empresse.
Eros. Sir, sir.
Ant. Yes my Lord, yes; he at Philippi kept
    His sword e'ne like a dancer, while I strooke
    The leane and wrinkled *Cassius,* and 'twas I
    That the mad *Brutus* ended: he alone
    Dealt on Lieutenantry, and no practise had
    In the braue squares of Warre: yet now: no matter.
Cleo. Ah stand by.

Liegt mein Besitztum. Nehmt es: O, dem folgt ich,
Das anzublicken mich erröten macht:
Die eignen Haare meutern; denn die grauen
Werfen den dunklen Leichtsinn vor, und diese
Jenen Furcht und Liebeswahn. Geht, Freunde,
Ich geb euch Briefe mit an ferne Freunde,
Die euch die Wege ebnen. Bitte, seid nicht traurig,
Noch ringt schwer nach Worten; folgt der Losung,
Die mein Verzweifeln ausgibt: laßt im Stich
Den, der sich selbst im Stich ließ! Ab mit euch
Zum Hafen, ich vermach euch Schiff und Schatz.
Verlaßt mich, bitte, kurz: hört ihr, ich bitte,
Tut's dennoch, denn mir fehlt Befehlsgewalt
Und so bitte ich. Wir sehn uns noch.
   Cleopatra, Charmian, Eros, Iras.
EROS Nein, liebe Madam, zu ihm, tröstet ihn.
IRAS Tut das, beste Königin.
CHARMIAN Tut's, was denn sonst?
CLEOPATRA Ich muß mich setzen. Juno, hilf!
ANTONIUS Nein, nein, nein, nein, nein.
EROS Seht Ihr das, Sir?
ANTONIUS O pfui, pfui, pfui!
CHARMIAN Madam!
IRAS Madam! O meine Herrscherin!
EROS Sir, Sir!
ANTONIUS Ja, mein Herr, ja; er, bei Philippi, schwang
 Sein Schwert recht wie ein Tänzer, derweil ich
 Den hagren, düstren Cassius schlug; ich war's,
 Der den verrückten Brutus fällte: er
 Hatte Leutnants und kein Fünkchen Praxis
 Im tapf'ren Kriegshandwerk: doch nun – gleichviel.
CLEOPATRA Ah, steht mir bei.

Eros. The Queene my Lord, the Queene.

Iras. Go to him, Madam, speake to him,
  Hee's vnqualited with very shame.

Cleo. Well then, sustaine me: Oh.

Eros. Most Noble Sir arise, the Queene approaches,
  Her head's declin'd, and death will cease her, but
  Your comfort makes the rescue.

Ant. I haue offended Reputation,
  A most vnnoble sweruing.

Eros. Sir, the Queene.

Ant. Oh whether hast thou lead me Egypt, see
  How I conuey my shame, out of thine eyes,
  By looking backe what I haue left behinde
  Stroy'd in dishonor.

Cleo. Oh my Lord, my Lord
  Forgiue my fearfull sayles, I little thought
  You would haue followed.

Ant. Egypt, thou knew'st too well,
  My heart was to thy Rudder tyed by'th'strings,
  And thou should'st stowe me after. O're my spirit
  The full supremacie thou knew'st, and that
  Thy becke, might from the bidding of the Gods
  Command mee.

Cleo. Oh my pardon.

Ant. Now I must
  To the young man send humble Treaties, dodge
  And palter in the shifts of lownes, who
  With halfe the bulke o'th'world plaid as I pleas'd,
  Making, and marring Fortunes. You did know
  How much you were my Conqueror, and that
  My Sword, made weake by my affection, would

EROS Die Königin, Mylord, die Königin.

IRAS Geht zu ihm, Madam, sprecht mit ihm.
Er ist vor tiefer Scham ganz außer sich.

CLEOPATRA Nun denn, so stützt mich: O!

EROS Hochedler Herr, erhebt Euch, denn es naht
Die Königin, das Haupt gesenkt, der Tod
Ergreift sie, Euer Trost allein bringt Rettung.

ANTONIUS Vernichtet ist der Ruf mir durch dies eine
Schandmanöver.

EROS   Sir, die Königin.

ANTONIUS O, wie weit hast du mich gebracht, Ägypten?
Sieh, deinem Blick entzieh ich meine Schmach
Und schau auf das zurück, was ich verließ,
Ehrlos verwüstet.

CLEOPATRA   O Mylord, Mylord,
Verzeiht den scheuen Segeln! Wer denn dachte,
Ihr würdet folgen.

ANTONIUS   Nur zu gut, Ägypten,
Hast du gewußt, wie fest vertäut mein Herz
Mit deinem Ruder war, und daß du nach
Mich schleppen mußtest. Daß du meine Seele
Ganz beherrschst, du wußtest es, und daß
Ein Wink vor dir mich dem Gebot der Götter
Ungehorsam macht.

CLEOPATRA   O, mir Vergebung!

ANTONIUS Gezwungen bin ich nun, dem jungen Mann
Demütige Verträge anzubieten,
Am Boden hinzukriechen und zu feilschen,
Ich, der die halbe Welt zum Spielball nahm
Und steigen ließ und fallen, wen ich wollte.
Du wußtest, ich war deine Kolonie,
Und daß mein Schwert, von Leidenschaft gestumpft,

Obey it on all cause.

Cleo. Pardon, pardon.

Ant Fall not a teare I say, one of them rates
All that is wonne and lost: Giue me a kisse,
Euen this repayes me.
We sent our Schoolemaster, is a come backe?
Loue I am full of Lead: some Wine
Within there, and our Viands: Fortune knowes,
We scorne her most, when most she offers blowes. *Exeunt*

Enter Cæsar, Agrippa, and Dollabello, with others.

Cæs. Let him appeare that's come from *Anthony*.
Know you him.

Dolla. Cæsar, 'tis his Schoolemaster,
An argument that he is pluckt, when hither
He sends so poore a Pinnion of his Wing,
Which had superfluous Kings for Messengers,
Not many Moones gone by.

        Enter Ambassador from Anthony.

Cæsar. Approach, and speake.

Amb. Such as I am, I come from *Anthony*:
I was of late as petty to his ends,
As is the Morne-dew on the Mertle leafe
To his grand Sea.

Cæs. Bee't so, declare thine office.

Amb. Lord of his Fortunes he salutes thee, and
Requires to liue in Egypt, which not granted
He Lessens his Requests, and to thee sues
To let him breath betweene the Heauens and Earth

156   III, xi, 76 - III, xii, 19

Ihr blind gehorchen muß.

CLEOPATRA   Pardon, Pardon!

ANTONIUS Vergieß nicht eine Träne, sag ich, eine
Wöge schon Gewinn auf wie Verlust:
Gib mir einen Kuß, ich bin entschädigt.
Ist unser Lehrer wieder da? Ihn sandten wir.
Ich komm mir vor wie'n Bleisoldat, Geliebte:
Bringt Wein und unser Fleisch! Du weißt, Kriegsglück,
Je härter du schlägst, schlagen wir zurück.

Zwölfte Szene

Caesar, Agrippa, Dolabella, Thidias.

CAESAR Ruft mir den Mann, den uns Antonius sendet.
Du kennst ihn?

DOLABELLA   Caesar, 's ist sein Hauslehrer.
Er muß schon sehr gerupft sein, schickt er uns
Aus seiner Schwinge nur die arme Feder,
Er, dem vor wenig Monden Könige
Als Boten dienten.

                Gesandter des Antonius.

CAESAR   Komm nur näher, sprich.

GESANDTER Antonius schickt mich her, so wie ich dasteh:
Klein war ich eben noch vor seinen Zwecken,
Wie Frühtau auf dem Myrtenblatt, verglichen
Mit dem Meer, das er darstellt.

CAESAR   Dein Auftrag.

GESANDTER Als Meister seiner Zukunft grüßt er dich,
Und bittet um ein Dasein in Ägypten,
Was er, gesetzt, daß es verweigert wird,
Vermindert dahingeh'nd, dich zu ersuchen,

A priuate man in Athens: this for him.
Next, *Cleopatra* does confesse thy Greatnesse,
Submits her to thy might, and of thee craues
The Circle of the *Ptolomies* for her heyres,
Now hazarded to thy Grace.

Cæs. For *Anthony*,
    I haue no eares to his request. The Queene,
    Of Audience, nor Desire shall faile, so shee
    From Egypt driue her all-disgraced Friend,
    Or take his life there. This if shee performe,
    She shall not sue vnheard. So to them both.
Amb. Fortune pursue thee.
Cæs. Bring him through the Bands:
    To try thy Eloquence, now 'tis time, dispatch,
    From *Anthony* winne *Cleopatra*, promise
    And in our Name, what she requires, adde more
    From thine inuention, offers. Women are not
    In their best Fortunes strong; but want will periure
    The ne're touch'd Vestall. Try thy cunning *Thidias*,
    Make thine owne Edict for thy paines, which we
    Will answer as a Law.

Thid. *Cæsar.* I go.
Cæsar. Obserue how *Anthony* becomes his flaw,
    And what thou think'st his very action speakes
    In euery power that mooues.
Thid. *Cæsar*, I shall.   *exeunt.*

Ihm, zwischen Erd und Himmel, als Privatmann
In Athen ein Leben zu vergönnen. Soviel
Zu ihm. Cleopatra, als nächstes, huldigt
Dir, beugt sich deiner Größe und erfleht
Aus deiner Hand die Ptolemäerkrone
Für ihre Erben, die nun deiner Gnade
Anheimstehn.
CAESAR   Was Antonius angeht,
   Bin ich taub. Der Königin soll es
   Nicht an Gehör und Großmut fehlen, treibt sie
   Aus Ägypten ihren faulen Freund aus
   Oder nimmt ihm da sein Leben. Glückt ihr
   Das, bleibt sie nicht ungehört. Dies an die zwei.
GESANDTER Das Glück sei mit dir.
CAESAR   Bringt ihn durch die Linien.
   Nun eil dich, deine Rednerkunst zu testen;
   Cleopatra gewinne dem Antonius
   Ab, versprich, und das in unserm Namen
   Ihr, was sie will; leg noch was drauf, nach eignem
   Gutdünken: stark sind Frauen auch in ihren
   Besten Zeiten nicht, doch Mangel bringt
   Selbst die prinzipienfesteste Vestalin
   Dazu, abzuschwören: tu, was du
   Vermagst, mein Thidias, bestimme selbst
   Den Preis für deine Mühn, wir nehmen ihn,
   Als wäre er Gesetz.
THIDIAS   Caesar, ich gehe.
CAESAR Beobachte Antonius, wie er den Hieb
   Erträgt und lies an seinem Äußren ab,
   Was in ihm vorgeht.
THIDIAS   Caesar, ich werd's tun.

Enter Cleopatra, Enobarbus, Charmian, & Iras.

Cleo. What shall we do, *Enobarbus*?
Eno. Thinke, and dye.
Cleo. Is *Anthony*, or we in fault for this?
Eno. *Anthony* onely, that would make his will
    Lord of his Reason. What though you fled,
    From that great face of Warre, whose seuerall ranges
    Frighted each other? Why should he follow?
    The itch of his Affection should not then
    Haue nickt his Captain-ship, at such a point,
    When halfe to halfe the world oppos'd, he being
    The meered question? 'Twas a shame no lesse
    Then was his losse, to course your flying Flagges,
    And leaue his Nauy gazing.

Cleo. Prythee peace.
        Enter the Ambassador, with Anthony.
Ant. Is that his answer?   *Amb.* I my Lord.

Ant. The Queene shall then haue courtesie,
    So she will yeeld vs vp.
Am. He sayes so.
Antho. Let her know't. To the Boy *Cæsar* send this
    grizled head, and he will fill thy wishes to the brimme,
    With Principalities.

Cleo. That head my Lord?
Ant. To him againe, tell him he weares the Rose

Dreizehnte Szene

Cleopatra, Enobarbus, Charmian, Iras.

CLEOPATRA Was tun wir, Enobarbus?
ENOBARBUS   Denken, sterben.
CLEOPATRA Wer trägt die Schuld, Antonius oder wir?
ENOBARBUS Antonius allein, der den Verstand
  Der Willkür unterjochte. Floht Ihr auch
  Des Krieges großes Antlitz, dessen Züge
  Einander schreckten, warum folgte er?
  Es durfte doch der Stich der Leidenschaft
  Nicht den Soldaten in ihm übertölpeln,
  An einem Punkt, wo sich die halbe Welt
  Der andern Hälfte gegenüber sah,
  Nur seinetwegen. Es war eine Schande,
  Groß wie seine Niederlage, als
  Er Eurer flücht'gen Flagge hinterdrein fuhr,
  Daß seine Flotte gaffte.
CLEOPATRA   Bitte schweig.
                Antonius, der Gesandte.
ANTONIUS Das ist die Antwort?
GESANDTER   Ja, Mylord.
ANTONIUS Die Königin kommt heil davon, wenn sie
  Uns fallen läßt?
GESANDTER   So sagt er.
ANTONIUS   Sie soll's wissen.
  Dem Knaben Caesar schick dies graue Haupt,
  Dann füllt er dir den Kelch der Wünsche randvoll
  Mit Fürstentümern.
CLEOPATRA   Dieses Haupt, Mylord?
ANTONIUS Zu ihm zurück und sag, er trüg die Rose

Of youth vpon him: from which, the world should note
Something particular: His Coine, Ships, Legions,
May be a Cowards, whose Ministers would preuaile
Vnder the seruice of a Childe, as soone
As i'th'Command of *Cæsar*. I dare him therefore
To lay his gay Comparisons a-part,
And answer me declin'd, Sword against Sword,
Our selues alone: Ile write it: Follow me.

Eno. Yes like enough: hye battel'd *Cæsar* will
Vnstate his happinesse, and be Stag'd to'th'shew
Against a Sworder. I see mens Iudgements are
A parcell of their Fortunes, and things outward
Do draw the inward quality after them
To suffer all alike, that he should dreame,
Knowing all measures, the full *Cæsar* will
Answer his emptinesse; *Cæsar* thou hast subdu'de
His iudgement too.
                    Enter a Seruant.
Ser. A Messenger from *Cæsar*.

Cleo. What no more Ceremony? See my Women,
Against the blowne Rose may they stop their nose,
That kneel'd vnto the Buds. Admit him sir.
Eno. Mine honesty, and I, beginne to square,
The Loyalty well held to Fooles, does make
Our Faith meere folly: yet he that can endure
To follow with Allegeance a falne Lord,
Does conquer him that did his Master conquer,
And earnes a place i'th'Story.

                    Enter Thidias.

Der Jugend auf sich, wovon doch die Welt
Auch etwas merken müsse: Schiffe, Truppen
Kann auch ein Feigling haben, dessen Helfer,
Befehligt auch ein Kind sie, grad so gut
Als unter Caesar siegen: darum sag ihm,
Ich fordere ihn auf, das abzutun,
Worauf er gar zu stolz ist, und mit mir
Gefallenem sich Schwert an Schwert zu messen,
Nur er und ich. Ich schreib's ihm: folge mir.

ENOBARBUS O ja! Sehr glaublich! Caesar, Herr der Lage,
Entläßt sein Glück und tritt in die Arena
Zum Schwertkampf an! Ich seh, der Menschen Urteil
Ist eins mit ihrem Los, und äußre Dinge
Ziehn innre nach sich, alles krankt zugleich.
Daß er, bei allem Witz, sich träumen läßt,
Der übervolle Caesar würd ein Wörtchen
Mit seiner Leere wechseln; Caesar, du
Hast ihm auch den Verstand besiegt.

Ein Diener.

ENOBARBUS   Ein Bote
Von Caesar.

CLEOPATRA   Wie, kein größrer Aufwand? Seht,
Der welken Rose rümpfen sie die Nase,
Die vor der Knospe knieten. Laßt ihn ein.

ENOBARBUS Mein Ehrgefühl und ich bekommen Streit.
Loyal an Narren festzuhalten, macht
Die Treue selbst zur Narrheit: allerdings,
Wer's über sich bringt, dem gefallnen Herrn
Ergeben nachzufolgen, der besiegt
Den, der den Herrn besiegte, und erwirbt
Sich einen Platz in der Geschichte.

Thidias.

Cleo. *Cæsars* will.

Thid. Heare it apart.

Cleo. None but Friends: say boldly.

Thid. So haply are they Friends to *Anthony*.

Enob. He needs as many (Sir) as *Cæsar* ha's,
   Or needs not vs. If *Cæsar* please, our Master
   Will leape to be his Friend: For vs you know,
   Whose he is, we are, and that is *Caesars*.

Thid. So. Thus then thou most renown'd, *Cæsar* intreats,
   Not to consider in what case thou stand'st
   Further then he is *Cæsars*.

Cleo. Go on, right Royall.

Thid. He knowes that you embrace not *Anthony*
   As you did loue, but as you feared him.

Cleo. Oh.

Thid. The scarre's vpon your Honor, therefore he
   Does pitty, as constrained blemishes,
   Not as deserued.

Cleo. He is a God,
   And knowes what is most right. Mine Honour
   Was not yeelded, but conquer'd meerely.

Eno. To be sure of that, I will aske *Anthony*.
   Sir, sir, thou art so leakie
   That we must leaue thee to thy sinking, for
   Thy deerest quit thee.   *Exit Enob.*

Thid. Shall I say to *Cæsar*,
   What you require of him: for he partly begges
   To be desir'd to giue. It much would please him,
   That of his Fortunes you should make a staffe
   To leane vpon. But it would warme his spirits

CLEOPATRA   Caesars Wille?
THIDIAS Hört allein.
CLEOPATRA   Nur Freunde: redet kühn.
THIDIAS Dann sind es wohl auch Freunde Marc Antons.
ENOBARBUS Er braucht so viele, wie sie Caesar hat,
    Sonst auch nicht uns. Beliebt es Caesar, springt
    Unser Herr, sein Freund zu sein: und wir,
    Wißt Ihr, sind's dem, dem er's ist, also Caesar.
THIDIAS So. Nun denn, ruhmvolle Königin,
    Caesar ersucht Euch, bei Betrachtung Eurer
    Lage nicht zu übersehen, daß
    Er Caesar ist.
CLEOPATRA   Recht königlich, nur weiter.
THIDIAS Er weiß, Ihr habt Antonius umarmt,
    Weil er Euch ängstigt, nicht aus Liebe.
CLEOPATRA   O!
THIDIAS Er sieht daher die Scharten Eurer Ehre
    Bedauernd als erzwungnen Makel an
    Und unverdient.
CLEOPATRA   Er ist ein Gott und kennt
    Die Wahrheit. Meine Ehre wurde nicht
    Gefragt, nein, schlicht genommen.
ENOBARBUS   Was Antonius
    Wohl dazu sagt. Sir, Sir, du schlugst so leck,
    Daß wir dich versinken lassen müssen,
    Denn dich verläßt dein Liebstes.   *Ab.*
THIDIAS   Darf ich Caesar
    Melden, worum Ihr ersucht? Er bittet gleichsam,
    Ihn sich als Gebenden zu wünschen. Ihm
    Wär's angenehm, wenn Ihr Euch seines Daseins
    Als eines Stabs bedientet, Euch darauf
    Zu stützen. Herzerwärmend wär's ihm,

To heare from me you had left *Anthony*,
And put your selfe vnder his shrowd, the vniuersal Land-
(lord.

Cleo. What's your name?

Thid. My name is *Thidias.*

Cleo. Most kinde Messenger,
Say to great *Cæsar* this in disputation,
I kisse his conqu'ring hand: Tell him, I am prompt
To lay my Crowne at's feete, and there to kneele.
Tell him, from his all-obeying breath, I heare
The doome of Egypt.

Thid. 'Tis your Noblest course:
Wisedome and Fortune combatting together,
If that the former dare but what it can,
No chance may shake it. Giue me grace to lay
My dutie on your hand.

Cleo. Your *Cæsars* Father oft,
(When he hath mus'd of taking kingdomes in)
Bestow'd his lips on that vnworthy place,
As it rain'd kisses.

Enter Anthony and Enobarbus.

Ant. Fauours? By Ioue that thunders. What art thou
(Fellow?

Thid. One that but performes
The bidding of the fullest man, and worthiest
To haue command obey'd.

Eno. You will be whipt.

Ant. Approch there: ah you Kite. Now Gods & diuels

Von mir zu hören, daß Ihr Marc Anton
Verlaßt und unter seinen, des Weltherrschers
Schutz Euch stellt.

CLEOPATRA   Wie heißt du?

THIDIAS   Thidias.

CLEOPATRA Lieber Bote, sag dem großen Caesar
In meinem Auftrag dies: ich küsse des
Erob'rers Hand; berichte ihm, ich sei
Gewillt, zu seinen Füßen meine Krone
Abzulegen und vor ihm zu knien:
Sag ihm, aus seinem Herrschermund will ich
Ägyptens Schicksal hören.

THIDIAS   Du beschreitest
Den edelsten der Pfade. Liegt die Weisheit
Mit dem Glück im Krieg und wagt nur alles,
So macht kein Mißgeschick sie wanken.
Laßt gnädig meine Ehrerbietung mich
Auf Eurer Hand bezeugen.

CLEOPATRA   Oft und oft
Hat Eures Caesars Vater seine Lippen,
Kam er von seinen Welteroberungsplänen,
Auf die bescheidne Stelle hier gedrückt,
Als regnete es Küsse.

Antonius, Enobarbus.

ANTONIUS   Wie? Ein Handkuß?
Beim Donnerer! Wer bist du, Bursche?

THIDIAS   Einer,
Der auf Geheiß des größten Mannes handelt,
Des meiner Dienste würdigsten.

ENOBARBUS   Paß auf,
Du wirst gepeitscht.

ANTONIUS   Kommt her, ihr! Ah, zum Geier!

Authority melts from me of late. When I cried hoa,
Like Boyes vnto a musse, Kings would start forth,
And cry, your will. Haue you no eares?
I am *Anthony* yet. Take hence this Iack, and whip him.

Enter a Seruant.

Eno. 'Tis better playing with a Lions whelpe,
    Then with an old one dying.
Ant. Moone and Starres,
    Whip him: wer't twenty of the greatest Tributaries
    That do acknowledge *Caesar*, should I finde them
    So sawcy with the hand of she heere, what's her name
    Since she was *Cleopatra*? Whip him Fellowes,
    Till like a Boy you see him crindge his face,
    And whine aloud for mercy. Take him hence.

Thid. Marke *Anthony.*

Ant. Tugge him away: being whipt
    Bring him againe, the Iacke of *Cæsars* shall
    Beare vs an arrant to him.   *Exeunt with Thidius.*
    You were halfe blasted ere I knew you: Ha?
    Haue I my pillow left vnprest in Rome,
    Forborne the getting of a lawfull Race,
    And by a Iem of women, to be abus'd
    By one that lookes on Feeders?

Cleo. Good my Lord.

Ant. You haue beene a boggeler euer,
    But when we in our viciousnesse grow hard
    (Oh misery on't) the wise Gods seele our eyes
    In our owne filth, drop our cleare iudgements, make vs
    Adore our errors, laugh at's while we strut

Mein Ansehen schmilzt ab: jüngst, wenn ich ›Ho!‹ schrie,
Rannten Könige wie rauflustige Buben,
Schreiend ›Was befehlt Ihr?‹ Habt ihr Ohren?
Noch bin ich Antonius. Nehmt den Schalk
Und peitscht ihn.

ENOBARBDUS Tja, mit dem jungen Löwen spielt sich's leichter,
  Als mit dem alten, der sein Ende fühlt.
ANTONIUS Mond und Sterne, peitscht ihn! Wären's auch
  Zwanzig von den größten Bündnisfürsten
  Aus Caesars Sammlung, träf ich sie so speichelnd
  Auf der Hand von ihr da an – wie heißt sie,
  Seit sie nicht Cleopatra mehr ist?
  Peitscht ihn, Freunde, bis er wie ein Schulbub
  Sein Gesicht verzieht und laut um Gnade winselt.
  Bringt ihn weg.
THIDIAS   Marcus Antonius!
ANTONIUS   Schleppt ihn weg:
  Habt ihr ihn gepeitscht, bringt ihn zurück
  Der Narr des Caesar soll ihm was bestellen.
  Ihr wart wohl im Bedarfsfall, eh Ihr mich traft?
  Wie? Ließ ich mein Bett in Rom nur leer,
  Versagte es mir, Erben mir zu zeugen,
  Und noch dazu mit dem Juwel der Frauen,
  Damit ich einer in die Hände falle,
  Die Sklaven nachschielt?
CLEOPATRA   Lieber, guter Herr –
ANTONIUS Ihr wart schon immer eine Spielerin,
  Doch wenn wir in Gemeinheit uns verhärten,
  O wärs nicht so! – dann blenden uns die Götter
  Und werfen den Verstand uns auf den Kehricht,
  Sie lassen unsern Irrtum uns bewundern

To our confusion.

Cleo. Oh, is't come to this?
Ant. I found you as a Morsell, cold vpon
   Dead *Cæsars* Trencher: Nay, you were a Fragment
   Of *Gneius Pompeyes*, besides what hotter houres
   Vnregistred in vulgar Fame, you haue
   Luxuriously pickt out. For I am sure,
   Though you can guesse what Temperance should be,
   You know not what it is.

Cleo. Wherefore is this?
Ant. To let a Fellow that will take rewards,
   And say, God quit you, be familiar with
   My play-fellow, your hand; this Kingly Seale,
   And plighter of high hearts. O that I were
   Vpon the hill of Basan, to out-roare
   The horned Heard, for I haue sauage cause,
   And to proclaime it ciuilly, were like
   A halter'd necke, which do's the Hangman thanke,
   For being yare about him. Is he whipt?

Enter a Seruant with Thidias.

Ser. Soundly, my Lord.
Ant. Cried he? and begg'd a Pardon?

Ser. He did aske fauour.
Ant. If that thy Father liue, let him repent
   Thou was't not made his daughter, and be thou sorrie
   To follow *Cæsar* in his Triumph, since
   Thou hast bin whipt. For following him, henceforth

Und lachen, wenn wir aufgebläht in unsern
Untergang stolziern.

CLEOPATRA   O, kam's so weit!

ANTONIUS Ich fand Euch, einen kaltgewordnen Bissen,
Auf Julius Caesars Teller: nein, als Rest
In des Pompejus Schüssel, ganz zu schweigen
Von all den schwülen Stunden, unerwähnt
In den Registern des gemeinen Ruhms,
Die Eure Gier sich gönnte. Ich bin sicher,
Wenn du auch ahnst, was Anstand wohl sein könnte,
Gekannt hast du ihn nicht.

CLEOPATRA   Was soll das mir?

ANTONIUS Daß so ein Bursche, der ein Trinkgeld nimmt,
Und sagt ›Vergelts Euch Gott!‹ vertraulich sich
An meine Spielgefährtin, Eure Hand,
Darf wagen; an dies königliche Siegel,
Den Herold hoher Freuden! O ich will
Auf Basans Hügel stehen, überbrüllen will ich
Das Hornvieh um mich her, denn wüsten Grund
Dazu hab ich, und ihn beherrscht verkünden,
Das wär, als würde der gehängte Hals
Dem Henker für die Mühewaltung danken.

Ist er gepeitscht?

DIENER   Gründlich, Mylord.

ANTONIUS   Und schrie er?
Bat um Gnade?

DIENER   Er erflehte Schonung.

ANTONIUS Lebt dir ein Vater noch, soll er's bereun,
Nicht eine Tochter sich gemacht zu haben;
Du sollst es leid sein, im Triumph des Caesar
Mitzulaufen, seit du für Mitlaufen

The white hand of a Lady Feauer thee,
Shake thou to looke on't. Get thee backe to *Cæsar*,
Tell him thy entertainment: looke thou say
He makes me angry with him. For he seemes
Proud and disdainfull, harping on what I am,
Not what he knew I was. He makes me angry,
And at this time most easie 'tis to doo't:
When my good Starres, that were my former guides
Haue empty left their Orbes, and shot their Fires
Into th'Abisme of hell. If he mislike,
My speech, and what is done, tell him he has
Hiparchus, my enfranched Bondman, whom
He may at pleasure whip, or hang, or torture,
As he shall like to quit me. Vrge it thou:
Hence with thy stripes, be gone.   *Exit Thid.*

Cleo. Haue you done yet?
Ant. Alacke our Terrene Moone is now Eclipst,
     And it portends alone the fall of *Anthony*.

Cleo. I must stay his time?
Ant. To flatter *Cæsar*, would you mingle eyes
     With one that tyes his points.
Cleo. Not know me yet?

Ant. Cold-hearted toward me?
Cleo. Ah (Deere) if I be so,
     From my cold heart let Heauen ingender haile,
     And poyson it in the sourse, and the first stone
     Drop in my necke: as it determines so
     Dissolue my life, the next Cæsarian smile,

Die Peitsche spürtest: und von nun an mache
Jede weiße Frauenhand dich fiebern,
Der Anblick schon dich zittern. Geh zu Caesar,
Erzähl von deinen Freuden: laß ihn wissen,
Daß er mich zornig macht. Es scheint, er will
Voll Hochmut mir das eine Lied nur singen,
Des, was ich war, nicht, wie er weiß, ich bin.
Er macht mich zornig, was ein Leichtes ist,
In dieser Zeit, da meine guten Sterne,
Die früher mich geleitet, ihre Bahn
Leer ließen und den Feuerglanz in alle
Höllentiefen warfen. Sollte ihm die Rede
Mißfallen, und was hier geschah, dann sag ihm,
Hipparchus sei, mein Freigelassner, bei ihm,
Den darf er, will er quitt sein, ganz nach Laune
Peitschen, foltern, hängen. Richt das aus:
Mit deinen Striemen, hebe dich hinweg!
CLEOPATRA Bist du soweit?
ANTONIUS   Ach, unser Erdenmond
    Hat sich verfinstert und er kündet einzig
    Des Antonius' Fall!
CLEOPATRA   Ich muß schon warten.
ANTONIUS Caesar schmeicheln willst du und liebäugelst
    Mit einem, der die Schuh ihm schnürt?
CLEOPATRA   Du kennst mich
    Noch nicht?
ANTONIUS   Kaltherzig wider mich?
CLEOPATRA   Ach, Liebster,
    Bin ichs, mag der Himmel mir mein kaltes
    Herz in einen gift'gen Hagel wandeln,
    Des erster Brocken meinen Nacken trifft:
    Und wie er wegtaut, so vergeh mein Leben;

Till by degrees the memory of my wombe,
Together with my braue Egyptians all,
By the discandering of this pelleted storme,
Lye grauelesse, till the Flies and Gnats of Nyle
Haue buried them for prey.

Ant. I am satisfied:
Cæsar sets downe in Alexandria, where
I will oppose his Fate. Our force by Land,
Hath Nobly held, our seuer'd Nauie too
Haue knit againe, and Fleete, threatning most Sea-like.
Where hast thou bin my heart? Dost thou heare Lady?
If from the Field I shall returne once more
To kisse these Lips, I will appeare in Blood,
I, and my Sword, will earne our Chronicle,
There's hope in't yet.
Cleo. That's my braue Lord.
Ant. I will be trebble-sinewed, hearted, breath'd,
And fight maliciously: for when mine houres
Were nice and lucky, men did ransome liues
Of me for iests: But now, Ile set my teeth,
And send to darkenesse all that stop me. Come,
Let's haue one other gawdy night: Call to me
All my sad Captaines, fill our Bowles once more:
Let's mocke the midnight Bell.

Cleo. It is my Birth-day,
I had thought t'haue held it poore. But since my Lord
Is *Anthony* againe, I will be *Cleopatra.*
Ant. We will yet do well.
Cleo. Call all his Noble Captaines to my Lord.
Ant. Do so, wee'l speake to them,

Ein zweiter soll Caesarion zerschmettern,
Bis endlich, was an meinen Schoß erinnert,
Mit allen meinen tapferen Ägyptern,
Vom Sturm, dem eisig körnigen, zerworfen,
Grablos liegt, bis es die Fliegenbrut
Des Nil als Beute eingräbt!
ANTONIUS   Ich bin still.
    Caesar sitzt in Alexandria,
    Da tret ich seinem Glück entgegen. Zuchtvoll
    Hält sich unsre Landmacht, unsre Flotte
    Hat sich neu formiert und droht zur See.
    Wo warst du nur, mein Herz? Hörst du mich, Lady?
    Kehr ich noch einmal aus dem Feld zurück,
    Den Mund zu küssen, komm ich ganz in Blut,
    Ich und mein Schwert sind Schnitter für die Chronik:
    Noch gibt es Hoffnung.
CLEOPATRA   Jetzt erkenn ich dich!
ANTONIUS Dreifach stark an Kraft und Mut und Atem
    Kämpf ich wie toll: in meinen besten Tagen,
    Da konnt ein Mann von mir sein Leben kaufen
    Mit einem Scherz: jetzt zeige ich die Zähne
    Und schick ins Schwarze, was mich aufhält. Kommt,
    Laßt uns noch eine wilde Nacht verbringen:
    Ruft meine tiefbetrübten Offiziere,
    Füllt uns noch einmal alle Becher voll;
    Der Mitternacht zum Spott.
CLEOPATRA   's ist mein Geburtstag,
    Ich wollt' ihn nicht groß feiern, doch da Ihr
    Antonius seid, bin ich Cleopatra.
ANTONIUS Wir schaffen das.
CLEOPATRA Ruft alle hohen Offiziere zu Mylord.
ANTONIUS Das tut, ich will zu ihnen sprechen, und

And to night Ile force
The Wine peepe through their scarres.
Come on (my Queene)
There's sap in't yet. The next time I do fight
Ile make death loue me: for I will contend
Euen with his pestilent Sythe.   *Exeunt.*

Eno. Now hee'l out-stare the Lightning, to be furious
Is to be frighted out of feare, and in that moode
The Doue will pecke the Estridge; and I see still
A diminution in our Captaines braine,
Restores his heart; when valour prayes in reason,
It eates the Sword it fights with: I will seeke
Some way to leaue him.   *Exeunt.*

Heut Nacht soll'n ihre Narben glühn vom Wein.
Komm, Königin, noch sind wir nicht am Ende.
Und fechte ich morgen, mache ich den Tod
In mich verliebt, denn gegen seine Sichel
Die abmäht wie die Pest, trete ich an.

ENOBARBUS Nun will er dem Blitz heimleuchten; derart
Tollkühn zu sein heißt, aus der Furcht geschreckt sein,
In solcher Laune hackt die Taube nach
Dem Habicht; und ich seh erneut, je mehr
Dem Feldherrn die Besinnung aufweicht, wächst ihm
Das Herz; wenn Tapferkeit sich den Verstand
Als Nahrung wählt, frißt sie das Schwert,
Mit dem sie kämpft: ich will nach Wegen suchen,
Ihn zu verlassen.

Enter Cæsar, Agrippa, & Mecenas with his Army,
Cæsar reading a Letter.

Cæs. He calles me Boy, and chides as he had power
    To beate me out of Egypt. My Messenger
    He hath whipt with Rods, dares me to personal Combat.
    Cæsar to *Anthony*: let the old Ruffian know,
    I haue many other wayes to dye: meane time
    Laugh at his Challenge.

Mece. *Cæsar* must thinke,
    When one so great begins to rage, hee's hunted
    Euen to falling. Giue him no breath, but now
    Make boote of his distraction: Neuer anger
    Made good guard for it selfe.
Cæs. Let our best heads know,
    That to morrow, the last of many Battailes
    We meane to fight. Within our Files there are,
    Of those that seru'd *Marke Anthony* but late,
    Enough to fetch him in. See it done,
    And Feast the Army, we haue store to doo't,
    And they haue earn'd the waste. Poore *Anthony*. *Exeunt*

Enter Anthony, Cleopatra, Enobarbus, Charmian,
Iras, Alexas, with others.

Ant. He will not fight with me, *Domitian*?
Eno. No?

VIERTER AKT
Erste Szene

Caesar, Agrippa, Maecenas.

CAESAR ›Knabe‹ nennt er mich, und spielt sich auf,
Als könne er mich aus Ägypten jagen.
Mein Bote wurde ausgepeitscht, und er
Fordert mich zum Zweikampf, Caesar gegen
Antonius: bestellt dem alten Raufbold,
Ich kann auf viele Weisen sterben; bis dahin
Verlach ich seine Ford'rung.
MAECENAS   Caesar, wißt,
Daß, rast ein Großer so, er sich gejagt sieht
Bis an den Rand. Gönnt ihm nicht Atem, nutzt
Seinen Irrsinn klug: noch nie stand Wut
Sich selber Wache.
CAESAR   Laßt die besten Führer
Wissen, daß wir morgen früh die letzte
Der vielen Schlachten auszukämpfen hoffen.
In unsern Reihen stehn genügend Männer,
Die gestern noch bei Marc Antonius dienten,
Und die ihn fangen können. Setzt das um,
Und gebt dem Heer ein Fest: wir haben Vorrat,
Und sie es sich verdient. Armer Antonius!

Zweite Szene

Antonius, Cleopatra, Enobarbus, Charmian, Iras, Alexas.

ANTONIUS Er schlägt den Zweikampf aus, Domitius?
ENOBARBUS   Ja.

Ant. Why should he not?

Eno. He thinks, being twenty times of better fortune,
    He is twenty men to one.

Ant. To morrow Soldier,
    By Sea and Land Ile fight: or I will liue,
    Or bathe my dying Honor in the blood
    Shall make it liue againe. Woo't thou fight well.

Eno. Ile strike, and cry, Take all.

Ant. Well said, come on:
    Call forth my Houshold Seruants, lets to night
                              Enter 3 or 4 Seruitors.
    Be bounteous at our Meale. Giue me thy hand,
    Thou hast bin rightly honest, so hast thou,
    Thou, and thou, and thou: you haue seru'd me well,
    And Kings haue beene your fellowes.

Cleo. What meanes this?

Eno. 'Tis one of those odde tricks which sorow shoots
    Out of the minde.

Ant. And thou art honest too:
    I wish I could be made so many men,
    And all of you clapt vp together, in
    An *Anthony*: that I might do you seruice,
    So good as you haue done.

Omnes. The Gods forbid.

Ant. Well, my good Fellowes, wait on me to night:
    Scant not my Cups, and make as much of me,
    As when mine Empire was your Fellow too,
    And suffer'd my command.

Cleo. What does he meane?

ANTONIUS Warum?

ENOBARBUS   Er meint, mit zwanzigmal mehr Chancen
Steht er wie zwanzig gegen einen.

ANTONIUS   Morgen,
Soldat, kämpf ich zu Wasser und zu Lande.
Entweder lebe ich oder ich bade
Die Ehre mir, die sterbende, in Blut,
Das sie neu leben läßt. Schlägst du dich gut?

ENOBARBUS Ich haue drein und schreie ›Auf sie!‹

ANTONIUS   Bestens.
Geh, ruf mir meine Fähnriche, heut Nacht
Woll'n einmal wir noch tafeln.

                    Sechs Fähnriche.

                          Deine Hand,
Du warst ein guter Kerl – du auch – und du –
Und du – und du: ihr habt mir treu gedient,
Und Könige war'n eure Kameraden.

CLEOPATRA Was bedeutet das?

ENOBARBUS   's ist einer jener Streiche,
Die Elend dem Gemüt spielt.

ANTONIUS   Du bist auch treu.
Könnt ich so viele Männer sein, und ihr
Zögt euch zu einem Marc Anton zusammen,
Daß ich euch dienen dürfte wie ihr mir.

ALLE Ihr guten Götter!

ANTONIUS   Kameraden, sorgt
Heut Nacht für mich und meinen Becher, achtet
Mich wie einst, als auch mein Weltreich noch
Euer Kamerad war und ich ihm
Befehlen konnte.

CLEOPATRA   Was will er erreichen?

Eno. To make his Followers weepe.

Ant. Tend me to night;
    May be, it is the period of your duty,
    Haply you shall not see me more, or if,
    A mangled shadow. Perchance to morrow,
    You'l serue another Master. I looke on you,
    As one that takes his leaue. Mine honest Friends,
    I turne you not away, but like a Master
    Married to your good seruice, stay till death:
    Tend me to night two houres, I aske no more,
    And the Gods yeeld you for't.

Eno. What meane you (Sir)
    To giue them this discomfort? Looke they weepe,
    And I an Asse, am Onyon-ey'd; for shame,
    Transforme vs not to women.

Ant. Ho, ho, ho:
    Now the Witch take me, if I meant it thus.
    Grace grow where those drops fall (my hearty Friends)
    You take me in too dolorous a sense,
    For I spake to you for your comfort, did desire you
    To burne this night with Torches: Know (my hearts)
    I hope well of to morrow, and will leade you,
    Where rather Ile expect victorious life,
    Then death, and Honor. Let's to Supper, come,
    And drowne consideration.   *Exeunt.*

Enter a Company of Soldiours.

1. *Sol.* Brother, goodnight: to morrow is the day.
2. *Sol.* It will determine one way: Fare you well.

ENOBARBUS Daß sein Anhang weint.

ANTONIUS   Heut Nacht seid gut
Zu mir; mag sein, das Ende eurer Fron
Ist nah, ihr seht mich schwerlich wieder oder
Wenn, dann als zerstücktes Schattenbild.
Morgen dient ihr einem neuen Herrn,
Vielleicht. Ich seh euch wie bei einem Abschied.
Ich will euch, meine Freunde, nicht verstoßen,
Nur eurem Dienst vermählt euch Treue halten
Bis zum Tod. Zwei Stunden noch, mehr nicht,
Und alle Götter mit euch!

ENOBARBUS   Sir, was treibt Euch,
Daß Ihr sie so entmutigt? Seht, sie weinen,
Selbst ich seh zwiebeläugig drein, ich Esel;
Macht uns nicht zu Weibern.

ANTONIUS   Ho, ho, ho!
Ich will verhext sein, wenn ich das gewollt!
Das Gnadenkraut wächst, wo die Tropfen fallen;
Ihr Herzensfreunde nehmt mich viel zu ernst,
Aufmuntern will ich euch, ich wünsche ja,
Daß ihr die Nacht mit Fackeln mir verbrennt:
Wißt, ich erhoffe mir von Morgen viel,
Und führen will ich euch, wo Sieg und Leben
Unsrer harrt, nicht Tod und Ehre. Kommt,
Tragt auf! Ertränken wir Bedenklichkeiten.   *Alle ab.*

Dritte Szene

Soldat 1, Soldat 2

SOLDAT 1 Schlaf gut, Bruder: morgen ist der Tag.
SOLDAT 2 So oder so entscheidet er. Leb wohl.

Heard you of nothing strange about the streets.

1 Nothing: what newes?

2 Belike 'tis but a Rumour, good night to you.

1 Well sir, good night.

They meete other Soldiers.

2 Souldiers, haue carefull Watch.

1 And you: Goodnight, goodnight.

They place themselues in euery corner of the Stage.

2 Heere we: and if to morrow
Our Nauie thriue, I haue an absolute hope
Our Landmen will stand vp.

1 'Tis a braue Army, and full of purpose.

Musicke of the Hoboyes is vnder the Stage.

2 Peace, what noise?

1 List list.

2 Hearke.

1 Musicke i'th'Ayre.

3 Vnder the earth.

4 It signes well, do's it not?

3 No.

1 Peace I say: What should this meane?

2 'Tis the God *Hercules*, whom *Anthony* loued,
Now leaues him.

1 Walke, let's see if other Watchmen
Do heare what we do?

2 How now Maisters?   *Speak together.*

Omnes. How now? how now? do you heare this?

Kam dir was Ungewöhnliches zu Ohren?

SOLDAT 1 Nichts: was denn?

SOLDAT 2   's wird nur ein Gerücht sein.
Gute Nacht.

SOLDAT 1   Dann dir das Gleiche, Sir.

              Soldat 3, Soldat 4.

SOLDAT 3 Bleibt wachsam, Leute.

SOLDAT 1   Ihr auch. Gute Nacht.

SOLDAT 3 Wir schon: und sollte unsre Flotte sich
Morgen halten, bin ich überzeugt,
Das Heer steht seinen Mann.

SOLDAT 4   Ein starkes Heer,
Und motiviert.

SOLDAT 2   Still, ein Geräusch.

SOLDAT 1   Halt's Maul!

SOLDAT 3 Horcht!

SOLDAT 4   Luftmusik.

SOLDAT 1   Nein, in der Erde unten.

SOLDAT 4 Ein gutes Zeichen, nicht?

SOLDAT 2   Nein.

SOLDAT 1   Ruhe, sag ich.

SOLDAT 3 Was bedeutet das?

SOLDAT 2 Antonius' Lieblingsahn, Held Herkules,
Verläßt ihn.

SOLDAT 1   Los, laßt sehn, ob andre Posten
Es auch hörn.

              Soldat 5, Soldat 6.

SOLDAT 1   Und, Leute?

SOLDAT 2   Und?

SOLDATEN 1, 2, 3, 4   Und? Hört ihr das?

1 I, is't not strange?
3 Do you heare Masters? Do you heare?

1 Follow the noyse so farre as we haue quarter.
   Let's see how it will giue off.
Omnes. Content: 'Tis strange.   *Exeunt.*

        Enter Anthony and Cleopatra, with others.

Ant. *Eros,* mine Armour *Eros.*
Cleo. Sleepe a little.
Ant. No my Chucke. *Eros,* come mine Armor *Eros.*
                    Enter Eros.
   Come good Fellow, put thine Iron on,
   If Fortune be not ours to day, it is
   Because we braue her. Come.
Cleo. Nay, Ile helpe too, *Anthony.*
   What's this for? Ah let be, let be, thou art
   The Armourer of my heart: False, false: This, this,

   Sooth-law Ile helpe: Thus it must bee.

Ant. Well, well, we shall thriue now.
   Seest thou my good Fellow. Go, put on thy defences.

Eros. Briefely Sir.
Cleo. Is not this buckled well?

Ant. Rarely, rarely:
   He that vnbuckles this, till we do please

186   IV, iii, 31 - IV, iv, 18

SOLDATEN 5, 6 Ja.

SOLDAT 5   's ist sonderbar.

SOLDAT 1   Was hörn wir, Leute?

SOLDAT 6 Gehn wir dem Ton nach bis zur Lagergrenze.
   Mal sehen, ob's da aufhört.

SOLDAT 2   Sicher. So was.   *Alle ab.*

Vierte Szene

Antonius, Cleopatra, Eros, Charmian, Iras

ANTONIUS Eros! Meine Rüstung, Eros!

CLEOPATRA   Ruht erst.

ANTONIUS Nein, Täubchen. Eros! Komm, die Rüstung, Eros!
                    Eros, mit der Rüstung.
   Komm, Bursche. Kleid mich in dein Eisenzeug:
   Läßt uns Fortuna heut im Stich, geschiehts,
   Weil wir ihr trotzen. Komm.

CLEOPATRA   Ich helfe auch.
   Wozu ist dies?

ANTONIUS   Ach laß nur, laß! Du wappnest
   Mir das Herz: falsch, falsch; so, so.

CLEOPATRA   Gemach,
   Schau, ich weiß schon: so gehörts.

ANTONIUS   Gut, gut,
   Es geht voran. Siehst du, mein guter Junge?
   Geh, rüste dich.

EROS   Sofort, Sir.

CLEOPATRA   Ist dies nicht
   Vorzüglich festgeschnallt?

ANTONIUS   Ganz ungewöhnlich;
   Den, der uns dies aufschnallt, eh wir selbst

187

To daft for our Repose, shall heare a storme.
Thou fumblest *Eros*, and my Queenes a Squire
More tight at this, then thou: Dispatch. O Loue,
That thou couldst see my Warres to day, and knew'st
The Royall Occupation, thou should'st see
A Workeman in't.

Enter an Armed Soldier.

Good morrow to thee, welcome,
Thou look'st like him that knowes a warlike Charge:
To businesse that we loue, we rise betime,
And go too't with delight.

Soul. A thousand Sir, early though't be, haue on their
Riueted trim, and at the Port expect you.   *Showt.*

Trumpets Flourish.

Enter Captaines, and Souldiers.

Alex. The Morne is faire: Good morrow Generall.
All. Good morrow Generall.
Ant. 'Tis well blowne Lads.
This Morning, like the spirit of a youth
That meanes to be of note, begins betimes.
So, so: Come giue me that, this way, well-sed.
Fare thee well Dame, what ere becomes of me,
This is a Soldiers kisse: rebukeable,
And worthy shamefull checke it were, to stand
On more Mechanicke Complement, Ile leaue thee.
Now like a man of Steele, you that will fight,
Follow me close, Ile bring you too't: Adieu.   *Exeunt.*
Char. Please you retyre to your Chamber?
Cleo. Lead me:
He goes forth gallantly: That he and *Caesar* might
Determine this great Warre in single fight;
Then *Anthony*; but now. Well on.   *Exeunt*

Zu kurzer Ruh es abzulegen wünschen,
Bläst es um. Du fummelst, Eros, schau,
Die Fürstin ist der bessre Knappe: geh jetzt.
O Liebste, sähst du heute meinen Krieg
Und kenntest dies Geschäft der Könige,
Du sähest einen guten Arbeitsmann.

Ein Soldat.

ANTONIUS Guten Morgen dir: sei mir willkommen:
Du siehst wie einer aus, der Krieg gelernt hat:
Ist uns das Handwerk lieb, stehn früh wir auf
Und gehn daran mit Lust.

SCARUS   Eintausend Mann, Sir,
Stehn, so jung der Tag auch ist, bewaffnet
Am Hafen unten und erwarten Euch.

Hauptleute, Soldaten.

HAUPTMANN Der Tag wird schön: Gut'n Morgen, General.

ALLE Gut'n Morgen, General.

ANTONIUS   Ihr stärkt mich, Männer.
Der Morgen gleicht der Seele eines Jünglings,
Die sich beweisen will und früh sich zeigt,
So, so; komm, gib das mir: nein, so herum;
In Ordnung. Meine Dame, lebt nun wohl,
Was immer auch mit mir geschieht: dies sei
Des Ritters Abschiedskuß: verwerflich wär's
Und einer Rüge wert, wenn wir uns länger
Mechanisch Höflichkeiten sagten; ich
Verlasse Euch, ein Mann aus Stahl. Adieu.

CHARMIAN Beliebts Euch, Euch zurückzuziehn?

CLEOPATRA   So führt mich:
Groß tritt er an: wenn ein Duell der beiden
Den Ausgang dieses Krieges könnt entscheiden,
Antonius würde – aber so – nun, gehn wir.

Trumpets sound. Enter Anthony, and Eros.

Eros. The Gods make this a happy day to *Anthony*.
Ant. Would thou, & those thy scars had once preuaild
　　To make me fight at Land.
Eros. Had'st thou done so,
　　The Kings that haue reuolted, and the Soldier
　　That has this morning left thee, would haue still
　　Followed thy heeles.
Ant. Whose gone this morning?
Eros. Who? one euer neere thee, call for *Enobarbus*,
　　He shall not heare thee, or from *Cæsars* Campe,
　　Say I am none of thine.
Ant. What sayest thou?
Sold. Sir he is with *Cæsar*.
Eros. Sir, his Chests and Treasure he has not with him.

Ant. Is he gone?
Sol. Most certaine.
Ant. Go *Eros*, send his Treasure after, do it,
　　Detaine no iot I charge thee: write to him,
　　(I will subscribe) gentle adieu's, and greetings;
　　Say, that I wish he neuer finde more cause
　　To change a Master. Oh my Fortunes haue
　　Corrupted honest men. Dispatch *Enobarbus*.　　　*Exit*

Fünfte Szene

Antonius, Eros, Alter Soldat.

ALTER SOLDAT Gebt heut, ihr Götter, dem Antonius Glück!
ANTONIUS Ich wollt, du hättst mit deinen Narben mich
    Zur Schlacht an Land bewogen!
ALTER SOLDAT   Hätt ich das,
    Die abgefall'nen Könige und der
    Soldat, der dich heut früh verließ, sie folgten
    Noch deinen Fersen.
ANTONIUS   Wer ging heute früh?
ALTER SOLDAT Wer? Einer, der dir nah war, Enobarbus!
    Rufst du ihn, er hört nicht oder sagt
    Aus Caesars Lager dir ›Nicht mich‹.
ANTONIUS   Was sagst du?
ALTER SOLDAT Sir, er ist bei Caesar.
EROS   Sir, was er
    Besaß an Kisten und an Geld, nahm er
    Nicht mit sich.
ANTONIUS   Er ist weg?
ALTER SOLDAT   Todsicher.
ANTONIUS Eros, send sein Gold ihm nach, tus gleich,
    Behalt kein Jota, das ist ein Befehl:
    Schreib einen Brief – ich will ihn unterzeichnen –
    Voll freundlicher Adieus und Grüße; sag ihm,
    Ich hoffe, er hat nie noch bessre Gründe,
    Den Herrn zu wechseln. O, mein Schicksal hat
    Auch Ehrliche bestochen. – Enobarbus.

Flourish. Enter Agrippa, Cæsar, with Enobarbus,
and Dollabella.

Cæs. Go forth *Agrippa*, and begin the fight:
  Our will is *Anthony* be tooke aliue:
  Make it so knowne.
Agrip. *Cæsar*, I shall.
Cæsar. The time of vniuersall peace is neere:
  Proue this a prosp'rous day, the three nook'd world
  Shall beare the Oliue freely.
                    Enter a Messenger.
Mes. *Anthony* is come into the Field.

Cæs. Go charge *Agrippa*,
  Plant those that haue reuolted in the Vant,
  That *Anthony* may seeme to spend his Fury
  Vpon himselfe.   *Exeunt.*
Enob. *Alexas* did reuolt, and went to Iewrij on
  Affaires of *Anthony*, there did disswade
  Great *Herod* to incline himselfe to *Cæsar*,
  And leaue his Master *Anthony*. For this paines,
  Cæsar hath hang'd him: *Camindius* and the rest
  That fell away, haue entertainment, but
  No honourable trust: I haue done ill,
  Of which I do accuse my selfe so sorely,
  That I will ioy no more.

                    Enter a Soldier of Cæsars.
Sol. *Enobarbus*, *Anthony*
  Hath after thee sent all thy Treasure, with

Sechste Szene

Caesar, Agrippa, Enobarbus, Dolabella.

CAESAR Rück vor, Agrippa, und beginn die Schlacht:
　　Antonius will ich lebend, mache das
　　Bekannt.
AGRIPPA　　Das werd ich, Caesar.
CAESAR Allen Kontinenten winkt der Frieden:
　　Gelingt uns dieser Tag, dann schmückt der Ölzweig
　　Die drei Enden dieser Welt.
　　　　　　　　　Ein Bote.
BOTE　　　　　　　　　Antonius
　　Ist aufmarschiert.
CAESAR　　　　　　Lauf, richt Agrippa aus,
　　Ganz vorn soll er die Überläufer aufstelln,
　　Dann sieht es aus, als ob Antonius' Wut
　　Ihm selbst gilt.　　　　*Alle ab, bis auf Enobarbus.*
ENOBARBUS Alexas revoltierte; von Antonius
　　Nach Judäa abgesandt, beschwatzte
　　Er den mächtigen Herodes, sich
　　Caesar anzuschließen und verriet
　　So den eignen Oberherrn. Die Mühe
　　Vergalt ihm Caesar mit dem Strick. Canidius
　　Und die andern Deserteure finden
　　Ein Unterkommen, aber kein Vertrauen:
　　Übel habe ich getan und klage
　　Mich so bitter an, daß nichts mehr mich
　　Noch freuen kann.
　　　　　　　　　Ein Soldat.
SOLDAT　　　　　　Ihr, Enobarbus,
　　Euch schickt Antonius Euer ganzes

His Bounty ouer-plus. The Messenger
Came on my guard, and at thy Tent is now
Vnloading of his Mules.

Eno. I giue it you.

Sol. Mocke not *Enobarbus*,
I tell you true: Best you saf't the bringer
Out of the hoast, I must attend mine Office,
Or would haue done't my selfe. Your Emperor
Continues still a Ioue.   *Exit*

Enob. I am alone the Villaine of the earth,
And feele I am so most. Oh *Anthony*,
Thou Mine of Bounty, how would'st thou haue payed
My better seruice, when my turpitude
Thou dost so Crowne with Gold. This blowes my hart,
If swift thought breake it not: a swifter meane
Shall out-strike thought, but thought will doo't. I feele
I fight against thee: No I will go seeke
Some Ditch, wherein to dye: the foul'st best fits
My latter part of life.   *Exit.*

Alarum, Drummes and Trumpets.
Enter Agrippa.

Agrip Retire, we haue engag'd our selues too farre:
Cæsar himselfe ha's worke, and our oppression
Exceeds what we expected.   *Exit.*

Alarums.
Enter Anthony, and Scarrus wounded.

Scar. O my braue Emperor, this is fought indeed,

Hab und Gut nach, obendrein mit Grüßen.
Ich steh da Posten, wo der Bote durchkam,
Der jetzt bei deinem Zelt die Mulis ablädt.
ENOBARBUS Ich schenk's dir.
SOLDAT   Werd nicht witzig, Enobarbus,
    Es ist, wie ich dir sage: sorg dafür,
    Daß der Mann heil raus kommt hier. Ich
    Muß zurück, sonst würd ich's selber machen.
    Dein Imperator bleibt ein Jupiter.   *Ab.*
ENOBARBUS Nie sah die Erde übleren Verrat
    Als meinen, und ich fühl es tief. Antonius,
    Du Berg der Milde, womit wolltest du
    Wohl bessren Dienst mir lohnen, wenn mit Gold
    Du meine Schandtat krönst! Es drückt das Herz
    Mir ab: bricht's der Gedanke mir nicht schnell,
    So tilgt ein schnellres Mittel den Gedanken,
    Doch ich fühle, der Gedanke bricht es.
    Ich dich bekriegen? Nein, ich geh und such mir
    Ein Loch, um drin zu sterben: passen wird es,
    Je stinkender es ist, nur desto besser
    Zum Ende meines Lebens.

                Siebte Szene

            Agrippa, Soldaten.

AGRIPPA Zieht euch zurück, wir sind fast abgeschnitten:
    Caesar selbst hat gut zu tun, der Druck
    Ist stärker als wir dachten.
                        Alle ab.
                    Antonius, Scarus.
SCARUS Das nenn ich Krieg, mein großer Imperator!

Had we done so at first, we had drouen them home
With clowts about their heads.   *Far off.*
Ant. Thou bleed'st apace.
Scar. I had a wound heere that was like a T,
    But now 'tis made an H.
Ant. They do retyre.
Scar. Wee'l beat'em into Bench-holes, I haue yet
    Roome for six scotches more.
                        Enter Eros.
Eros. They are beaten Sir, and our aduantage serues
    For a faire victory.
Scar. Let vs score their backes,
    And snatch 'em vp, as we take Hares behinde,
    'Tis sport to maul a Runner.

Ant. I will reward thee
    Once for thy sprightly comfort, and ten-fold
    For thy good valour. Come thee on.
Scar. Ile halt after.   *Exeunt*

        Alarum. Enter Anthony againe in a March.
            Scarrus, with others.

Ant. We haue beate him to his Campe: Runne one
    Before, & let the Queen know of our guests: to morrow
    Before the Sun shall see's, wee'l spill the blood
    That ha's to day escap'd. I thanke you all,
    For doughty handed are you, and haue fought
    Not as you seru'd the Cause, but as't had beene
    Each mans like mine: you haue shewne all *Hectors.*

Das gleich so, und wir hätten sie mit Pflastern
Auf den Köpfen heimgeschickt.
ANTONIUS   Du blutest.
SCARUS Erst sah die Schramme wie groß T aus, aber
    Jetzt gleicht sie mehr groß H.
ANTONIUS   Sie blasen Rückzug.
SCARUS Wir prügeln sie in alle Scheißhauslöcher,
    Hier haben noch sechs Kratzer Platz.
                            Eros.
EROS Sie sind geschlagen, Sir; und unser Vorteil
    Reicht gut für einen Sieg.
SCARUS   Den Buckel laßt uns
    Ihnen kerben und sie wie die Hasen
    Bei den Fersen packen, Jagdsport ist es
    Was wegrennt, zu vermöbeln.
ANTONIUS   Das macht Mut,
    Den ich dir lohnen will, und zehnmal mehr
    Noch deinen eignen. Vorwärts.
SCARUS   Ich hink nach.

Achte Szene

Antonius, Scarus.

ANTONIUS Bis in sein Camp ist er zurückgeworfen.
    Lauf einer vor, der Königin zu melden,
    Was wir vollbrachten: morgen früh, eh uns
    Die Sonne sieht, vergießen wir das Blut,
    Das heut entkam, Dank sei euch allen, denn
    Beherzte Hände habt ihr, habt gekämpft,
    Als dientet ihr nicht irgendeiner Sache,
    Sondern Eurer: alle wart ihr Hektors.

Enter the Citty, clip your Wiues, your Friends,
Tell them your feats, whil'st they with ioyfull teares
Wash the congealement from your wounds, and kisse
The Honour'd-gashes whole.

Giue me thy hand,
To this great Faiery, Ile commend thy acts,
Make her thankes blesse thee. Oh thou day o'th'world,
Chaine mine arm'd necke, leape thou, Attyre and all
Through proofe of Harnesse to my heart, and there
Ride on the pants triumphing.

Cleo. Lord of Lords.
Oh infinite Vertue, comm'st thou smiling from
The worlds great snare vncaught.
Ant. Mine Nightingale,
We haue beate them to their Beds.
What Gyrle, though gray
Do somthing mingle with our yonger brown, yet ha we
A Braine that nourishes our Nerues, and can
Get gole for gole of youth. Behold this man,
Commend vnto his Lippes thy fauouring hand,
Kisse it my Warriour: He hath fought to day,
As if a God in hate of Mankinde, had
Destroyed in such a shape.
Cleo. Ile giue thee Friend
An Armour all of Gold: it was a Kings.

Ant. He has deseru'd it, were it Carbunkled
Like holy Phœbus Carre. Giue me thy hand,
Through Alexandria make a iolly March,

Zieht in die Stadt ein, eure Frauen schließt,
Schließt eure Freunde wieder in die Arme,
Erzählt die Heldentaten, derweil sie
Das Blut euch ab mit Freudentränen waschen
Und Küsse eure Ehrenwunden schließen.

Deine Hand. Der großen Zauberin
Sing ich dein Heldenlied, auf daß
Ihr Dank dich segne. O du Tag der Welt,
Umschling den erz'nen Nacken, springe du,
Geschmückt und alles, durch den harten Panzer
An mein Herz und reit auf seinen Schlägen
Im Triumph.
CLEOPATRA   Mein Mann der Männer,
    O Tapferkeit unsagbar, kommst du lächelnd
    Vom großen Netz der Welt und ungefangen?
ANTONIUS Meine Nachtigall, wir haben sie
    Zu Bett geklopft. Was, Mädchen, mischt sich auch
    Hier und da Grau uns in das jüngre Braun,
    Ein Hirn besitzen wir einstweilen noch,
    Das seine Nerven nährt und mit der Jugend
    Gleichzieht Zug um Zug. Merk dir den Mann:
    Dem befiehl den Kuß der hohen Hand:
    Küß sie, mein Krieger: er hat heut gefochten,
    Als sei ein Gott, der Männer haßt, erschienen,
    In Mannsgestalt sie zu verheeren.
CLEOPATRA   Freund,
    Ich schenk dir eine gold'ne Rüstung; vor dir
    Trug ein König sie.
ANTONIUS   Er hat's verdient,
    Strahlte sie auch hell wie Phoebus Wagen.
    Reich mir deine Hand, und wir marschieren

Beare our hackt Targets, like the men that owe them.
Had our great Pallace the capacity
To Campe this hoast, we all would sup together,
And drinke Carowses to the next dayes Fate
Which promises Royall perill, Trumpetters
With brazen dinne blast you the Citties eare,
Make mingle with our ratling Tabourines,
That heauen and earth may strike their sounds together,
Applauding our approach.   *Exeunt.*

Enter a Centerie, and his Company, Enobarbus followes.

Cent. If we be not releeu'd within this houre,
    We must returne to'th'Court of Guard: the night
    Is shiny, and they say, we shall embattaile
    By'th'second houre i'th'Morne.
1. *Watch.* This last day was a shrew'd one too's.

Enob. Oh beare me witnesse night.
2 What man is this?
1 Stand close, and list him.
Enob. Be witnesse to me (O thou blessed Moone)
    When men reuolted shall vpon Record
    Beare hatefull memory: poore *Enobarbus* did
    Before thy face repent.

Cent. *Enobarbus?*
2 Peace: Hearke further.
Enob. Oh Soueraigne Mistris of true Melancholly,

Vergnügt durch Alexandria und zeigen
Unsre Schilde, schartig wie die Träger.
Wär der Palast nur groß genug, das Heer
Einzuquartieren, speisten wir da alle,
Und tränken reihum auf den nächsten Tag,
Der königlich Gefahren uns verheißt.
Trompeter, sprengt das Ohr der Stadt mit Blechlärm,
Vermischt mit dem Gedröhn von unsern Trommeln,
Bis Erd und Himmel aufeinander schlagen
Im Beifall, den sie unsrer Ankunft spenden.   *Alle ab.*

Neunte Szene

Posten 1, Posten 2, Enobarbus.

POSTEN 1 Werden wir nicht bald hier abgelöst,
    Müssen wir ins Wachlokal zurück:
    Die Nacht ist mondhell, und es heißt, die Schlacht
    Beginnt um zwei Uhr früh.
POSTEN 2   Der letzte Tag
    War bös für uns.
ENOBARBUS   O sei mir Zeugin, Nacht –
POSTEN 2 Wer ist der Kerl?
POSTEN 1   Bleib, wo du bist. Und Ruhe.
ENOBARBUS Sei meine Zeugin, keusche Göttin du
    Des heilig stillen Monds, wird einst die Liste
    Treuvergessner Männer haßerfüllt
    Gelesen: hier vor deinem Antlitz
    Bereute Enobarbus.
POSTEN 2   Enobarbus?
POSTEN 1 Still!
ENOBARBUS   O hohe Herrin echter Schwermut,

The poysonous dampe of night dispunge vpon me,
That Life, a very Rebell to my will,
May hang no longer on me. Throw my heart
Against the flint and hardnesse of my fault,
Which being dried with greefe, will breake to powder,
And finish all foule thoughts. Oh *Anthony*,
Nobler then my reuolt is Infamous,
Forgiue me in thine owne particular,
But let the world ranke me in Register
A Master leauer, and a fugitiue:
Oh *Anthony*! Oh *Anthony*!

1 Let's speake to him.

Cent. Let's heare him, for the things he speakes
    May concerne *Cæsar*.

2 Let's do so, but he sleepes.

Cent. Swoonds rather, for so bad a Prayer as his
    Was neuer yet for sleepe.

1 Go we to him.

2 Awake sir, awake, speake to vs.

1 Heare you sir?

Cent. The hand of death hath raught him.
                Drummes afarre off.
    Hearke the Drummes demurely wake the sleepers:
    Let vs beare him to'th'Court of Guard: he is of note:
    Our houre is fully out.

2 Come on then, he may recouer yet.   *exeunt*

Benetze mich mit gift'gem Nachttau, mach,
Daß das Leben, Erzfeind meines Willens,
Mich länger nicht umklammert hält. Mein Herz
Wirf an den harten Felsen meiner Schuld,
Es wird, vom Gram gedörrt, zu Staub zerfallen
Und alles kranke Denken enden. O
Antonius, der du so hoch stehst, daß ich
So tief nicht sinken kann, vergib du mir,
Doch laß die Welt mich im Register führen
Der Fahnenflüchtigen und Überläufer.
O Antonius! Antonius!
POSTEN 2 Reden wir ihn an?
POSTEN 1   Wir lauschen, 's könnt
Wichtig sein für Caesar.
POSTEN 2   Machen wir.
Jetzt ist er eingeschlafen.
POSTEN 1   Fiel wohl mehr
In Ohnmacht, weil, so übel betet keiner
Der gut schlafen möchte.
POSTEN 2   Gehn wir zu ihm.
POSTEN 1 Wacht auf, Sir! Sir, wacht auf und sprecht mit uns.
POSTEN 2 He, Sir!
POSTEN 1   Die Faust des Tods hat ihn gerafft.

POSTEN 2 Horch, die Trommeln schlagen dumpf und wecken,
Was noch zu wecken ist. Wir tragen ihn
Ins Wachlokal, er ist 'ne Größe, und
Unser Dienst ist 'rum.
POSTEN 1 Faß an. Vielleicht erholt er sich.

Enter Anthony and Scarrus, with their Army.

Ant. Their preparation is to day by Sea,
    We please them not by Land.
Scar. For both, my Lord.
Ant. I would they'ld fight i'th'Fire, or i'th'Ayre,
    Wee'ld fight there too. But this it is, our Foote
    Vpon the hilles adioyning to the Citty
    Shall stay with vs. Order for Sea is giuen,
    They haue put forth the Hauen:
    Where their appointment we may best discouer,
    And looke on their endeuour.   *exeunt*

Enter Cæsar, and his Army.

Cæs. But being charg'd, we will be still by Land,
    Which as I tak't we shall, for his best force
    Is forth to Man his Gallies. To the Vales,
    And hold our best aduantage.   *exeunt.*

Alarum afarre off, as at a Sea-fight.
Enter Anthony, and Scarrus.

Ant. Yet they are not ioyn'd:
    Where yon'd Pine does stand, I shall discouer all.
    Ile bring thee word straight, how 'tis like to go.   *exit.*

Zehnte Szene

Antonius, Scarus.

ANTONIUS Heut rüsten sie zum Seekrieg, denn zu Lande
  Woll'n wir nicht gefallen.
SCARUS   Weder noch, Herr.
ANTONIUS Und kämpften sie in Feuer oder Luft
  Tun wir das auch. Bis dahin faßt das Fußvolk
  Mit uns gemeinsam Posten auf den Hügeln
  Rings um die Stadt (die Flotte hat Befehle
  Und lief schon aus), von wo wir ihre Stärke
  Und ihre Taktik gut erkennen können.

Elfte Szene

Caesar, Heerführer.

CAESAR Erfolgt kein Angriff, halten wir die Stellung,
  Und so wird's, denk ich, werden, denn
  Seine besten Truppen sind zum Kampf
  Auf die Galeeren kommandiert. Besetzt
  Die Ebene und seht auf unsern Vorteil.

Zwölfte Szene

Antonius, Scarus.

ANTONIUS Noch keine Schlacht zu sehn: dort bei der Pinie
  Hab ich mehr Übersicht: gleich meld ich dir,
  Wie es sich anläßt.

Scar. Swallowes haue built
    In *Cleopatra's* Sailes their nests. The Auguries
    Say, they know not, they cannot tell, looke grimly,
    And dare not speake their knowledge. *Anthony*,
    Is valiant, and deiected, and by starts
    His fretted Fortunes giue him hope and feare
    Of what he has, and has not.

                        Enter Anthony.
Ant. All is lost:
    This fowle Egyptian hath betrayed me:
    My Fleete hath yeelded to the Foe, and yonder
    They cast their Caps vp, and Carowse together
    Like Friends long lost. Triple-turn'd Whore, 'tis thou
    Hast sold me to this Nouice, and my heart
    Makes onely Warres on thee. Bid them all flye:
    For when I am reueng'd vpon my Charme,
    I haue done all. Bid them all flye, be gone.

    Oh Sunne, thy vprise shall I see no more,
    Fortune, and *Anthony* part heere, euen heere
    Do we shake hands? All come to this? The hearts
    That pannelled me at heeles, to whom I gaue
    Their wishes, do dis-Candie, melt their sweets
    On blossoming *Cæsar.* And this Pine is barkt,
    That ouer-top'd them all. Betray'd I am.
    Oh this false Soule of Egypt! this graue Charme,
    Whose eye beck'd forth my Wars, & cal'd them home:
    Whose Bosome was my Crownet, my chiefe end,
    Like a right Gypsie, hath at fast and loose
    Beguil'd me, to the very heart of losse.

SCARUS Schwalben bauten Nester
In Ägyptens Segeln. Die Auguren
Wissen nichts Genaues, können es
Nicht sagen, blicken finster drein, und sind
Zu ängstlich, um ihr Wissen kundzutun.
Antonius ist tapfer und verzagt,
Schubweise läßt sein morsches Glück ihn hoffen
Und fürchten, es sei nicht, wie's ist.

Antonius.

ANTONIUS Hin, alles:
Die schändliche Ägypterin betrog mich,
Dem Feind ergibt sich meine Flotte, schon
Werfen sie die Mützen in die Luft
Und besaufen sich wie alte Freunde
Nach langer Trennung. Dreifachhure du,
Du hast mich diesem Anfänger verkauft,
Und nur mein Herz ist noch dein Feind. Die Losung
Lautet Flucht, verbreite das, denn ich
Will nur noch eines: an ihr Rache nehmen,
Die mich behexte: Flucht die Losung, geh!
O Sonne, nie mehr seh ich dein Erwachen,
Das Glück nimmt von Antonius hier Abschied,
Hier schütteln wir die Hände. Kam's dahin?
Die Hundeherzen, die mir wedelten,
Denen ich ihr Wünschen andressierte,
Liegen nun zu Füßen, lecken nun
Die Hand des blüh'nden Caesar: und die Fichte
Die alle überragte, liegt geschält.
Betrogen bin ich. O das falsche Herz
Ägyptens! Schwüler Zauber, dessen Auge
Mich in den Krieg entsandte und zurückrief,
Deine Brust das Kriegsziel und die Krone,

What *Eros, Eros*?

Enter Cleopatra.

Ah, thou Spell! Auaunt.

Cleo. Why is my Lord enrag'd against his Loue?

Ant. Vanish, or I shall giue thee thy deseruing,
And blemish *Cæsars* Triumph. Let him take thee,
And hoist thee vp to the shouting Plebeians,
Follow his Chariot, like the greatest spot
Of all thy Sex. Most Monster-like be shewne
For poor'st Diminitiues, for Dolts, and let
Patient *Octauia*, plough thy visage vp
With her prepared nailes.   *exit Cleopatra.*
'Tis well th'art gone,
If it be well to liue. But better 'twere
Thou fell'st into my furie, for one death
Might haue preuented many. *Eros*, hoa?
The shirt of *Nessus* is vpon me, teach me
Alcides, thou mine Ancestor, thy rage.
Let me lodge *Licas* on the hornes o'th'Moone,
And with those hands that graspt the heauiest Club,
Subdue my worthiest selfe: The Witch shall die,
To the young Roman Boy she hath sold me, and I fall
Vnder this plot: She dyes for't. *Eros* hoa?   *exit.*

Enter Cleopatra, Charmian, Iras, Mardian.

Cleo. Helpe me my women: Oh hee's more mad
Then *Telamon* for his Shield, the Boare of Thessaly

Gleich 'ner Zigeunerin hast du, als gält's
Nichts als 'nen Kartentrick, mich ausgenommen.
Was, Eros, Eros!

Cleopatra.

Ah, du Blendwerk, weiche!

CLEOPATRA Was tobt Mylord so gegen seine Liebe?

ANTONIUS Hinweg! Sonst geb ich dir, was du verdienst,
Und Caesar ist blamiert. Soll er dich nehmen,
An seinem Mast, der Pöbel johlt, dich hissen,
Folg seinem Wagen als die Ausgeburt
Deines Geschlechts. Gleich einem Monster zeig er
Den Gaffern dich, dem Abschaum, und Octavia
Die sanfte, soll mit spitzen Nägeln dir
Die Fratze pflügen. Gehst du? Das ist gut,
Wenns gut ist, daß du lebst. Viel besser wärs,
Du fielest meiner Wut, der eine Tod
Bewahrte viele Leben. Eros, he!
Ich steck im Nessushemd, jetzt, Herkules,
Mein Ahnherr, lehr mich deinen Zorn.
Hoch zum gehörnten Mond schlag ich den Lichas,
Und Hände, von der schwersten Keule hart,
Zerstör'n, was von mir blieb. Die Hexe sterbe,
Verkauft hat sie mich an Roms Milchgesicht
Das fällt mich, und sie stirbt dafür: He, Eros!

Dreizehnte Szene

Cleopatra, Charmian, Iras, Mardian.

CLEOPATRA Helft, meine Fraun! O, er rast mehr als Ajax
Um des Achilles' Schild, Thessaliens Eber

Was neuer so imbost.

Char. To'th'Monument, there locke your selfe,
And send him word you are dead:
The Soule and Body riue not more in parting,
Then greatnesse going off.

Cleo. To'th'Monument:
Mardian, go tell him I haue slaine my selfe:
Say, that the last I spoke was *Anthony*,
And word it (prythee) pitteously. Hence Mardian,
And bring me how he takes my death to'th'Monument.

Exeunt.

Enter Anthony, and Eros.

Ant. *Eros*, thou yet behold'st me?

Eros. I Noble Lord.

Ant. Sometime we see a clowd that's Dragonish,
A vapour sometime, like a Beare, or Lyon,
A toward Cittadell, a pendant Rocke,
A forked Mountaine, or blew Promontorie
With Trees vpon't, that nodde vnto the world,
And mocke our eyes with Ayre.
Thou hast seene these Signes,
They are blacke Vespers Pageants.

Eros. I my Lord.

Ant. That which is now a Horse, euen with a thoght
the Racke dislimes, and makes it indistinct
As water is in water.

Eros. It does my Lord.

Ant. My good Knaue *Eros*, now thy Captaine is

Hat nicht so geschäumt.

CHARMIAN Zum Grabmal,
Da schließt Euch ein und sagt ihm, Ihr seid tot.
Die Seele trennt sich schwerer nicht vom Körper,
Als wir uns von der Größe.

CLEOPATRA Auf zum Grabmal!
Mardian, du gehst und sagst ihm, ich erstach mich:
Mein letzter Seufzer war ›Antonius!‹
Und bitte, stells ergreifend dar. Mardian!
Komm ja zurück und bring mir, wie er's nimmt.
Zum Grabmal.

Vierzehnte Szene

Antonius, Eros.

ANTONIUS Eros, du siehst mich noch?

EROS Ja, edler Herr.

ANTONIUS Manchmal scheint eine Wolke drachenhaft,
Ein Dunst sieht wie ein Bär aus oder Löwe,
Wie eine Burg mit Türmen, wie ein Felsen,
Wie Gipfelzacken, Vorgebirge, blau
Mit Tannen drauf, die sich zur Erde neigen.
So täuscht das Auge Luft. Du kennst die Zeichen,
Der Dämm'rung Festzug ist's.

EROS Jawohl, Mylord.

ANTONIUS Was ein Pferd war, in Gedankenschnelle
Löst es sich auf, nicht mehr zu unterscheiden,
Wie im Wasser Wasser.

EROS Das ist wahr.

ANTONIUS Eros, mein Junge, hier dein General

Euen such a body: Heere I am *Anthony*,
Yet cannot hold this visible shape (my Knaue)
I made these warres for Egypt, and the Queene,
Whose heart I thought I had, for she had mine:
Which whil'st it was mine, had annext vntoo't
A Million moe, (now lost:) shee *Eros* has
Packt Cards with *Cæsars*, and false plaid my Glory
Vnto an Enemies triumph.
Nay, weepe not gentle *Eros*, there is left vs
Our selues to end our selues.

Enter Mardian.

Oh thy vilde Lady, she has rob'd me of my Sword.

Mar. No *Anthony*,
My Mistris lou'd thee, and her Fortunes mingled
With thine intirely.
Ant. Hence sawcy Eunuch peace, she hath betraid me,
And shall dye the death.
Mar. Death of one person, can be paide but once,
And that she ha's discharg'd. What thou would'st do
Is done vnto thy hand: the last she spake
Was *Anthony*, most Noble *Anthony*.
Then in the midd'st a tearing grone did breake
The name of *Anthony*: it was diuided
Betweene her heart, and lips: she rendred life
Thy name so buried in her.

Ant. Dead then?
Mar. Dead.
Ant. Vnarme *Eros*, the long dayes taske is done,
And we must sleepe: That thou depart'st hence safe
Does pay thy labour richly: Go.   *exit Mardian.*

Ist auch aus solchem Stoff: ich hier, Antonius,
Kann meinen Umriß nicht mehr halten, Junge,
Ich war Soldat der Königin Ägyptens,
Ihr Herz, dacht ich, war mein, denn meins war ihres:
Solang es meins war, hingen Millionen
An ihm, wo sind sie jetzt? Sie, Eros, spielte
Caesars Farbe, ich warf meine Karten
Zu meines Gegners Trumpf.
Nicht weinen, Eros, wir sind ja noch übrig,
Um mit uns Schluß zu machen.

     Mardian.

        Diese Hündin,
Deine Lady, stahl mein Schwert.

ALEXAS   Antonius,
Nein, Euch liebte meine Herrin, innigst
War ihr Geschick dem Eurigen verwoben.

ANTONIUS Weg, schmieriger Kastrat! Wirst du wohl schweigen!
Betrogen hat sie mich, sie ist des Todes.

ALEXAS Pro Person kommt man auf einen Tod,
Den hat sie hinter sich. Was du getan sehn willst,
Getan ist's ohne dich: ihr letztes Wort
›Antonius, liebster, edelster Antonius‹,
Sodann brach reißend' Stöhnen deinen Namen
Mitten durch, je eine Hälfte blieb
In ihrem Herzen stecken wie auf ihren Lippen,
Sie gab ihr Leben hin, begrub den Namen
Sozusagen in sich selbst.

ANTONIUS   Ist tot?

ALEXAS   Tot.

ANTONIUS Eros, die Waffen weg. Der Tag, lang hell,
Ist um. Wir müssen schlafen. Geh du, wie
Du kamst. Dein Lohn ist das. Herunter damit!

Off, plucke off,
The seuen-fold shield of *Aiax* cannot keepe
The battery from my heart. Oh cleaue my sides.
Heart, once be stronger then thy Continent,
Cracke thy fraile Case. Apace *Eros*, apace;
No more a Soldier: bruised peeces go,
You haue bin Nobly borne. From me awhile.   *exit Eros*
I will o're-take thee *Cleopatra*, and
Weepe for my pardon. So it must be, for now
All length is Torture: since the Torch is out,
Lye downe and stray no farther. Now all labour
Marres what it does: yea, very force entangles
It selfe with strength: Seale then and all is done.
Eros? I come my Queene. *Eros*? Stay for me,
Where Soules do couch on Flowers, wee'l hand in hand,
And with our sprightly Port make the Ghostes gaze:
Dido, and her *Aeneas* shall want Troopes,
And all the haunt be ours. Come *Eros*, *Eros*.

                    Enter Eros.

Eros. What would my Lord?
Ant. Since *Cleopatra* dyed,
I haue liu'd in such dishonour, that the Gods
Detest my basenesse. I, that with my Sword,
Quarter'd the World, and o're greene Neptunes backe
With Ships, made Cities; condemne my selfe, to lacke
The Courage of a Woman, lesse Noble minde
Then she which by her death, our *Cæsar* telles
I am Conqueror of my selfe. Thou art sworne *Eros*,
That when the exigent should come, which now
Is come indeed: When I should see behinde me
Th'ineuitable prosecution of disgrace and horror,
That on my command, thou then would'st kill me.

Des Ajax siebenhäut'ger Schild wehrt nicht
Den Sturm ab auf dies Herz. O fallt, ihr Mauern!
Sei einmal stärker, Herz, als deine Schale,
Brich aus! Beeil dich, Eros, mach schon!
Soldat nicht wieder: Blech, samt deinen Beulen
Geh, mit Glanz getragen wardst du. Laß mich.
Ich überhole dich, Cleopatra,
Und weine um Vergebung. Das muß sein.
Abstand ist Qual. Die Fackel ist erloschen,
Ruh aus, irr nicht umher. Noch mehr der Mühe
Macht alles hin: Kraft stolpert über Stärke,
Drum Siegel drauf, und alles ist getan.
Eros! – Ich komme, meine Königin! –
Eros! – Erwarte mich, da wo die Seelen
Auf Blumenbetten ruhn, Hand in Hand
Wolln wir mit unserm lebensvollen Auftritt
Die Schatten staunen machen: Dido und Aeneas
Wird's an Gefolgschaft fehlen und ihr Schwarm
Läuft uns nach. Eros, Eros, komm!
EROS Was wünscht mein Herr?
ANTONIUS   Cleopatra ist tot,
Und seither lebe ich in Schande, so tief,
Daß Götter meine Niedrigkeit verabscheun.
Ich, der mit dem Schwert die Welt vierteilte,
Ich, der Neptuns grünen Rücken reitend,
Aus Schiffen Städte schuf, sprech mir mein Urteil:
Den Mut der Frau nicht hab ich, noch den Rang
Wie sie, die unserm Caesar durch den Tod
Die Botschaft schickt ›Erobert habe ich mich‹.
Du schwurst es, Eros, daß du, wenn das Unheil
Käme und jetzt ist es da, wenn ich
Gehetzt mich nur von Schmach und Schrecken sähe,

Doo't, the time is come: Thou strik'st not me,
'Tis *Cæsar* thou defeat'st. Put colour in thy Cheeke.

Eros. The Gods with-hold me,
  Shall I do that which all the Parthian Darts,
  (Though Enemy) lost ayme, and could not.
Ant. Eros,
  Would'st thou be window'd in great Rome, and see
  Thy Master thus with pleacht Armes, bending downe
  His corrigible necke, his face subdu'de
  To penetratiue shame; whil'st the wheel'd seate
  Of Fortunate *Cæsar* drawne before him, branded
  His Basenesse that ensued.
Eros. I would not see't.
Ant. Come then: for with a wound I must be cur'd.
  Draw that thy honest Sword, which thou hast worne
  Most vsefull for thy Country.
Eros. Oh sir, pardon me.
Ant. When I did make thee free, swor'st yu not then
  To do this when I bad thee? Do it at once,
  Or thy precedent Seruices are all
  But accidents vnpurpos'd. Draw, and come.
Eros. Turne from me then that Noble countenance,
  Wherein the worship of the whole world lyes.
Ant. Loe thee.
Eros. My sword is drawne.
Ant. Then let it do at once
  The thing why thou hast drawne it.
Eros. My deere Master,
  My Captaine, and my Emperor. Let me say
  Before I strike this bloody stroke, Farwell.

Daß du dann, wenn ich es dir befehle,
Mich töten würdest. Tu's, die Zeit ist reif.
Du schlägst nicht mich, dem Caesar gilt der Hieb.
Tu Farbe auf die Wangen.

EROS   Niemals, Götter!
Soll ich können, was die Partherpfeile
Feindlich nicht gekonnt?

ANTONIUS   Mein Eros,
Willst du in Rom am Fenster stehn und zusehn,
Wie dein Herr so, mit stillgelegten Armen
Den gezähmten Nacken beugt, die Stirn
Von Scham verbrüht, indes der Siegeswagen
Caesars ihm vorausrollt und zum Nichts
Den stempelt, der ihm folgt?

EROS   Das will ich nicht.

ANTONIUS Dann komm: du heilst mich nur mit einer Wunde.
Zieh das brave Schwert, das deinem Land
Schon nützlich war.

EROS   O, Sir, wollt mir vergeben.

ANTONIUS Als ich dich frei erklärte, schwurst du nicht,
Mir dies zu tun, wenn ich dich bäte? Tu es
Jetzt! Sonst ist dein früherer Verdienst
Nichts als ein Zufall, grundlos. Zieh und komm.

EROS So wendet Euer Angesicht von mir,
Die Welt verehrt es, wie denn nicht auch ich?

ANTONIUS Nun los!

EROS   Ich zog das Schwert.

ANTONIUS   Dann laß es tun,
Wozu du es gezogen.

EROS   Liebster Herr,
Mein General und Kaiser: Euch sag ich,
Eh ich blutig zuschlag, Lebewohl.

Ant. 'Tis said man, and farewell.

Eros. Farewell great Chiefe. Shall I strike now?

Ant. Now *Eros*.   *Killes himselfe.*

Eros. Why there then:

    Thus I do escape the sorrow of Anthonies death.

Ant. Thrice-Nobler then my selfe,

    Thou teachest me: Oh valiant *Eros*, what

    I should, and thou could'st not, my Queene and *Eros*

    Haue by their braue instruction got vpon me

    A Noblenesse in Record. But I will bee

    A Bride-groome in my death, and run intoo't

    As to a Louers bed. Come then, and *Eros*,

    Thy Master dies thy Scholler; to do thus

    I learnt of thee. How, not dead? Not dead?

    The Guard, how? Oh dispatch me.

Enter a Guard.

1. *Guard.* What's the noise?

Ant. I haue done my worke ill Friends:

    Oh make an end of what I haue begun.

2 The Starre is falne.

1 And time is at his Period.

All. Alas, and woe.

Ant. Let him that loues me, strike me dead.

1 Not I.

2 Nor I.

3 Nor any one.   *exeunt*

Dercetus. Thy death and fortunes bid thy folowers fly

    This sword but shewne to *Cæsar* with this tydings,

    Shall enter me with him.

Enter Diomedes.

ANTONIUS Es ist gesagt, Mann, lebe wohl.

EROS Lebt wohl, mein Held. Jetzt soll ich schlagen?

ANTONIUS   Jetzt.

EROS Warum auch nicht: entgeh' ich doch der Trauer
    Um des Antonius' Tod.   *Er ersticht sich.*

ANTONIUS   Du dreifach Edler,
    Du lehrtest mich, o kühner Eros, was ich
    Selbst tun mußte und du drum nicht konntest.
    Die Königin und Eros haben sich,
    Indem sie mich so mutig instruierten,
    Unsterblichkeit gesichert. Ich jedoch
    Will Bräutigam sein meines Todesengels,
    Seine Brust mein Hochzeitsbett. Und, Eros,
    Dein Herr stirbt als dein Schüler: dies ist's,
    Was ich lernte. Wie, nicht tot? Nicht tot?
    Wache, he! O, helft mir weg!
       Wache 1, Wache 2, Wache 3, Decretas.

WACHE 1   Wer ruft?

ANTONIUS Ich machte schlechte Arbeit, Freunde: O
    Beendet, was ich anfing.

WACHE 2   Unser Stern
    Erlischt.

WACHE 1 Die Zeit steht still.

ALLE   Weh uns! Weh allen!

ANTONIUS Wer mich liebt, der schlägt mich tot.

WACHE 1   Ich nicht.

WACHE 2 Ich auch nicht.

WACHE 3   Und auch sonst kein Mensch. *Wachen ab.*

DECRETAS Dein Tod und Ende gibt Befehl zur Flucht.
    Dies Schwert, gezeigt dem Caesar, samt der Nachricht,
    Führn mich bei ihm ein.
       Diomedes.

Dio. Where's *Anthony*?

Decre. There *Diomed* there.

Diom. Liues he: wilt thou not answer man?

Ant. Art thou there *Diomed*?
Draw thy sword, and giue mee,
Suffising strokes for death.

Diom. Most absolute Lord:
My Mistris *Cleopatra* sent me to thee.

Ant. When did shee send thee?

Diom. Now my Lord.

Anth. Where is she?   (feare

Diom. Lockt in her Monument: she had a Prophesying
Of what hath come to passe: for when she saw
(Which neuer shall be found) you did suspect
She had dispos'd with *Cæsar*, and that your rage
Would not be purg'd, she sent you word she was dead:
But fearing since how it might worke, hath sent
Me to proclaime the truth, and I am come
I dread, too late.

Ant. Too late good *Diomed*: call my Guard I prythee.

Dio. What hoa: the Emperors Guard,
The Guard, what hoa? Come, your Lord calles.
   Enter 4. or 5. of the Guard of Anthony.

Ant. Beare me good Friends where *Cleopatra* bides,
'Tis the last seruice that I shall command you.

1 Woe, woe are we sir, you may not liue to weare
All your true Followers out.

All. Most heauy day.

Ant. Nay good my Fellowes, do not please sharp fate
To grace it with your sorrowes. Bid that welcome
Which comes to punish vs, and we punish it

DIOMEDES Antonius?

DECRETAS   Da, Diomedes, da.

DIOMEDES Lebt er? Kannst du nicht reden, Mann?

ANTONIUS Bist du das, Diomedes? Zieh dein Schwert,
     Und schlag so oft zu, bis ich tot bin.

DIOMEDES   Herr,
     Cleopatra schickt, meine Herrin, mich.

ANTONIUS Wann schickte sie dich?

DIOMEDES   Eben jetzt, Mylord.

ANTONIUS Wo ist sie?

DIOMEDES   In ihr Grabmal eingeschlossen;
     Ein fürchterliches Ahnen kam ihr dessen,
     Was vor sich geht: denn als sie sah, Ihr argwöhnt –
     Wofür es niemals Grund wird geben – sie
     Hielte es mit Caesar und Eu'r Zorn
     War unauslöschlich, gab sie sich für tot aus;
     Seither in Sorge, was dies wohl bewirke,
     Schickt sie nun mich, die Wahrheit zu berichten,
     Und ich, so steht zu fürchten, komm zu spät.

ANTONIUS Zu spät, mein Guter. Ruf mir meine Wachen.

DIOMEDES He, Wache! Wache! He! Wo steckt ihr denn?
     Was macht ihr, kommt, der Imperator ruft.

                    Wachen.

ANTONIUS Cleopatra, tragt, Freunde, mich zu ihr:
     Dann habe ich euch nichts mehr zu befehlen.

WACHE 1 Wir sind in Angst, Sir, Euer Gnaden könnte
     Uns versterben.

ALLE   Allerschwerster Tag!

ANTONIUS Nein, Kameraden, den Gefallen tut
     Dem Unheil nicht, es auch noch zu bejammern:
     Begrüßen wir, was uns zu strafen naht,

Seeming to beare it lightly. Take me vp,
I haue led you oft, carry me now good Friends,
And haue my thankes for all.   *Exit bearing Anthony*

Enter Cleopatra, and her Maides aloft, with
Charmian & Iras.

Cleo. Oh *Charmian*, I will neuer go from hence.
Char. Be comforted deere Madam.
Cleo. No, I will not:
    All strange and terrible euents are welcome,
    But comforts we dispise; our size of sorrow
    Proportion'd to our cause, must be as great
    As that which makes it.

Enter Diomed.
    How now? is he dead?
Diom. His death's vpon him, but not dead.
    Looke out o'th other side your Monument,
    His Guard haue brought him thither.
                Enter Anthony, and the Guard.
Cleo. Oh Sunne,
    Burne the great Sphere thou mou'st in, darkling stand

    The varrying shore o'th'world. O *Antony, Antony, Antony*

    Helpe *Charmian*, helpe *Iras* helpe: helpe Friends
    Below, let's draw him hither.
Ant. Peace,
    Not *Cæsars* Valour hath o'rethrowne *Anthony*,
    But *Anthonie*'s hath Triumpht on it selfe.

Dann strafen wir es durch den Schein des Gleichmuts.
Nehmt mich auf: tragt, liebe Freunde, mich,
Der euch so oft voran zog. Und habt Dank.   *Alle ab.*

Fünfzehnte Szene

Cleopatra, Charmian, Iras.

CLEOPATRA O Charmian, hier bleibe ich für immer.
CHARMIAN Seid zuversichtlich, Madam.
CLEOPATRA   Nein, ich will nicht:
    Alles Schlimme, alle Übel finden
    Einlaß, Zuversicht wird abgewiesen;
    Der Umfang unsres Grams muß, seinem Grund
    Entsprechend, so gewaltig sein wie das,
    Was ihn verursacht.
                              Diomedes.
CLEOPATRA   Und nun? Ist er tot?
DIOMEDES Sein Tod ist über ihm, tot ist er nicht.
    Seht nach der andern Seite Eures Grabmals,
    Da bringt ihn seine Wachmannschaft.

CLEOPATRA   O Sonne,
    Die große Sphäre, an der du dich drehst,
    Verschmore, eingedunkelt liegen sollen
    Die Ufer, die verschiedenen, der Welt.
    Antonius! Antonius! Antonius!
    Hilf, Charmian, hilf, Iras, hilf: helft, Freunde,
    Wir wollen ihn heraufziehn.
ANTONIUS   Nein, gebt Ruhe!
    Nicht Caesars Glanz macht den Antonius blaß,
    Antonius feiert eigenen Triumph.

Cleo. So it should be,
   That none but *Anthony* should conquer *Anthony*,
   But woe 'tis so.
Ant. I am dying Egypt, dying; onely
   I heere importune death a–while, vntill
   Of many thousand kisses, the poore last
   I lay vpon thy lippes.
Cleo. I dare not Deere,
   Deere my Lord pardon: I dare not,
   Least I be taken: not th'Imperious shew
   Of the full-Fortun'd *Cæsar*, euer shall
   Be brooch'd with me, if Knife, Drugges, Serpents haue
   Edge, sting, or operation. I am safe:
   Your Wife *Octauia*, with her modest eyes,
   And still Conclusion, shall acquire no Honour
   Demuring vpon me: but come, come *Anthony*,
   Helpe me my women, we must draw thee vp:
   Assist good Friends.

Ant. Oh quicke, or I am gone.
Cleo. Heere's sport indeede:
   How heauy weighes my Lord?
   Our strength is all gone into heauinesse,
   That makes the waight. Had I great *Iuno*'s power,
   The strong wing'd Mercury should fetch thee vp,
   And set thee by Ioues side. Yet come a little,
   Wishers were euer Fooles. Oh come, come, come,
                    They heaue Anthony aloft to Cleopatra.
   And welcome, welcome. Dye when thou hast liu'd,
   Quicken with kissing: had my lippes that power,
   Thus would I weare them out.
All. A heauy sight.

CLEOPATRA So sollt' es sein, daß niemand als Antonius
Antonius schlägt, doch weh, daß es so kam.

ANTONIUS Ich sterbe dir, Ägypten, sterbe; nur
Reiß ich hier dem Tod noch aus, bis ich
Von abertausend Küssen dir den armen
Letzten auf die Lippen drückte.
CLEOPATRA   Ich
Wag es nicht, Geliebter, Liebster, Gnade:
Ich wag es nicht, sie fangen mich: die Schau
Der Herrschgewalt des glücksgeschwellten Caesar
Schmück ich nicht, wo Messer, Schlangen, Gifte
Noch schneiden, stechen, Wirkung tun. Ich bin
Gerettet hier: Octavia, die Gattin,
Kommt dadurch nicht zu Ehren, daß ihr Blick
Kalt auf mir ruht, in schweigender Verachtung.
Doch komm, komm du, Antonius – helft, ihr Frauen –
Wir müssen hoch dich ziehen: liebe Freunde,
Legt Hand an.
ANTONIUS   O, nur schnell, sonst bin ich hin.
CLEOPATRA Das ist ein Sport! Wie schwer Mylord doch wiegt!
Die Kraft hat sich zu Schwermut uns gewandelt,
Das schafft Gewicht. Wär ich an Junos Stelle,
Dich höbe der gefiederte Merkur,
Und Jupiter zur Seite setzt' er dich.
Nur noch ein wenig, die Zeit ist vorbei,
Da Wünsche noch geholfen haben, komm,
O komm, komm, komm. Willkommen!
Willkommen! Stirb nicht, eh du lebtest,
Geheilt von Küssen: hätten meine Lippen
Die Macht, ich nutzte so sie ab.
ALLE   Das sehen!

Ant. I am dying Egypt, dying.
   Giue me some Wine, and let me speake a little.
Cleo. No, let me speake, and let me rayle so hye,
   That the false Huswife Fortune, breake her Wheele,
   Prouok'd by my offence.
Ant. One word (sweet Queene)
   Of *Cæsar* seeke your Honour, with your safety. Oh.

Cleo. They do not go together.
Ant. Gentle heare me,
   None about *Cæsar* trust, but *Proculeius.*
Cleo. My Resolution, and my hands, Ile trust,
   None about *Cæsar.*
Ant. The miserable change now at my end,
   Lament nor sorrow at: but please your thoughts
   In feeding them with those my former Fortunes
   Wherein I liued. The greatest Prince o'th'world,
   The Noblest: and do now not basely dye,
   Not Cowardly put off my Helmet to
   My Countreyman. A Roman, by a Roman
   Valiantly vanquish'd. Now my Spirit is going,
   I can no more.
Cleo. Noblest of men, woo't dye?
   Hast thou no care of me, shall I abide
   In this dull world, which in thy absence is
   No better then a Stye? Oh see my women:
   The Crowne o'th'earth doth melt. My Lord?
   Oh wither'd is the Garland of the Warre,
   The Souldiers pole is falne: young Boyes and Gyrles
   Are leuell now with men: The oddes is gone,
   And there is nothing left remarkeable
   Beneath the visiting Moone.

ANTONIUS Ich sterbe dir, Ägypten, sterbe.
Gebt mir Wein und laßt mich etwas sagen.
CLEOPATRA Nein, mich laßt etwas sagen, laßt mich lauthals
Auf Fortuna schimpfen, bis das falsche Weib,
Von mir gereizt, sein Rad zerbricht.
ANTONIUS   Ein Wort noch,
Süße Königin: bei Caesar suche
Für dich nach Sicherheit und Ehre. O!
CLEOPATRA Die gehen nicht zusammen.
ANTONIUS   Warte, hör mich:
An Caesars Hof trau nur dem Proculeius.
CLEOPATRA Mir selbst und meinen Händen trau ich, keinem
Von Caesars Hof.
ANTONIUS Die armselige Wendung meines Endes
Beklag nicht, noch betraure: dein Gedenken,
Hell es auf mit all dem früh'ren Glück,
In dem ich schwamm, der höchste Fürst der Welt,
Der nobelste, der hier nicht ehrlos stirbt,
Nicht feig den Helm abzieht vor seinem Landsmann,
Vielmehr römisch sich besiegt, den Römer.
Geist, du gehst. Ich kann nicht mehr.

CLEOPATRA   Stirbst du,
Herrlichster der Männer? Was wird dann
Aus mir, soll ich in dieser öden Welt
Ausharren, die, bist du erst fort, nicht besser
Als ein Viehstall ist? O, seht, ihr Frauen,
Das Diadem der Erde schmilzt. Mylord?
O, welk ist aller Schmuck des Kriegs, verglüht
Der Leitstern des Soldaten: Knaben, Mädchen
Gehn jetzt als Männer durch, das Maß kam um,
Und nichts, das nennenswert, bleibt uns erhalten

Char. Oh quietnesse, Lady.
Iras. She's dead too, our Soueraigne.
Char. Lady.
Iras. Madam.
Char. Oh Madam, Madam, Madam.
Iras. Royall Egypt: Empresse.

Char. Peace, peace, *Iras.*
Cleo. No more but in a Woman, and commanded
  By such poore passion, as the Maid that Milkes,
  And doe's the meanest chares. It were for me,
  To throw my Scepter at the iniurious Gods,
  To tell them that this World did equall theyrs,
  Till they had stolne our Iewell. All's but naught:
  Patience is sottish, and impatience does
  Become a Dogge that's mad: Then is it sinne,
  To rush into the secret house of death,
  Ere death dare come to vs. How do you Women?
  What, what good cheere? Why how now *Charmian*?
  My Noble Gyrles? Ah Women, women! Looke
  Our Lampe is spent, it's out. Good sirs, take heart,
  Wee'l bury him: And then, what's braue, what's Noble,
  Let's doo't after the high Roman fashion,
  And make death proud to take vs. Come, away,
  This case of that huge Spirit now is cold.
  Ah Women, Women! Come, we haue no Friend
  But Resolution, and the breefest end.
        Exeunt, bearing of Anthonies body.

Unter dem Wechselmond.

CHARMIAN   O, still doch, Lady.

IRAS Sie ist mit tot, unser Oberhaupt.

CHARMIAN   Mylady!

IRAS Madam!

CHARMIAN   O Madam, Madam, Madam!

IRAS   Ganz
   Ägypten: Kaiserin!

CHARMIAN   Still, Iras, still.

CLEOPATRA Nur eine Frau von vielen, und die Beute
   Von Leidenschaften, einer Kuhmagd gleichend,
   Die melkt und kehrt. Wär's anders, müßte ich
   Mein Szepter nach den schlimmen Göttern schleudern,
   Daß sie wissen, diese Welt kam ihrer gleich,
   Bis sie die Krone stahlen. Alles nichts:
   Geduld ist blöde, Ungeduld ist etwas
   Für tolle Hunde: ist es also sündhaft,
   In das geheime Haus des Tods zu brechen,
   Eh er an uns sich wagt? Wie geht's euch, Mädchen?
   Was denn, lächelt! Wie, was ist dir, Charmian?
   Ihr Guten! Ah, ihr Himmel, Weiber! Weiber!
   Seht doch, unser Licht erlosch, 's ist aus.
   Ihr lieben Herrn, faßt Mut, wir wollen ihn
   Begraben: und nach Art der Römer tun wir
   Dann, was groß und nobel ist und geben
   Dem Tod drei Gründe stolz zu sein. Kommt mit mir,
   Kalt ist die Hülle dieser Riesenseele.
   Ah, Weiber! Weiber! Kommt, zum schnellen Ende
   Braucht es nur Tapferkeit und ruhige Hände.

Enter Cæsar, Agrippa, Dollabella, Menas, with
his Counsell of Warre.

Cæsar. Go to him *Dollabella*, bid him yeeld,
    Being so frustrate, tell him,
    He mockes the pawses that he makes.
Dol. *Cæsar*, I shall.
        Enter Decretas with the sword of Anthony.
Cæs. Wherefore is that? And what art thou that dar'st
    Appeare thus to vs?

Dec. I am call'd *Decretas*,
    Marke Anthony I seru'd, who best was worthie
    Best to be seru'd: whil'st he stood vp, and spoke
    He was my Master, and I wore my life
    To spend vpon his haters. If thou please
    To take me to thee, as I was to him,
    Ile be to *Cæsar:* if yu pleasest not, I yeild thee vp my life.

Cæsar. What is't thou say'st?
Dec. I say (Oh *Caesar*) *Anthony* is dead.
Cæsar. The breaking of so great a thing, should make
    A greater cracke. The round World
    Should haue shooke Lyons into ciuill streets,
    And Cittizens to their dennes. The death of *Anthony*
    Is not a single doome, in the name lay
    A moity of the world.
Dec. He is dead *Cæsar*,
    Not by a publike minister of Iustice,
    Nor by a hyred Knife, but that selfe-hand

FÜNFTER AKT
Erste Szene

Caesar, Agrippa, Dolabella, Maecenas, Gallus, Proculeius.

CAESAR Geh zu ihm, Dolabella, er soll aufhörn.
Sag ihm, erledigt wie er ist, macht ihn
Sein Geziere zum Gespött.

DOLABELLA   Mein Caesar.   *Ab*

CAESAR   Was
Bedeutet das? Wer bist du, daß du dich
Uns so zu nahen wagst?

DECRETAS   Decretas heiß ich,
Ich diente Marc Anton, der es wohl wert war,
Daß ich ihm diente: als er stand und sprach,
War er mein Herr, mein Leben hatt' ich gegen
Seine Hasser. Wenn es dir gefällt,
Mich aufzunehmen, bin ich, was ich ihm war,
Caesar. Wenn's dir nicht gefällt, leg ich
In deine Hand mein Leben.

CAESAR   Was sagst du?

DECRETAS Ich sage, Caesar, Marc Anton ist tot.

CAESAR Warum, wenn ein so riesig Ding zerbricht,
Kracht es nicht lauter? Unsre runde Erde
Muß doch Löwen in die Städte schütteln
Und Bürger in die Wüste! Dieser Tod
Ist mehr als eines Einz'gen Fall, da starb
Die halbe Welt.

DECRETAS   Tot ist er, Caesar, nicht
Durch Schergen der Justiz, noch auch durch ein
Gekauftes Messer, nein, dieselbe Hand,

Which writ his Honor in the Acts it did,
Hath with the Courage which the heart did lend it,
Splitted the heart. This is his Sword,
I robb'd his wound of it: behold it stain'd
With his most Noble blood.

Cæs. Looke you sad Friends,
The Gods rebuke me, but it is Tydings
To wash the eyes of Kings.

Dol. And strange it is,
That Nature must compell vs to lament
Our most persisted deeds.

Mec. His taints and Honours, wag'd equal with him.

Dola. A Rarer spirit neuer
Did steere humanity: but you Gods will giue vs
Some faults to make vs men. *Cæsar* is touch'd.

Mec. When such a spacious Mirror's set before him,
He needes must see him selfe.

Cæsar. Oh *Anthony*,
I haue followed thee to this, but we do launch
Diseases in our Bodies. I must perforce
Haue shewne to thee such a declining day,
Or looke on thine: we could not stall together,
In the whole world. But yet let me lament
With teares as Soueraigne as the blood of hearts,
That thou my Brother, my Competitor,
In top of all designe; my Mate in Empire,
Friend and Companion in the front of Warre,
The Arme of mine owne Body, and the Heart
Where mine his thoughts did kindle; that our Starres

Die tätig ihm Annalen schrieb des Ruhms,
Hat, vom Herzen Kampfesmut sich borgend,
Sein Herz zerschnitten. Dies sein Schwert, ich raubte
Es seiner Wunde: seht, es ist befleckt
Mit seinem edlen Blut.

CAESAR   Ihr trauert, Freunde?
Strafen mich die Götter, diese Nachricht
Wäscht Königsaugen.

AGRIPPA   Und es ist schon seltsam,
Daß die Natur uns nötigt, zu beseufzen,
Was wir so heiß verfolgten.

MAECENAS   Licht und Schatten
War'n in ihm gleich verteilt.

AGRIPPA   Nie ward die Menschheit
Von einem edlern Mann gelenkt. Doch ihr, ihr Götter
Baut Fehler ein, auf daß wir Menschen bleiben.
Caesar ist bewegt.

MAECENAS   Hält man ihm einen
Derart geräum'gen Spiegel vor, muß er
Sich selbst erblicken.

CAESAR   O Antonius,
Ich machte das aus dir, doch wird das Kranke
Geschnitten aus dem Körper. 's war ein Zwang,
Dir deinen Tag zu zeigen, wollte ich
Nicht meinen sehn. Kein Platz war in der Welt
Für dich und mich. Jetzt aber laß mich klagen
Mit Tränen, die dem Herzblut in nichts nachstehn,
Daß du mein Bruder, du mein Mitbeherrscher,
Mein Kamerad am Gipfel des Imperiums,
Freund und Genosse an der Front des Kriegs,
Arm meines Körpers, Herz, an dem das meine
Sich Funken schlug – daß droben unsre Sterne

Vnreconciliable, should diuide our equalnesse to this.
Heare me good Friends,
But I will tell you at some meeter Season,
The businesse of this man lookes out of him,
Wee'l heare him what he sayes.

Enter an Ægyptian.

Whence are you?

Ægyp. A poore Egyptian yet, the Queen my mistris
Confin'd in all, she has her Monument
Of thy intents, desires, instruction,
That she preparedly may frame her selfe
To'th'way shee's forc'd too.

Cæsar. Bid her haue good heart,
She soone shall know of vs, by some of ours,
How honourable, and how kindely Wee
Determine for her. For *Cæsar* cannot leaue to be vngentle

Ægypt. So the Gods preserue thee.   *Exit.*

Cæs. Come hither *Proculeius.* Go and say
We purpose her no shame: giue her what comforts
The quality of her passion shall require;
Least in her greatnesse, by some mortall stroke
She do defeate vs. For her life in Rome,
Would be eternall in our Triumph: Go,
And with your speediest bring vs what she sayes,
And how you finde of her.

Pro. *Cæsar* I shall.   *Exit Proculeius.*

Cæs. *Gallus*, go you along: where's *Dolabella*, to se-
cond *Proculeius*?

All. *Dolabella.*

So unversöhnlich unser Einssein schieden,
Wie sie's getan. Hört, meine Freunde, ich –
Doch sag ich's lieber zu gegebner Zeit.
            Ein Ägypter.
Der Mann dampft ja vor lauter Botschaft. Laßt uns
Hören, was er sagt. Wo kommst du her?

ÄGYPTER Von wo Ägypten war. Die Königin
    Die mir gebietet, wünscht, in was ihr blieb,
    Ihr Grabmal, eingeschlossen, zu erfahren,
    Wie deine Pläne lauten, auf daß sie
    Beizeiten sich in das zu fügen lernt,
    Was ihr bevorsteht.
CAESAR   Rate ihr zu Ruhe;
    Wir werden zu ihr senden, bald schon weiß sie,
    Wie hochanständig und wie gütig wir
    Über sie beschließen. Caesar lebt
    Der Milde.
ÄGYPTER   So erhalten dich die Götter!   *Ab.*
CAESAR Komm, Proculeius. Lauf und red ihr zu,
    Daß wir nicht ihre Schande wollen. Haben
    Soll sie, wonach sie verlangt, damit
    Sie sich, sie hat Format, nichts antut und
    Uns mit. Denn sieht Rom sie nicht unbeschädigt
    Beim Triumph, wird der nicht dauern. Geh jetzt,
    Und mit dem Schnellsten melde, was sie sagt
    Und wie du Sie fand'st.
PROCULEIUS   Mein Caesar.   *Ab.*
CAESAR   Gallus,
    Ihr geht mit. Und wo ist Dolabella,
    Als Proculeius' Beistand?
ALLE   Dolabella!

Cæs. Let him alone: for I remember now
   How hee's imployd: he shall in time be ready.
   Go with me to my Tent, where you shall see
   How hardly I was drawne into this Warre,
   How calme and gentle I proceeded still
   In all my Writings. Go with me, and see
   What I can shew in this.   *Exeunt.*

   Enter Cleopatra, Charmian, Iras, and Mardian.

Cleo. My desolation does begin to make
   A better life: Tis paltry to be *Cæsar.*
   Not being Fortune, hee's but Fortunes knaue,
   A minister of her will: and it is great
   To do that thing that ends all other deeds,
   Which shackles accedents, and bolts vp change;
   Which sleepes, and neuer pallates more the dung,
   The beggers Nurse, and *Cæsars.*
                    Enter Proculeius.
Pro. *Cæsar* sends greeting to the Queene of Egypt,
   And bids thee study on what faire demands
   Thou mean'st to haue him grant thee.
Cleo. What's thy name?
Pro. My name is *Proculeius.*
Cleo. *Anthony*
   Did tell me of you, bad me trust you, but
   I do not greatly care to be deceiu'd
   That haue no vse for trusting. If your Master
   Would haue a Queene his begger, you must tell him,
   That Maiesty to keepe *decorum*, must

CAESAR Laßt nur: denn ich weiß jetzt schon, was ich ihm
Zu tun auftrug. Er wird gleich wieder da sein.
Folgt mir in mein Zelt. Dort sollt ihr sehn,
Daß dieser Krieg mir aufgezwungen wurde,
Und wie besonnen und gelassen ich
Gleichwohl verfuhr. Kommt mit mir, seht
Die schriftlichen Beweise.

Zweite Szene

Cleopatra, Charmia, Iras.

CLEOPATRA Schon verhilft mein Absturz mir zu einem
Bessren Leben. Caesar sein ist nichts:
Er, der Fortuna spielt, ist nur ihr Fuhrknecht,
Handlanger ihrer Launen: groß ist das Tun,
Das alles Tun zum Schluß bringt, das den Zufall
In Fesseln legt, Veränderung verriegelt,
Was Schlaf schenkt, nicht Geschmack mehr hat am Kot,
Der Bettler nährt und Caesar.
    Proculeius, Gallus, Soldaten.
PROCULEIUS Caesar grüßt die Königin Ägyptens,
Und bittet dich, erwäge, welche Wünsche
Er dir erfüllen darf.
CLEOPATRA   Wie ist dein Name?
PROCULEIUS Proculeius ist mein Name.
CLEOPATRA   Marc Anton
Sprach mir von dir, bat mich, dir zu vertrauen:
Doch ich, die sich nicht sorgt, ob sie getäuscht wird,
Brauche kein Vertrauen. Wünscht dein Herr
Eine Königin vor sich zu sehen
Als Bettelweib, sag ihm, die Majestät

No lesse begge then a Kingdome: If he please
To giue me conquer'd Egypt for my Sonne,
He giues me so much of mine owne, as I
Will kneele to him with thankes.

Pro. Be of good cheere:
Y'are falne into a Princely hand, feare nothing,
Make your full reference freely to my Lord,
Who is so full of Grace, that it flowes ouer
On all that neede. Let me report to him
Your sweet dependacie, and you shall finde
A Conqueror that will pray in ayde for kindnesse,
Where he for grace is kneel'd too.
Cleo. Pray you tell him,
I am his Fortunes Vassall, and I send him
The Greatnesse he has got. I hourely learne
A Doctrine of Obedience, and would gladly
Looke him i'th'Face.
Pro. This Ile report (deere Lady)
Haue comfort, for I know your plight is pittied
Of him that caus'd it.

Pro. You see how easily she may be surpriz'd:
Guard her till *Cæsar* come.

Iras. Royall Queene.
Char. Oh *Cleopatra*, thou art taken Queene.
Cleo. Quicke, quicke, good hands.
Pro. Hold worthy Lady, hold:
Doe not your selfe such wrong, who are in this
Releeu'd, but not betraid.

Darf, um Dekor zu wahren, sich nicht wen'ger
Als ein Reich erbetteln: wenn er gütig
Mir das eroberte Ägypten ließe
Für meinen Sohn, so gäb er mir von dem,
Was meines ist, soviel, daß ich es ihm
Auf Knien dankte.

PROCULEIUS Seid unbesorgt. In eine Herrscherhand
Seid Ihr gefallen. Überlaßt Euch frei
Der Gnade meines Herrn, die überfließt
Auf die Bedürftigen. Ich geb Bericht
Von Eurem freundlichen Entgegenkommen,
Und ein Eroberer tritt vor Euch, der
Von Euch die Huld erbittet, die Ihr knieend
Von ihm erfleht.

CLEOPATRA   Sag ihm, ich sei Vasallin
Seiner Allmacht und begegne ihm
Wie's seiner Größe ansteht. Jede Stunde
Lehrt neu mich den Gehorsam und zu gerne
Würd ich sein Gesicht sehn.

PROCULEIUS   Genau das,
Verehrte Lady, werde ich berichten.
Seid getrost, denn ich weiß, Eure Not
Rührt den, der sie verursacht hat.

GALLUS   Seht ihr,
Ein Kinderspiel wars, sie zu überrumpeln.
Bis Caesar kommt, laßt sie nicht aus dem Auge.

IRAS Königliche Herrin!

CHARMIAN Cleopatra, man fing dich, Königin.

CLEOPATRA Schnell, schnell, ihr lieben Hände.

PROCULEIUS   Nicht doch, Lady:
Begeht an Euch kein Unrecht: Schutz ist dies,
Nicht Strafe.

Cleo. What of death too that rids our dogs of languish

Pro. *Cleopatra*, do not abuse my Masters bounty, by
Th'vndoing of your selfe: Let the World see
His Noblenesse well acted, which your death
Will neuer let come forth.

Cleo. Where art thou Death?
Come hither come; Come, come, and take a Queene
Worth many Babes and Beggers.
Pro. Oh temperance Lady.
Cleo. Sir, I will eate no meate, Ile not drinke sir,
If idle talke will once be necessary
Ile not sleepe neither. This mortall house Ile ruine,
Do *Cæsar* what he can. Know sir, that I
Will not waite pinnion'd at your Masters Court,
Nor once be chastic'd with the sober eye
Of dull *Octauia*. Shall they hoyst me vp,
And shew me to the showting Varlotarie
Of censuring Rome? Rather a ditch in Egypt.
Be gentle graue vnto me, rather on Nylus mudde
Lay me starke-nak'd, and let the water-Flies
Blow me into abhorring; rather make
My Countries high pyramides my Gibbet,
And hang me vp in Chaines.

Pro. You do extend
These thoughts of horror further then you shall
Finde cause in *Cæsar*.
                    Enter Dolabella.
Dol. *Proculeius*,

CLEOPATRA   Wie denn, vorm Tod auch, der selbst
Den lahmen Hund erlöst?
PROCULEIUS   Cleopatra,
Mißbraucht die Güte meines Herrn nicht dadurch,
Daß Ihr Euch auslöscht: laßt die Welt es sehen,
Was seine Großmut tut, die Euer Tod
Verdunkeln würde.
CLEOPATRA   Tod, wo bist du? Komm,
Komm hierher! Komm, hol eine Königin,
Die viele Säuglinge und Bettler aufwiegt!
PROCULEIUS Mäßigung, Lady!
CLEOPATRA   Sir, ich esse nicht,
Ich trinke nicht, Sir, noch, wenn das der Klatsch
Benötigt, schlafe ich. Dies Haus aus Staub
Lege ich in Trümmer, Euer Caesar
Tue, was er kann. Wißt, Sir, aus mir
Wird nie ein Käfigvogel Eures Chefs,
Noch wird der nasse Fischblick mich der faden
Octavia bestarren. Wollt ihr mich
Hochzieh'n im eitlen Rom vor dem Geschmeiß
Der Gaffer? Besser in Ägypten ein
Dunghaufen freundlich mir als Grab,
Besser legt mich nackt im Nilschlamm ab,
Als Fliegenbeute, gräßlich aufgebläht;
Die steilen Pyramiden meines Reichs
Macht besser mir zum Galgen, mich daran
In Ketten aufzuhängen.
PROCULEIUS   Euch derart
In Schreckensphantasien hineinzusteigern,
Gibt Caesar Euch nicht Anlaß.
                    Dolabella.
DOLABELLA   Proculeius,

What thou hast done, thy Master *Cæsar* knowes,
And he hath sent for thee: for the Queene,
Ile take her to my Guard.

Pro. So *Dolabella*,
It shall content me best: Be gentle to her,
To *Cæsar* I will speake, what you shall please,
If you'l imploy me to him.   *Exit Proculeius*

Cleo. Say, I would dye.

Dol. Most Noble Empresse, you haue heard of me.

Cleo. I cannot tell.

Dol. Assuredly you know me.

Cleo. No matter sir, what I haue heard or knowne:
You laugh when Boyes or Women tell their Dreames,
Is't not your tricke?

Dol. I vnderstand not, Madam.

Cleo. I dreampt there was an Emperor *Anthony.*
Oh such another sleepe, that I might see
But such another man.

Dol. If it might please ye.

Cleo. His face was as the Heau'ns, and therein stucke
A Sunne and Moone, which kept their course, & lighted
The little o'th'earth.

Dol. Most Soueraigne Creature.

Cleo. His legges bestrid the Ocean, his rear'd arme
Crested the world: His voyce was propertied
As all the tuned Spheres, and that to Friends:
But when he meant to quaile, and shake the Orbe,
He was as ratling Thunder. For his Bounty,
There was no winter in't. An *Anthony* it was,
That grew the more by reaping: His delights
Were Dolphin-like, they shew'd his backe aboue
The Element they liu'd in: In his Liuery

Caesar, dein Herr, weiß dein Verdienst zu schätzen
Und hat nach dir gesandt: die Königin
Steht unter meiner Obhut.

PROCULEIUS   Dolabella,
Das kommt mir sehr zupaß: seid gut zu ihr;
Entlaßt Ihr mich, so richt ich Caesar aus,
Was Ihr verlangt.

CLEOPATRA   Sagt ihm, ich wolle sterben.

DOLABELLA Ihr hörtet schon von mir, hochedle Fürstin?

CLEOPATRA Kann ich nicht sagen.

DOLABELLA   Ganz gewiß, Ihr kennt mich.

CLEOPATRA Egal, Sir, was ich hörte oder kenne:
Erzählen Kinder ihre Träume, oder Weiber,
Lacht ihr sie aus.

DOLABELLA   Was wollt Ihr sagen, Madam?

CLEOPATRA Von einem Feldherrn Marc Anton träumt' ich.
O solch ein Schlaf noch einmal, einmal noch
Zu sehen solchen Mann.

DOLABELLA   Wenn's Euch gefiele –

CLEOPATRA Sein Antlitz glich den Himmeln, Mond und Sonne
Zogen darin Kreise und erhellten
Das kleine O, die Erde.

DOLABELLA   Hohes Wesen –

CLEOPATRA Ein Schritt, ein Ozean. Sein starker Arm
Die Zier am Helm der Welt und seine Stimme
Sphärenklang den Freunden, Feinden aber
Donner, der den Erdkreis schüttelt. Frost
War seiner Güte fremd, sie war ein Herbst,
Der mit der Ernte reift: Delphinen ähnlich
Hoben seine Freuden ihm den Rücken
Aus ihrem Lebenselement: in seinen Farben
Gingen Kronen neben Krönchen: Reiche

Walk'd Crownes and Crownets: Realms & Islands were
As plates dropt from his pocket.
Dol.   *Cleopatra.*
Cleo.   Thinke you there was, or might be such a man
As this I dreampt of?

Dol.   Gentle Madam, no.
Cleo.   You Lye vp to the hearing of the Gods:
But if there be, nor euer were one such
It's past the size of dreaming: Nature wants stuffe
To vie strange formes with fancie, yet t'imagine
An *Anthony* were Natures peece, 'gainst Fancie,
Condemning shadowes quite.

Dol.   Heare me, good Madam:
Your losse is as your selfe, great; and you beare it
As answering to the waight, would I might neuer
Ore-take pursu'de successe: But I do feele
By the rebound of yours, a greefe that suites
My very heart at roote.
Cleo.   I thanke you sir:
Know you what *Cæsar* meanes to do with me?
Dol.   I am loath to tell you what, I would you knew.
Cleo.   Nay pray you sir.
Dol.   Though he be Honourable.

Cleo.   Hee'l leade me then in Triumph.
Dol.   Madam he will, I know't.   *Flourish.*
          Enter Proculeius, Cæsar, Gallus, Mecenas,
                  and others of his Traine.
All.   Make way there *Cæsar.*
Cæs.   Which is the Queene of Egypt.

Fielen ihm und Inseln aus den Taschen
Wie's Münzen tun.
DOLABELLA   Cleopatra!
CLEOPATRA   Glaubt Ihr,
Daß je ein Mann war oder sein wird, dem gleich
Von dem ich träumte?
DOLABELLA   Madam, nein.
CLEOPATRA   Das lügt Ihr
Bis hinauf ans Ohr der Götter. Aber
Wäre so wer oder wär gewesen,
So sprengt das jeden Traum. Natur braucht Stoff,
Um unsre Phantasie zu überflügeln,
Antonius war ihr Meisterstück, kein Traum,
Und alle Schatten schlagend.
DOLABELLA   Hört mich, Madam:
Wie Ihr seid, ist, was Ihr verloren, groß,
Und wie Ihr's tragt, macht deutlich, was es wiegt.
Du schlaue Politik, fahr hin, hier dies mein Herz
Hallt mir von Eurer Trauer wider bis
Zum Zerspringen.
CLEOPATRA   Sir, ich danke Euch.
Euch ist bekannt, was Caesar mit mir vorhat?
DOLABELLA Was Ihr nicht wißt, ich mag es Euch nicht sagen.
CLEOPATRA Nein, Sir, ich bitte Euch –
DOLABELLA   So höflich er
Auch ist –
CLEOPATRA Er zeigt mich im Triumph.
DOLABELLA   Das, Madam,
Will er, wie ich weiß.
STIMME   Platz da für Caesar!
    Proculeius, Caesar, Gallus, Maecenas.
CAESAR Welche ist die Königin Ägyptens?

Dol. It is the Emperor Madam.   *Cleo. kneeles.*
Cæsar. Arise, you shall not kneele:
  I pray you rise, rise Egypt.
Cleo. Sir, the Gods will haue it thus,
  My Master and my Lord I must obey,

Cæsar. Take to you no hard thoughts,
  The Record of what iniuries you did vs,
  Though written in our flesh, we shall remember
  As things but done by chance.
Cleo. Sole Sir o'th'World,
  I cannot proiect mine owne cause so well
  To make it cleare, but do confesse I haue
  Bene laden with like frailties, which before
  Haue often sham'd our Sex.
Cæsar. *Cleopatra* know,
  We will extenuate rather then inforce:
  If you apply your selfe to our intents,
  Which towards you are most gentle, you shall finde
  A benefit in this change: but if you seeke
  To lay on me a Cruelty, by taking
  Anthonies course, you shall bereaue your selfe
  Of my good purposes, and put your children
  To that destruction which Ile guard them from,
  If thereon you relye. Ile take my leaue.
Cleo. And may through all the world: tis yours, & we
  your Scutcheons, and your signes of Conquest shall
  Hang in what place you please. Here my good Lord.
Cæsar. You shall aduise me in all for *Cleopatra.*
Cleo. This is the breefe: of Money, Plate, & Iewels
  I am possest of, 'tis exactly valewed,
  Not petty things admitted. Where's *Seleucus?*

DOLABELLA Es ist der Imperator, Madam.

CAESAR Steht auf, Ihr sollt nicht knien: ich bitte Euch,
Steh auf, steh auf, Ägypten.

CLEOPATRA   Sir, die Götter
Wollens so, doch meinem Herrn und Meister
Muß ich gehorchen.

CAESAR   Denkt nicht hart von uns;
Die Liste der Vergehen gegen uns
Obgleich in unser Fleisch gekerbt, gilt uns
Als nebensächlich.

CLEOPATRA   Einz'ger Weltenherrscher,
Hier meine Sache führen und erklären
Kann ich nicht, jedoch gestehe ich,
Beladen war auch ich mit jener Schwäche,
Die mein Geschlecht beschämt.

CAESAR   Cleopatra,
Wir wollen Milde, nicht Gewalt. Von Vorteil
Wird's für Euch sein, fügt Ihr Euch unsern wahrhaft
Rücksichtsvollen Plänen. Zieht Ihr's vor,
Mich in ein schiefes Licht zu setzen, wie
Antonius es tat, raubt Ihr Euch jede
Vergünstigung und liefert Eure Kinder
Dem Untergang aus, vor dem ich sie rette,
Wenn Ihr mir vertraut. Ich muß jetzt gehn.

CLEOPATRA Das könnt Ihr, in die weite Welt: 's ist Eure!
Und uns hängt als Trophäen Ihr und Beute
Hin, wo Ihr wollt. Für Euch, mein edler Herr.

CAESAR Mein Fachmann für Cleopatra seid Ihr.

CLEOPATRA Das Verzeichnis: Geld, Geschirr, Juwelen,
Was ich besitze, ist exakt notiert hier,
Bis auf Flitterkram. Wo ist Seleucus?

Seleu. Heere Madam.

Cleo. This is my Treasurer, let him speake (my Lord)
    Vpon his perill, that I haue reseru'd
    To my selfe nothing. Speake the truth *Seleucus.*

Seleu. Madam, I had rather seele my lippes,
    Then to my perill speake that which is not.

Cleo. What haue I kept backe.

Sel. Enough to purchase what you haue made known

Cæsar. Nay blush not *Cleopatra*, I approue
    Your Wisedome in the deede.

Cleo. See *Cæsar*: Oh behold,
    How pompe is followed: Mine will now be yours,
    And should we shift estates, yours would be mine.
    The ingratitude of this *Seleucus*, does
    Euen make me wilde. Oh Slaue, of no more trust
    Then loue that's hyr'd? What goest thou backe, yu shalt
    Go backe I warrant thee: but Ile catch thine eyes
    Though they had wings. Slaue, Soule-lesse, Villain, Dog.
    O rarely base!

Cæsar. Good Queene, let vs intreat you.

Cleo. O *Cæsar*, what a wounding shame is this,
    That thou vouchsafing heere to visit me,
    Doing the Honour of thy Lordlinesse
    To one so meeke, that mine owne Seruant should
    Parcell the summe of my disgraces, by
    Addition of his Enuy. Say (good *Cæsar*)
    That I some Lady trifles haue reseru'd,
    Immoment toyes, things of such Dignitie

Seleucus.

SELEUCUS Hier bin ich, Madam.

CLEOPATRA Er ist mein Kämmerer, ihn laßt, Mylord,
Bei Strafe sprechen, daß ich nichts für mich
Zurückbehielt. Seleucus, sag die Wahrheit.

SELEUCUS Madam, eher ließ ich mir den Mund
Zunähen, als bei Strafe hier zu sagen,
Was unwahr ist.

CLEOPATRA   Was hielt ich denn zurück?

SELEUCUS Genug, um das zu kaufen, was Ihr angebt.

CAESAR Nein, kein Rot, Cleopatra, ich schätze
Die Umsicht Eures Tuns.

CLEOPATRA   Seht, Caesar! O
Merkt, wie Größe zwingt: Meins ist nun Euer,
Und käms zum Umschwung, wäre Eures mein.
Von dem der Undank aber, dem Seleucus,
Der macht mich wild. O Schuft, war deine Treue
Bloß Gunst, die man sich mietet? Du weichst aus?
Weich aus, Grund dazu hast du: deine Augen
Kratz ich dir weg und wenn sie Flügel hätten.
Schuft! Herzloser Gauner! Hund! O Prunkstück
An Gemeinheit!

CAESAR   Beste Königin,
Gestattet mir, Euch zu besänftigen.

CLEOPATRA O Caesar, mich verwundet Scham, daß du,
Geruhend, mich hier zu besuchen, mir
Die Ehre gebend deiner Herrlichkeit,
Die ich so arm daran bin, Zeuge sein mußt,
Wie einer meiner Sklaven mir das Bündel
Meiner Übel schwerer macht durch seine
Niedertracht. Und selbst wenn ich, mein Caesar,
Ein wenig Frauentand zur Seite schaffte,

As we greet moderne Friends withall, and say
Some Nobler token I haue kept apart
For *Liuia* and *Octauia*, to induce
Their mediation, must I be vnfolded
With one that I haue bred: The Gods! it smites me
Beneath the fall I haue. Prythee go hence,
Or I shall shew the Cynders of my spirits
Through th'Ashes of my chance: Wer't thou a man,
Thou would'st haue mercy on me.

Cæsar. Forbeare *Seleucus.*
Cleo. Be it known, that we the greatest are mis-thoght
    For things that others do: and when we fall,
    We answer others merits, in our name
    Are therefore to be pittied.
Cæsar. *Cleopatra,*
    Not what you haue reseru'd, nor what acknowledg'd
    Put we i'th' Roll of Conquest: still bee't yours,
    Bestow it at your pleasure, and beleeue
    Cæsars no Merchant, to make prize with you
    Of things that Merchants sold. Therefore be cheer'd,
    Make not your thoughts your prisons: No deere Queen,
    For we intend so to dispose you, as
    Your selfe shall giue vs counsell: Feede, and sleepe:
    Our care and pitty is so much vpon you,
    That we remaine your Friend, and so adieu.
Cleo. My Master, and my Lord.
Cæsar. Not so: Adieu.   *Flourish.*
            Exeunt Cæsar, and his Traine.
Cleo. He words me Gyrles, he words me,

Unwichtiges Spielzeug, Dinge der Art,
Die wir entfernteren Bekannten schenken,
Und selbst wenn ich das eine oder andre
Von Wert mir aufgehoben hätte, um
Livia und Octavia als Vermittler
Mir zu gewinnen, muß darum gleich einer,
Den ich groß gemacht, mich öffentlich
Verschreien? Gute Götter! Das stürzt mich
Noch unter meinen Fall. Geh bitte weg,
Sonst stieben aus der Asche meines Glücks
Noch Funken meines Lebensmuts. Ein Mann
Wär mitleidsvoller.

CAESAR   Geh, Seleucus.

CLEOPATRA Die Welt muß wissen, wir, die Größten, halten
Den Kopf für Klein're hin; und wenn wir fallen,
Steht unser Name ein für ihr Verfehlen:
Darum habt Nachsehn.

CAESAR   Nichts, Cleopatra,
Das Einbehaltne nicht, noch Aufgeführte
Fällt uns zu: es ist Euer, nach Gutdünken
Verfügt darüber, und seid sicher, Caesar
Ist kein Krämer, daß er mit Euch feilschte
Um Kram, von Krämern feilgeboten. Freut Euch,
Baut Euch kein Gefängnis aus Gedanken:
Nicht, beste Königin, denn Euer Ratschlag
Legt fest, wie mit Euch umzugehen ist:
Eßt und ruht. Wir fühlen mit und sorgen
Für Euch wie ein Freund. Alsdann Adieu.

CLEOPATRA Mein Herr und Meister!

CAESAR   Das nun nicht: Adieu.

CLEOPATRA Er beschwatzt mich, Mädchen, er beschwatzt mich,

That I should not be Noble to my selfe.
But hearke thee *Charmian*.

Iras. Finish good Lady, the bright day is done,
And we are for the darke.

Cleo. Hye thee againe,
I haue spoke already, and it is prouided,
Go put it to the haste.

Char. Madam, I will.

Enter Dolabella.

Dol. Where's the Queene?

Char. Behold sir.

Cleo. Dolabella.

Dol. Madam, as thereto sworne, by your command
(Which my loue makes Religion to obey)
I tell you this: *Cæsar* through Syria
Intends his iourney, and within three dayes,
You with your Children will he send before,
Make your best vse of this. I haue perform'd
Your pleasure, and my promise.

Cleo. *Dolabella*, I shall remaine your debter.

Dol. I your Seruant:
Adieu good Queene, I must attend on *Cæsar*.   *Exit*

Cleo. Farewell, and thankes.
Now *Iras*, what think'st thou?
Thou, an Egyptian Puppet shall be shewne
In Rome aswell as I: Mechanicke Slaues
With greazie Aprons, Rules, and Hammers shall
Vplift vs to the view. In their thicke breathes,
Ranke of grosse dyet, shall we be enclowded,
And forc'd to drinke their vapour.

V, ii, 227–256

Nicht nobel zu mir selbst zu sein. Hör, Charmian.

IRAS Schluß, beste Lady, aus der helle Tag,
    Und wir sind für das Dunkel.
CLEOPATRA   Eil dich, ich
    Hab's eingefädelt, und es ist besorgt,
    Dräng du auf Lieferung.
CHARMIAN   Das werd ich, Madam.
                  Dolabella.
DOLABELLA Wo ist die Königin?
CHARMIAN   Seht hin, Sir.
CLEOPATRA   Dolabella!
DOLABELLA Madam, wie geschworen, sag ich Euch,
    Gemäß Eurem Befehl, dem zu gehorchen
    Mitleid mir als Glaubensgrundsatz vorschreibt:
    Caesar zieht durch Syrien, und Euch
    Und Eure Kinder sendet er nach Rom
    In spätestens drei Tagen. Macht aus dem
    Das Beste. Euer Wunsch war's und mein Wort,
    Was mich das tun hieß.
CLEOPATRA   Dolabella, ich
    Bleibe Eure Schuldnerin,
DOLABELLA   Eu'r Diener.
    Adieu, Hoheit, zu Caesar ruft die Pflicht mich.   *Ab*
CLEOPATRA Lebt wohl und Dank. Was hältst du davon, Iras?
    Du und ich als zwei Ägypterpüppchen
    Auf allen Rummelplätzen Roms: stupider Pöbel,
    Verschmierte Schürzen, Latten, Eisenhämmer,
    Will uns erhöht sehn, um uns anzuglotzen,
    Ihr Atem stinkend, fetten Fraß aufstoßend,
    Umwölkt uns, und wir trinken Schweißgeruch.

Iras. The Gods forbid.

Cleo. Nay, 'tis most certaine Iras: sawcie Lictors
    Will catch at vs like Strumpets, and scald Rimers
    Ballads vs out a Tune. The quicke Comedians
    Extemporally will stage vs, and present
    Our Alexandrian Reuels: *Anthony*
    Shall be brought drunken forth, and I shall see
    Some squeaking *Cleopatra* Boy my greatnesse
    I'th'posture of a Whore.

Iras. O the good Gods!

Cleo. Nay that's certaine.

Iras. Ile neuer see't? for I am sure mine Nailes
    Are stronger then mine eyes.

Cleo. Why that's the way to foole their preparation,
    And to conquer their most absurd intents.

                  Enter Charmian.

    Now *Charmian*.
    Shew me my Women like a Queene: Go fetch
    My best Attyres. I am againe for *Cidrus*,
    To meete *Marke Anthony*. Sirra *Iras*, go
    (Now Noble *Charmian*, wee'l dispatch indeede,)
    And when thou hast done this chare, Ile giue thee leaue
    To play till Doomesday: bring our Crowne, and all.

                        A noise within.

    Wherefore's this noise?

                Enter a Guardsman.

Gards. Heere is a rurall Fellow,
    That will not be deny'de your Highnesse presence,
    He brings you Figges.

Cleo. Let him come in.   *Exit Guardsman.*
    What poore an Instrument
    May do a Noble deede: he brings me liberty:

IRAS Die Götter hindern's.

CLEOPATRA   Nein, das tun sie nicht.
  Amtliche Pfoten greifen uns wie Dirnen,
  Verseschmiede reimen uns zu Tod,
  Die schnellen Komödianten spielen uns,
  Und zeigen Alexandria bei Nacht:
  Antonius tritt betrunken auf, und mich
  Seh ich von irgendeinem Jüngling kreischend
  Als Hure dargestellt.

IRAS   Ihr guten Götter!

CLEOPATRA Nein, das sind sie nicht.

IRAS Ich werd's nicht sehn, solange meine Nägel
  Mir härter als die Augen sind.

CLEOPATRA   Wozu das?

                    Charmian.

  Hier kommt der Weg, der ihre Absicht narrt,
  Und ihre ganz absurde Planung umwirft.
  Nun also, Charmian! Macht mich, ihr Frauen,
  Zu einer Königin: holt mir, was mir
  Am besten steht. Zum Cydnus will ich wieder,
  Dort Marc Anton zu treffen. Los, Freund Iras.
  (Jetzt, meine liebe Charmian, geht's zuende.)
  Und tatst du mir den Dienst noch, hast du frei
  Und spielst bis an den Jüngsten Tag. Vergeßt
  Das Diadem nicht und all das. Welch Lärm?

                    Wache.

WACHE Da ist ein Bauernbursche, der partout
  Zu Eurer Hoheit selber will. Er bringt
  Euch Feigen.

CLEOPATRA   Laßt ihn ein. Wie schlicht
  Das Werkzeug ist, das Schönes schaffen kann!
  Er bringt mir Freiheit: mein Entschluß steht fest,

My Resolution's plac'd, and I haue nothing
Of woman in me: Now from head to foote
I am Marble constant: now the fleeting Moone
No Planet is of mine.

Enter Guardsman, and Clowne.

Guards. This is the man.

Cleo. Auoid, and leaue him.   *Exit Guardsman.*
Hast thou the pretty worme of Nylus there,
That killes and paines not?

Clow. Truly I haue him: but I would not be the par-
tie that should desire you to touch him, for his byting is
immortall: those that doe dye of it, doe seldome or neuer recouer.

Cleo. Remember'st thou any that haue dyed on't?

Clow. Very many, men and women too. I heard of
one of them no longer then yesterday, a very honest woman, but something giuen to lye, as a woman should not
do, but in the way of honesty, how she dyed of the byting of it, what paine she felt: Truely, she makes a verie
good report o'th'worme: but he that wil beleeue all that
they say, shall neuer be saued by halfe that they do: but
this is most falliable, the Worme's an odde Worme.

Cleo. Get thee hence, farewell.

Clow. I wish you all ioy of the Worme.

Cleo. Farewell.

Clow. You must thinke this (looke you,) that the
Worme will do his kinde.

Cleo. I, I, farewell.

Clow. Looke you, the Worme is not to bee trusted,
but in the keeping of wise people: for indeede, there is
no goodnesse in the Worme.

Und nichts an mir ist weiblich: fest wie Marmor
Bin ich von Kopf bis Fuß: der Wechselmond
Ist mein Gestirn nicht mehr.

Wache mit einem Clown, der einen Korb trägt.

WACHE Hier ist der Mann.

CLEOPATRA Geh weg, und ihn laß hier. Hast du den netten
Nilwurm mit, der tötet ohne Wehtun?

CLOWN Aber sicher doch: nur gehör ich nich zu dem Verein,
der sich wünscht, Ihr sollt ihm anpacken, weil, sein Biß hält
ewig: die dran eingehn, komm' selten wieder hoch oder
nie.

CLEOPATRA Kennst du wen, der dran starb?

CLOWN Jede Menge, Männlein wie Weiblein. Gestern erst hat
mir wieder eine erzählt, eine hochanständige Dame, nurn
bisschen verlogen, was 'ne Dame nicht sein soll, außer es
geht um ihren Ruf, wie sie verstorben ist von dem Beißen
und komplett ohne Schmerzen: sie empfiehlt den Wurm
unbedingt weiter: aber wer alles glaubt, was die Großkopfe-
ten so von sich geben, den hält nicht die Hälfte von dem
über Wasser, was sie dann machen. Auf jeden
Unfall: der Wurm hats in sich.

CLEOPATRA Entferne dich, leb wohl.

CLOWN Wünsche viel Freude an dem Wurm.

CLEOPATRA Leb wohl.

CLOWN Denkt immer dran, der Wurm, nich wahr, tut, was er
muß.

CLEOPATRA Ja, ja, leb wohl.

CLOWN Nich wahr, auf den Wurm is kein Verlaß nich, außer
man genießt ihn mit Vorsicht: denn ehrlich, in dem Wurm
steckt nix Guts.

Cleo. Take thou no care, it shall be heeded.

Clow. Very good: giue it nothing I pray you, for it
   is not worth the feeding.

Cleo. Will it eate me?

Clow. You must not think I am so simple, but I know
   the diuell himselfe will not eate a woman: I know, that
   a woman is a dish for the Gods, if the diuell dresse her
   not. But truly, these same whorson diuels doe the Gods
   great harme in their women: for in euery tenne that they
   make, the diuels marre fiue.

Cleo. Well, get thee gone, farewell.

Clow. Yes forsooth: I wish you ioy o'th'worm.   *Exit*

Cleo. Giue me my Robe, put on my Crowne, I haue
   Immortall longings in me. Now no more
   The iuyce of Egypts Grape shall moyst this lip.
   Yare, yare, good *Iras*; quicke: Me thinkes I heare
   Anthony call: I see him rowse himselfe
   To praise my Noble Act. I heare him mock
   The lucke of *Cæsar*, which the Gods giue men
   To excuse their after wrath. Husband, I come:
   Now to that name, my Courage proue my Title.
   I am Fire, and Ayre; my other Elements
   I giue to baser life. So, haue you done?
   Come then, and take the last warmth of my Lippes.
   Farewell kinde *Charmian*, *Iras*, long farewell.

   Haue I the Aspicke in my lippes? Dost fall?
   If thou, and Nature can so gently part,
   The stroke of death is as a Louers pinch,
   Which hurts, and is desir'd. Dost thou lye still?
   If thus thou vanishest, thou tell'st the world,

CLEOPATRA Keine Sorge, wir passen auf.

CLOWN Sehr schön: bitte auf keinen Fall füttern, das ist er nicht
wert.

CLEOPATRA Würde er mich fressen?

CLOWN Glaubt Ihr, ich bin so deppert und weiß nicht, daß selbst
der Teufel nie nich keine Frau frißt? Eine Frau, das is Götter-
speise, vorausgesetzt, sie is nich vom Teufel gezuckert. Aber
unter uns, diese Hurensöhne von Teufeln machen den Göttern, was die Frauen anlangt, ganz hübsch zu schaffen: von
zehn, wo die zusammenbasteln, versaubeuteln die Teufel fünf.

CLEOPATRA Nun denn, heb dich hinweg, leb wohl. *Gibt ihm Geld.*

CLOWN Ja, hiermit gern: viel Spaß noch mit dem Wurm.

CLEOPATRA Gebt mir mein Kleid, die Krone setzt mir auf,
Ich habe Lust auf die Unsterblichkeit.
Nach dem Rebensaft Ägyptens dürsten
Diese Lippen nicht mehr. Iras, nimm dich
Zusammen, und das flink: mir ist, als rief
Antonius mich, ich seh ihn sich erheben
Zum Lobe meiner Heldentat. Verspotten
Hör ich ihn Caesarenglück, gespendet
Von Göttern, deren Zorn nachfolgt. Ich komme,
Mein Gemahl: das Recht, dich so zu nennen,
Erwirbt mir meine Stärke! Feuer bin ich,
Luft: die andern Elemente weih ich
Dem, was unten lebt. Seid ihr soweit?
Dann kommt, nehmt mir die Wärme von den Lippen.
Leb wohl, Charmian, Iras, leb wohl für lange.
Hab ich Natternlippen? Bist du tot?
Kannst du von der Natur so leicht dich trennen,
So ist der Würgegriff des Tods, als kniffe
Der Liebste uns im Scherz, 's tut weh und freut.
Liegst du ganz still? Gehst du so von uns, heißt das,

It is not worth leaue-taking.

Char. Dissolue thicke clowd, & Raine, that I may say
   The Gods themselues do weepe.

Cleo. This proues me base:
   If she first meete the Curled *Anthony*,
   Hee'l make demand of her, and spend that kisse
   Which is my heauen to haue. Come thou mortal wretch,
   With thy sharpe teeth this knot intrinsicate,
   Of life at once vntye: Poore venomous Foole,
   Be angry, and dispatch. Oh could'st thou speake,
   That I might heare thee call great *Cæsar* Asse, vnpolicied.

Char. Oh Easterne Starre.

Cleo. Peace, peace:
   Dost thou not see my Baby at my breast,
   That suckes the Nurse asleepe.

Char. O breake! O breake!

Cleo. As sweet as Balme, as soft as Ayre, as gentle.
   O *Anthony*! Nay I will take thee too.
   What should I stay————   *Dyes.*

Char. In this wilde World? So fare thee well:
   Now boast thee Death, in thy possession lyes
   A Lasse vnparalell'd. Downie Windowes cloze,
   And golden Phœbus, neuer be beheld
   Of eyes againe so Royall: your Crownes away,
   Ile mend it, and then play————
         Enter the Guard rustling in, and Dolabella.

1 *Guard.* Where's the Queene?

Char. Speake softly, wake her not.

1 *Cæsar* hath sent

Char. Too slow a Messenger.

Die Welt hat keinen Abschiedsgruß verdient.
CHARMIAN Unglückswolke, brich entzwei und regne,
   Als weinten selbst die Götter!
CLEOPATRA   Das geniert mich:
   Trifft sie den schön gelockten Marc Anton
   Vor mir, sieht er nur sie, und schenkt den Kuß weg,
   Der mir den Himmel gibt. Komm, armes Kriechtier,
   Tödliches, mit deinem scharfen Zahn
   Mach den verworr'nen Lebensknoten auf:
   Giftiger Narr, werd böse und mach Schluß.
   O, sprächst du, daß ich hören dürfte, wie du
   Den großen Caesar einen Esel nennst,
   Einen Politiker.
CHARMIAN   O Stern des Ostens!
CLEOPATRA   Still doch!
   Siehst du nicht, wie das Kind an meiner Brust
   In Schlaf die Amme saugt?
CHARMIAN   O, brich! O, brich!
CLEOPATRA Balsamisch süß, wie Luft so sanft, so freundlich.
   O Antonius! Nein, dich nehm ich auch.
   Was soll ich hier –
CHARMIAN Im Kot der Welt? Leb wohl denn. Nun darfst du
   Dich brüsten, Tod, im Arm hältst du ein Mädchen
   Ohnegleichen. Schließt euch, Fleisches Fenster,
   Und niemals wieder schaun dich, goldner Phoebus,
   So herrscherliche Augen! Deine Krone
   Ist verrutscht, ich richte sie, und spiele.
                  Wache 1.
WACHE 1 Wo ist die Königin?
CHARMIAN   Sprich leise, weck sie nicht.
WACHE Caesar sendet –
CHARMIAN   Allzu lahme Boten.

Oh come apace, dispatch, I partly feele thee.
1 Approach hoa,
   All's not well: Cæsar's beguild.
2 There's *Dolabella* sent from *Cæsar*: call him.
1 What worke is heere *Charmian*?
   Is this well done?

Char. It is well done, and fitting for a Princesse
   Descended of so many Royall Kings.
   Ah Souldier.   *Charmian dyes.*

                 Enter Dolabella.

Dol. How goes it heere?
2. Guard. All dead.
Dol. Cæsar, thy thoughts
   Touch their effects in this: Thy selfe art comming
   To see perform'd the dreaded Act which thou
   So sought'st to hinder.

          Enter Cæsar and all his Traine, marching.

All. A way there, a way for *Cæsar*.
Dol. Oh sir, you are too sure an Augurer:
   That you did feare, is done.
Cæsar. Brauest at the last,
   She leuell'd at our purposes, and being Royall
   Tooke her owne way: the manner of their deaths,
   I do not see them bleede.
Dol. Who was last with them?
1. Guard. A simple Countryman, that broght hir Figs:
   This was his Basket.

Cæsar. Poyson'd then.
1. Guard. Oh *Cæsar*:
   This *Charmian* liu'd but now, she stood and spake:
   I found her trimming vp the Diadem;

O, flink, vollende, mach mich völlig fühllos.

WACHE 1   Hierher! Mist! Und Caesar ist der Dumme.

Wache 2.

WACHE 2   Sein Dolabella ist noch da. Ich hol ihn.

WACHE 1   Was geht hier vor? Ist das in Ordnung, Charmian?

CHARMIAN   Das ist in Ordnung, passend zu der Tochter
So vieler stolzer Könige.
Ah, mein Soldat!

Dolabella.

DOLABELLA   Was ist hier los?

WACHE 2   Tot, alle.

DOLABELLA   Deine Ahnung,
Caesar, hiermit wird sie wahr: du kommst,
Den bösen letzten Akt zu sehn, den du
Vermeiden wolltest.

STIMME   Platz da, Platz da für den Kaiser!

Caesar, Gefolge.

DOLABELLA   O Sir, Ihr seid ein allzu sichrer Augur:
Ihr befürchtet, es trifft ein.

CAESAR   Im Ziel noch
Schlägt sie uns, errechnet unsre Zwecke,
Und nimmt höchst königlich den eignen Weg.
Was ist die Todesart? Ich seh kein Blut.

DOLABELLA   Wer war zuletzt bei ihr?

WACHE 1   Ein Bauer bloß,
Der ihr Feigen brachte: das hier ist
Der Korb.

CAESAR   Vergiftet also.

WACHE 1   Aber, Caesar,
Charmian, die hier, lebte eben noch,
Stand da und sprach: ich sah, wie sie den Haarreif

On her dead Mistris tremblingly she stood,
And on the sodaine dropt.
Cæsar. Oh Noble weakenesse:
If they had swallow'd poyson, 'twould appeare
By externall swelling: but she lookes like sleepe,
As she would catch another *Anthony*
In her strong toyle of Grace.
Dol. Heere on her brest,
There is a vent of Bloud, and something blowne,
The like is on her Arme.
1. *Guard.* This is an Aspickes traile,
And these Figge-leaues haue slime vpon them, such
As th'Aspicke leaues vpon the Caues of Nyle.
Cæsar. Most probable
That so she dyed: for her Physitian tels mee
She hath pursu'de Conclusions infinite
Of easie wayes to dye. Take vp her bed,
And beare her Women from the Monument,
She shall be buried by her *Anthony*.
No Graue vpon the earth shall clip in it
A payre so famous: high euents as these
Strike those that make them: and their Story is
No lesse in pitty, then his Glory which
Brought them to be lamented. Our Army shall
In solemne shew, attend this Funerall,
And then to Rome. Come *Dolabella*, see
High Order, in this great Solmemnity.   *Exeunt omnes*

FINIS.

V, ii, 411–438

Auf ihrer toten Herrin grade rückte;
Sie zitterte, und plötzlich fiel sie um.
CAESAR O feine Rücksicht! Aßen sie das Gift,
So lägen sie verfärbt da und gedunsen:
Doch sie sieht schlafend aus, als wolle sie
Mit dem Versprechen lieblichsten Erwachens
Sich einen anderen Antonius fangen.
DOLABELLA Auf ihrer Brust hier findet etwas Blut sich,
Und eine Schwellung, hier am Arm das Gleiche.

WACHE 1 Das ist 'n Schlangenbiß, und hier die Blätter
Zeigen Schleimspur'n, wie die Nattern sie
Im Gesträuch des Nilstroms hinterlassen.
CAESAR Vermutlich starb sie so: ihr Leibarzt sagte,
Die Frage nach schmerzarmen Todesarten
Sei ihr von größter Wichtigkeit gewesen.
Nehmt sie mit ihrem Bett auf und entfernt
Mir ihre Frauen aus dem Monument.
Seite an Seite mit Antonius
Soll sie bestattet werden. Es umschließt
Kein zweites Grab auf Erden solch ein Paar:
Ereignisse wie dieses haben Wirkung
Auf ihre Macher auch: es ruft ihr Los
In gleichem Maße Mitgefühl hervor,
Wie Anerkennung dessen, der den Grund,
Sie zu betrauern, gab. Das ganze Heer
Wohnt dem Begräbnis bei in voller Wehr,
Und dann nach Rom. Hab, Dolabella, Acht,
Auf dieser hohen Feier ernste Pracht.

Dramatis Personae

ANTONIUS	)
OCTAVIUS CAESAR	) Triumvirn
LEPIDUS	)

SEXTUS POMPEJUS

DOMITIUS ENOBARBUS	)
VENTIDIUS	)
EROS	)
SCARUS	) Freunde des Antonius
DECRETAS	)
DEMETRIUS	)
PHILO	)

MAECENAS	)
AGRIPPA	)
DOLABELLA	)
PROCULEIUS	) Freunde Caesars
THIDIAS	)
GALLUS	)
MENAS	)
MENECRATES	)
VARRIUS	)

TAURUS   Caesars Oberleutnant

CANIDIUS   Oberleutnant des Antonius

SILIUS   Offizier des Ventidius

SCHULMEISTER   Botschafter des Antonius bei Caesar

ALEXAS   )
MARDIAN ein Eunuch   ) Hofleute Cleopatras
DIOMEDES   )

SELEUCUS   Schatzmeister Cleopatras

LAMPRIUS   ein Wahrsager

BAUER

CLEOPATRA   Königin Ägyptens

OCTAVIA   Schwester Caesars

CHARMIAN   Hofdame Cleopatras

IRAS   Zofe Cleopatras

Offiziere, Soldaten, Boten

Die Szene bilden verschiedene Teile des Römischen Reiches

Anmerkungen

I, i, 1   *Actus Primus. Scœna Prima.*
In den originalen Quartoausgaben gab es keine Einteilung in Akte/ Szenen, in der Folioausgabe wurde sie in einigen Fällen durchgeführt, in anderen (wie in diesem Stück) nur angekündigt

I, i, 5   *Ore* – steht immer für o'er (over)

I, i, 12   *reneages* – reneges

I, i, 31   *scarse-bearded Cæsar*
scarce-bearded; hier ist Gaius Octavius gemeint, der spätere Antonius, Cäsars Adoptivsohn. Siehe Personenverzeichnis

I, i, 33   *Infranchise* – enfranchise

I, i, 45   *raing'd* – ranged

I, i, 50   *One paine* – Var. On paine F2

I, i, 63   *who euery passion* – Var. whose every passion F2

I, ii, 1   *Lamprius, ... Rannius, Lucillius*
daß diese drei in der Szene nichts sagen läßt zwar nicht zwingend den Schluß zu, daß sie gar nicht auftreten, weist aber auf einen teilweise nonchalanten Umgang mit Regieanweisungen hin, der Generationen von Editoren (zu denen auch die der *Folio* zu rechnen sind) mit Arbeit versorgt hat

I, ii, 7   *change* – Var. charge (Theobald)

I, ii, 27   *Liuer* – die Leber wurde durch Liebe erhitzt (AE 96)

I, ii, 40   *foretell* – Var. fertile (Theobald)

I, ii, 54   *I cannot scratch mine eare* – dann bin ich keine Frau (AE 98)

I, ii, 55   *worky day* – workaday

I, ii, 65   *mary* – marry

I, ii, 69   *waight* – weight

I, ii, 71   *prayer of the people*
Anspielung auf das *Book of Common Pryer* (AE 99)

I, ii, 83   *Saue you,* – Var. saw you F2 (DF)

I, ii, 87   *sodaine* – sudden (auch I, iii, 8)

I, ii, 88   *strooke* – struck

I, ii, 102 *ioynting* – jointing

I, ii, 124 *windes* – Var. minds (Hanmer), DF

I, ii, 124 *illes* – ills

I, ii, 148 *shou'd* – shoved

I, ii, 173 *showre* – shower

I, ii, 190   *greefe* – grief
I, ii, 203   *loue* – Var. leave (Pope)
I, ii, 217   *heire* – Var. hair (Row)
        vgl. Fußnote AE 106
I, iii, 15   *farre* – far
I, iii, 34   *first* – korrigiert aus fitst (DF)
I, iii, 52   *Lyar* – liar
I, iii, 58   *Seruicles* – Var. services (F2)
I, iii, 62   *Domesticke* – domestic
I, iii, 76   *Garboyles* – garboiles
I, iii, 79   *Violles* – vials (Lacrimarium)
I, iii, 124   *Lawrell* – laurel
I, iii, 128   *reciding* – residing
I, iv, 10   *vouchsafe* – Var. vouchsafed (Johnson)
I, iv, 14   *enow* – enough
I, iv, 16   *fierie* – fiery
I, iv, 17   *purchaste* – purchased
I, iv, 19   *graunt* – grant
I, iv, 27   *foyles* – foiles
I, iv, 30   *surfets* – surfeits
I, iv, 30   *the drinesse of his bones*
        Symptom von Syphillis AE 115, Beleg Thomas Middleton
I, iv, 51   *fear'd* – Var. deared (Theobald)
I, iv, 58   *inrodes* – inroads
I, iv, 63   *Warre* – war (häufig verwendet)
I, iv, 65   *Vassailes* – Var. wassailes (Pope) statt vassals (Vasallen)
I, iv, 72   *pallat ... daine* – pallate ... deign
I, iv, 74   *Stagge* – stag
I, v, 4   *Mandragora* – Quelle lt. OE 119 ist hier Apulejus
I, v, 14   *ought ... ha's* – aught .. has
I, v, 27   *moou'st* – mov'st
I, v, 28   *demy* – demi
I, v, 29   *Burganet* – burgonet (Sturmhaube)
I, v, 36   *Monarke* – monarch
I, v, 43   *great Med'cine*
        alchemistische Flüssigkeit zur Goldgewinnung (OE 122)
I, v, 48   *Orient Pearle* – vgl. MND u.a. Stellen bei S.
I, v, 53   *peece* – piece

I, v, 56	*Arme-gaunt Steede* – wurde von den Editoren angezweifelt, da der Ausdruck nur hier auftaucht; eher Zeichen von enger Vertrautheit mit zeittypischen Militaria und Pferden
I, v, 57	*hye* – high
I, v, 58	*dumbe* – Var. dumbed (Theobald), DF
I, v, 70	*mans* – Var. man (F2)
I, v, 82	*Paragon againe* – korr. aus Paragonagaine (DF)
II, i, 7	*sutors* – suitors
II, i, 10	*Powres* – powers
II, i, 15	*Cressent* – crescent
II, i, 18	*without doores* – vor den Türen
II, i, 22	*Mene.* – Var. Menas (Malone)
II, i, 28	*wand* – Var. waned (Steevens)
II, i, 32	*sawce* – sauce
II, i, 34	*Lethied* – Leth'd
II, i, 43	*Surfetter* – surfeiter
II, i, 48	*neere* – Var. never (Theobald)
II, i, 52	*war'd* – gemäß F2 korrigiert aus wan'd
II, i, 60	*Ciment* – cement
II, ii, 3	*intreat* – entreat
II, ii, 11	*stomacking* – stomaching
II, ii, 15	*small* – korrigiert aus fmall (DF)
II, ii, 22	*Hearke* – Hark
II, ii, 31	*tearmes* – termes
II, ii, 51	*practise on my State* – verschwören
II, ii, 55	*heere* – here
II, ii, 57	*Theame* – theme
II, ii, 63	*stomacke* – stomach
II, ii, 83	*Shrodenesse* – shrewdness
II, ii, 119	*attone* – atone
II, ii, 152	*Ielousies* – jealousies
II, ii, 169	*shewes* – shows
II, ii, 189	*Mesena* – in Norths' Plutarch Misena
II, ii, 191	*encreasing* – increasing
II, ii, 210	*disgested* – Var. digested F2
II, ii, 220	*purst* – pursed
II, ii, 221	*Sidnis* – Var. Cydnus F2 (entspricht North)
II, ii, 226	*Poope* – Achterdeck

II, ii, 229   *Owers* – oars
II, ii, 235   *Venus* – korrigiert aus Venns (DF)
II, ii, 239   *gloue* – Var. glow (Rowe)
II, ii, 242   *Gentlewomen* – korrigiert aus Gentlewoman gemäß F2
II, ii, 249   *adiacent* – adjacent
II, ii, 252   *Whisling* – Var. Whistling (DF)
II, ii, 271   *powre* – pour
II, iii, 5   *prayers* – korrigiert aus ptayers (DF)
II, iii, 10   *Good night Sir.*
               von Octavia gesprochen (DF, Korrektur aus F2 übernommen)
II, iii, 22   *Thy Dæmon that thy spirit which keepes thee ... thy Angell*
               wie in V, ii, 126 *ein direkter* Anklang an *Arte of English Poesie* (1589)
               »consider of the substances ... which we call ... good *Angels (Demones)*«
               (Malim 131)
II, iii, 25   *a feare* – Var. afeared (Collier)
II, iii, 34   *alway* – Var. away (Pope), DF
II, iii, 36   *Ventigius* – Var. Ventidius (F2), wohl auch ein DF in diesem
               druckfehlerreichen Abschnitt
II, iii, 41   *Battaile* – battle (frz.)
II, iii, 43   *in hoopt* – inhooped
II, iii, 48   *reciue't* – receive it
II, v, 6   *Billards*
               es wird vermutet, daß S. die Idee der billardspielenden Ägypter aus
               einem Stück Chapmans von 1598 übernommen hat (AE 147)
II, v, 16   *Tawny fine* – Var. tawny-finned (Theobald)
II, v, 35   *yeild* – yield
II, v, 37   *vaines* – veines
II, v, 65   *alay* – allay
II, v, 67   *Iaylor* – jailer (AE: gaoler)
II, v, 85   *Wyer* – wire
II, v, 92   *guift* – gift
II, v, 103   *byte* – bite
II, v, 124   *Cesterne* – cistern
II, v, 133   *art* – Var. act, eine von zahlreichen nicht »wholly satisfactory«
               (AE 153) Vorschlägen
II, v, 134   *Marchandize* – merchandise
II, vi, 11   *Cicelie* – auch Cicilie; mehrfach für Sicily (in F2 geändert)
II, vi, 24   *is* – in F2 korrigert aus his (DF)

II, vi, 25   *rigge* – rig
II, vi, 26   *fomes* – foames
II, vi, 36   *maist* – mayst
II, vi, 41   *too* – Var. to
II, vi, 42   *waigh* – weigh
II, vi, 56   *your Brother* – Antonius' Bruder
II, vi, 71   *vassaile* – vassal
II, vi, 74   *composition* – in F2 korrigert aus composion (DF)
II, vi, 84   *meaning* – Var. meanings (Rowe)
II, vi, 87   *Appolodorus*

spielt auf eine intime Anekdote an, die nur durch Plutarchs Schilderung (vgl. AE 159) verständlich wird: Appolodorus »schickte Cleopatra zu Caesar in 'nem Teppich.« (s.u.)

II, vi, 90   *Matris* – mattress
II, vi, 100   *Inioy* – enjoy
II, vi, 102   *Aboord my Gally* – aboard my galley
II, vi, 112   *thogh* – though
II, vi, 138   *wold* – would
II, vii, 2   *Banket* – banquet
II, vii, 6   *Coulord* – in F2 korrigert aus Conlord (DF)
II, vii, 7   *Almes drinke* – Bedeutung unklar (AE 162)
II, vii, 11   *greater* – in F2 korrigert aus greatet (DF)
II, vii, 14   *liue* – Var. lief (Capell)
II, vii, 23   *Pyramid* – hier im Sinne von Obelisk (AE 164)
II, vii, 25   *Foizon* – foison
II, vii, 52   *Transmigrates* – Pythagoräisches Gedankengut, vgl. AE 165
II, vii, 59   *Epicure* – vgl. Peter Moores Aufsatz
II, vii, 68   *Quicke-sands* – Treibsand
II, vii, 92   *betraide* – betrayed
II, vii, 96   *paul'd* – polled
II, vii, 114 *strike the Vessells* – Bedeutung unklar
II, vii, 117 *grow* – Var. grows F2
II, vii, 122 *Backenals* – Bacchanals
II, vii, 136 *Fattes* – Var. vats (Pope)
II, vii, 155 *No to my Cabin*

diese 4 Zeilen werden Menas zugesprochen (Var. Capell)

III, i, 1   *Pacorus* – Sohn des Partherkönigs Orodes II. (Orades), besiegte Marcus Crassus bei Carrhae (53-)

III, i, 3   *darting* – bezieht sich auf den erfolgreichen militärischen Gebrauch von Pfeilen durch die Parther (AE 171)

III, i, 3   *stroke* – Var. struck F3

III, i, 11   *whether* – whither

III, i, 16   *A lower* – korrigiert aus Alower (DF)

III, i, 19   *serues* – serve's

III, i, 24   *atchiu'd* – achieved

III, ii, 2   *the Brothers* – gemeint sind die Triumvirn

III, ii, 7   *Greene-Sicknesse* hypochrome Anämie, Blutarmut aus Eisenmangel (AE 174)

III, ii, 20   *number* – im Sinne von versifizieren (AE 175)

III, ii, 24   *They are his Shards, and he their Beetle* AE verweist auf das Sprichwort »the beetle flies over many sweet flowers and lights in a cowshard« (175)

III, ii, 31   *Band* – bond

III, ii, 33   *Vertue* – virtue

III, ii, 34   *Cyment* – cement

III, ii, 68   *year indeed* – korrigiert aus yearindeed (DF)

III, ii, 68   *trobled* – troubled

III, ii, 70   *weepe* – Var. wept (Theobald)

III, ii, 75   *wrastle* – wrestle

III, iii, 6   *Iury* – Jewry

III, iii, 25 *gate* – gait

III, iii, 39 *hearke* – hark

III, iv, 8   *tearmes* – termes

III, iv, 10   *look't* – Var. look't (Theobald)

III, iv, 15   *deuision* – division

III, iv, 27   *your* – Var. yours F2

III, iv, 34   *You* – Var.your F2

III, iv, 36   *soader* – solder

III, iv, 42   *he's* – Var. has F2

III, v, 13   *would* – Var. world (Hanmer)

III, v, 15   *the other* – Var. the one the other (Capell)

III, v, 20   *rig'd* – Var. rigges

III, vi, 13   *shew place* – showplace

III, vi, 14   *hither* – Var. he there (Johnson)

III, vi, 18   *abiliments* – habiliments

III, vi, 22   *queazie* – queasy

III, vi, 43   *my L.* – Var. my Lord (F3); der Plural (lords) der älteren AE ist denkbar, aber nicht zwingend

II, vi, 67   *abstract* – Var. obstruct (Theobald), wird von AE nicht mehr unterstützt

III, vi, 79   *Manchus* – korrigiert aus Mauchus (DF)

III, vi, 79   *King of Pont* – Pontus, damals Königreich

III, vi, 86   *does* – 3. Pers. Plural (AE 191, dort weitere Beispiele)

III, vi, 102   *abhominations* – abominations

III, vii, 5   *it is not fit* – AE korrigiert stillschweigend aus *it it not fit* (DF)

III, vii, 7   *If not* – Var. Is't not (Rowe)

III, vii, 45   *Muliters* – korrigiert aus Militers (F2: muleteers)

III, vii, 89   *Ven.* – Var. Canidius (Pope)

III, viii, 7   *Scroule* – scroll

III, x, 17   *ribaudred* – dieses Wort erscheint einzig und allein an dieser Stelle, »a corrupt reading ... which has not yet been satisfactorily emended« (OED, AE 201)

III, x, 21   *Iune* – in F2 korrigiert aus Inne

III, x, 38   *his* – Var. he F2

III, x, 43   *toot* – to't

III, xi, 50   *cease* – Var. seize F2

III, xi, 64   *stowe* – Var. tow (Rowe), wird mit Wiederholung des »st« aus dem letzten Wort erklärt

III, xi, 71   *lownes* – lowness

III, xii, 13 *Mertle* – myrtle

III, xii, 18 *Lessens* – in F2 korrigiert aus lessons

III, xiii, 7 *seuerall ranges* – Truppenteile

III, xiii, 10 *nickt* – nicked

III, xiii, 12 *meered* – mered

III, xiii, 31 *Comparisons* – Var. caparisons (Pope)

III, xiii, 34 *hye* – high

III, xiii, 41 *subdu'de* – subdued

III, xiii, 51 *falne* – fallen

III, xiii, 70 *scarre's* – scars

III, xiii, 86 *shrowd* – shroud

III, xiii, 90 *disputation* – Var. deputation (Theobald)

III, xiii, 112 *musse* – ein Spiel, bei dem Kinder nach auf dem Boden liegenden Sachen krabbeln (AE 217)

III, xiii, 114 *Iack* – vgl. die Anekdote, die über den Earl of Oxford

berichtet wird: when Jacks go up... (unsere *Macbeth*-Edition 207)

III, xiii, 123   *crindge* – cringe

III, xiii, 128   *arrant* – errand

III, xiii, 132   *Iem* – gem

III, xiii, 137   *seele* – Begriff aus der Falknerei (AE 219)

III, xiii, 154   *Basan* – vgl. Psalm 22:12

III, xiii, 176   *Abisme* – abysm

III, xiii, 191   *ingender* – engender

III, xiii, 192   *sourse* – source

III, xiii, 194   *smile* – Var. smite Rowe

III, xiii, 197   *discandering* – Var. discandying (Theobald)

III, xiii, 204   *Fleete* – are afloat (AE 223)

III, xiii, 228   *sap* – Saft, Leben

III, xiii, 233   *Estridge* – Habicht

IV, ii, 11   *Woo't* – wilt

IV, iii, 12   *Heere* – here

IV, iii, 16   *Hoboyes* – hautboys

IV, iv, 9   *Cleo. Nay, Ile helpe too, Anthony.*
die nachfolgenden Verse sind nicht Cleopatra, sondern zumindest teilweise Antonius zuzuschreiben, was schon Malone bemerkte. Zur Zuordnung siehe die Übersetzung. Vermutet wird, daß der *Anthony* hier als Anrede mißverstanden wurde

IV, iv, 12   *Sooth-law* – sooth, la

IV, iv, 19   *daft* – doff't

IV, iv, 34   *Alex.* – Da Alexas (vgl. IV, vi, 16ff.) bereits übergelaufen war, wird diese Ansprache einem Hauptmann zugeordnet

IV, iv, 39   *well-sed* – well said

IV, iv, 43   *Complement* – compliment

IV, v, 2   *Eros.* – seit Theobald werden einige Verse dieser Szene statt Eros dem später auftretenden Soldaten zugeschrieben, da hier auf dessen Warnung III, vii, 76ff. zurückgekommen wird.

IV, v, 23   *Enobarbus* – Var. Eros F2

IV, vi, 13   *Vant* – van

IV, vi, 16   *Iewrij* – Jewry

IV, vi, 17   *disswade* – dissuade

IV, vi, 23   *sorely* – korrigiert aus forely (DF), ebenso wie das *more* der folgenden Zeile, das in F wohl als *mote* gesetzt wurde

IV, vi, 41   *hart* – heart

IV, vii, 10   *clowts* – clouts

IV, viii, 4   *guests* – Var. gests (Theobald). Das wäre dann allerdings die einzige Stelle bei S., bei der dieses Wort verwendet wird (AE 242)

IV, viii, 16   *Faiery* – fairy

IV, viii, 20   *Ride on the pants triumphing.*
AE 243 wird auf eine dieses Bild imitierende (m.E. schwache) Parallele in Fletchers *The False One* (ca. 1619–23 lt. wkipedia) hingewiesen

IV, viii, 24   *Mine* – Var. My F2

IV, viii, 27   *ha* – have (keine Var., wohl nur Kurzform)

IV, viii, 29   *gole* – goal

IV, viii, 30   *fauouring* – Var. savouring (Theobald)

IV, viii, 42   *Carowses* – carouses

IV, viii, 44   *dinne* – din

IV, viii, 45   *Tabourines* – taborins

IV, ix, 1   *Centerie* – Sentry

IV, ix, 6   *too's* – to's

IV, ix, 17   *dispunge* – disponge

IV, ix, 32   *Swoonds* – swoons

IV, x, 11   *endeuour* – endeavour

IV, xii, 5   *'tis* – korrigiert aus 'ris (DF, Verwechselung r/t)

IV, xii, 26   *pannelled* – Var. spanieled (spannelled), (Hanmer)

IV, xii, 33   *fast and loose* – ein Spiel/Trick, bei dem etwas vermeintlich festes tatsächlich locker ist. Vgl. Lyly, *Euphues and his England* (1580, Oxford gewidmet): »Thus with the Aegyptian thou playest fast or loose.« (AE 251; www.elizabethanauthors.org/euphues-england-02.htm)

IV, xii, 52   *Alcides* – Herakles

IV, xiii, 3   *the Boar of Thessaly* – seit *Venus und Adonis* ist der Eber (boar), hier in mythologischer Gestalt, in S.s Werk allgegenwärtig

IV, xiii, 4   *imbost* – embossed

V, xiv, 6   *toward* – Var. towered (Rowe)

V, xiv, 6   *pendant* – pendent

IV, xiv, 7   *blew* – blue

IV, xiv, 13   *thoght* – thought

IV, xiv, 14   *dislimes* – Var. dislimns (Rowe)

IV, xiv, 32   *intirely* – entirely

IV, xiv, 39   *grone* – groan

IV, xiv, 41   *rendred* – rendered

IV, xiv, 88   *subdu'de* – subdued
IV, xiv, 97   *yu* – y mit hochgestelltem u, hier nicht darstellbar
IV, xiv, 136   *Dercetus* – identisch mit Decretas
IV, xiv, 145   *Suffising* – sufficing
IV, xv, 7   *dispise* – despise
IV, xv, 57   *hye* – high
IV, xv, 79   *Stye* – sty
IV, xv, 82   *falne* – fallen
IV, xv, 93   *in a Woman* – Var. e'en a Woman (Capell/Johnson)
V, i, 5   *pawses* – pauses
V, i, 22   *dennes* – dens
V, i, 24   *moity* – moiety
V, i, 36   *Dol.* – diese und die nachfolgenden Verse wurden Dolabella
abgesprochen, da er V, i, 6 bereits die Bühne verließ
V, i, 72   *leaue* – hier wurden mehrere Varianten versucht: lean (AE),
live (Rowe), learn (Dyce)
V, i, 92   *shew* – show
V, ii, 7   *accedents* – accidents
V, ii, 20   *Queene* - korrigiert aus Queece (DF)
V, ii, 31   *dependacie* – dependency
V, ii, 32   *ayde* – aid
V, ii, 42   *Pro.* – zwischen dieser und der vorherigen Rede Peroculeius
ist eine offensichtliche Lücke, die (nicht nur?) aus Regieanweisungen
bestehen könnte. Dennoch gibt es keinen zwingenden Grund, hier
Gallus sprechen zu lassen
V, ii, 63   *pinnion'd* – pinioned
V, ii, 64   *chastic'd* – chastised
V, ii, 66   *Varlotarie* – varletry
V, ii, 84   *imploy* – employ
V, ii, 99   *The little o'th'earth* – Var. the little O, the earth (Steevens).
Nur mit dem Hinweis auf eine parallele S.-Stelle (AE 282) m.E. nicht
zu rechtfertigen
V, ii, 106   *An Anthony it was* – die AE, obwohl sie diese weitreichende
Var. Theobalds noch übernimmt, liefert auch gute Argumente, beim
Originaltext zu bleiben (AE 305)
V, ii, 114   *dreampt* – dreamt (DF?)
V, ii, 126   *suites* – Var. smites (Capell); Pope versucht shoots.
Die Lesart smites wird gestützt durch die wörtlichen Anklang an die

Erläuterung zur rhetorischen Figur »Atanaclasis or Rebound« aus der *Arte of English Poesie* (1589): »Ye have another figure which by his nature we may call the *Rebound*, alluding to the tennis ball which being *smitten* by the racket rebounds back again« (Malim 128)

V, ii, 154   *inforce* – enforce

V, ii, 168   *valewed* – valued

V, ii, 174   *seele* – s.o. III, xiii, 137

V, ii, 204   *Cynders* – cinders

V, ii, 252   *Mechanicke Slaues* – Handwerker, auf die nicht nur hier in aristokratscher Erhabenheit herabgesehen wird

V, ii, 260   *Ballads* – Var. Ballad F2

V, ii, 260   *a Tune* – Var. o'tune (Theobald)

V, ii, 268   *mine* – Var. my F2

V, ii, 275   *Cidrus* – Var. Cidnus (Rowe); Vgl. II, ii, 221 Sidnis

V, ii, 328   *tenne* – ten

V, ii, 336   *rowse* – rouse

V, ii, 345   *Haue I the Aspicke in my lippes? Dost fall?* – Iras stirbt

V, ii, 363   *rowse* – bei Plutarch sticht die Schlange noch in den Arm; die Vorstellung, daß die Schlange an die Brust gesetzt wurde entstand lt. AE (297) zur Entstehungszeit des Stückes. Als Beleg wird Thomas Nashe (*Christ's Tears Over Jerusalem*, 1593) angeführt: »At thy breasts (as at Cleopatraes) aspisses shall be put out to nurse« (ebd.)

V, ii, 369   *wilde* – Var. vile (Capell)

V, ii, 371   *Lasse* – lass

V, ii, 373   *away* – Var. awry (Rowe)

V, ii, 417   *toyle* – toil

V, ii, 419   *Bloud* – blood

Nachwort

Zu dieser Edition

Im Nachwort zum ersten Band dieser Ausgabe (*Timon aus Athen*) haben wir die Prinzipien unserer Edition dargelegt und ausführlicher begründet, insbesondere die Entscheidung, auf den englischen Originaltext zurückzugehen (was auch in der aktuellen Arden-Edition (AE) an vielen Stellen geschieht: im Zweifelsfall *pro Folio*). Zusammengefaßt:

- als englischer Text wird der (in diesem Falle einzige) Originaltext des Stücks weitgehend wort- und zeichengetreu dargeboten: der der ersten Shakespeare-Sammelausgabe (»First Folio«, F) von 1623.
- Die deutsche Übersetzung ist auch immer als Kommentar zum englischen Text zu verstehen, die den Leser in der Regel schnell den Sinn des Originaltextes erfassen läßt und bei Zweifelsfällen erläuternd wirkt.
- Bei fehlenden Vokabeln hilft meist ein einfaches Nachschlagen in Wörterbüchern (online oder offline), die wir hier nicht ersetzen wollen
- Fast alle – bei Shakespeare bekanntlich häufiger als bei jedem anderen Autor zu findenden – seltenen Ausdrücke sind in der Orthographie (nahezu) identisch mit der heutigen Schreibweise, was daran liegen mag, daß die sperrigen Vokabeln des Urtextes heute immer noch imgrunde dieselben sind wie vor mehr als 400 Jahren – und heute genauso selten wie zur Shakespeare-Zeit. Mit anderen Worten: altertümlich anmutende Wörter sind eher nicht durch altertümliche Schreibweise fremd, sondern durch ihre Seltenheit, ja Einzigartigkeit.

- Im Anhang wird bei einigen orthographisch abweichenden Wörtern zusätzlich die moderne Schreibweise angegeben. Offensichtliche Druckfehler und von verschiedenen Herausgebern vorgeschlagene denkbare Varianten werden ebenfalls vermerkt und ggf. diskutiert

Das Prinzip der wort-und zeichengenauen Wiedergabe des Quarto- bzw. Folio-Textes sollte nicht in dem Sinne mißverstanden werden, daß man sich hier auch in jedem äußerlichen Detail an diese Vorlage hält; dann müßte man letztlich auch im selben Format zweispaltig drucken etc. Hierzu sei auf die Folio-Reprints verwiesen und auf die im Internet (z. B. bei internetshakespeare.uvic.ca) bereitgestellten Reproduktionen. Die Folioausgabe ist zwar das Original, aber eben doch nur in Sinne einer postumen Ausgabe, deren Beweiskraft im Zweifelsfall, z.B. bei der Schreibweise eines Wortes, auch nur begrenzt ist. Gerade anhand von *Anthonie and Cleopatra* lassen sich die Grenzen der Shakespeare-Philologie bis ins Detail nachverfolgen; an einigen Stellen ist auch nach seitenlangen Diskussionen immer noch der Weisheit letzter Schluß: ignoramus – wir wissen es nicht.

Da dies so ist, hat auch eine Korrektur eines offensichtlichen Druck- oder Lesefehlers, den die *zweite Folioausgabe* von 1632 (noch zu Lebzeiten Ben Jonsons und 30 Jahre vor der nächsten, nahezu völlig irrelevanten Ausgabe) vorgenommen hat, eine Aussagekraft, die nicht immer zurückzuweisen ist. In den Anmerkungen wird darauf hingewiesen, wenn in einigen wenigen Fällen die F2-Variante vorgezogen wurde, um die Lesbarkeit des Textes nicht durch zufallsbedingte Stolpersteine prinzipienreiterisch zu erschweren.

Zum Stück

Textgrundlage

Einziger Quelltext ist die »First Folio« von 1623. Bei dem Stück handelt es sich also um eine aus dem Nachlaß des Verfassers (wem immer man die Verfasserschaft zuschreibt) herausgegebene Schrift; daher kann es nicht genügend betont werden, daß alle Aussagen über Entstehungsgeschichte, redaktionelle Eingriffe, Quellenbezüge etc. letztlich nichts als Spekulationen sind.

Der Eindruck, daß der Setzer im Falle von *Anthonie and Cleopatra* nicht immer sehr sorgfältig gearbeitet hat, ist dennoch nicht zu leugnen. Sich an Spekulationen über die Eigenheiten verschiedener Setzer, die vermuteten Charakteristika imaginärer *foul papers* etc. zu beteiligen, wie sie die traditionelle Shakespeare-Philologie (bewundernswerter Scharfsinn, der über Jahrhunderte aufgeboten wurde) bis zum Überdruß auch des literarisch Interessierten betrieben hat, halte ich jedoch für wenig sinnvoll. Das Stück ist sehr lang, es wird also mühevoll zu setzen gewesen sein – sehr viel mehr kann aus diesen Studien nicht mit Sicherheit gefolgert werden.

»Diese Merkmale [inkonsistente Regieanweisungen etc.] weisen stark darauf hin, daß eine Abschrift des Verfassermanuskripts als Satzvorlage für den Folio-Text genommen wurde; wie auch bestimmte Shakespeare-unspezifische Schreibweisen, insbesondere der vorherrschende Gebrauch des ›oh‹ statt des kürzeren ›o‹« (Wells, AE 78). Wäre es da nicht logisch, wenn dann die stilometrischen Erbsenzähler Werke wie z. B. *Anthonie and Cleopatra* aus ihren Betrachtungen ausklammern würden?

Quellen

»In einem Kontenbuch, in dem verschiedene für die königlichen Wards [vaterlos gewordene minderjährige Adlige, die in königliche Vormundschaft genommen wurden, d. Hrsg.] bestrittene Ausgaben verzeichnet sind, findet sich für die Zeit zwischen dem 1. Januar und 30. September 1570 „zugunsten des Earl of Oxford" folgender Eintrag: „An William Seres, Schreibwarenhändler, für eine vergoldete Geneva-Bibel, einen Chaucer, Plutarchs Werke auf französisch und andere Bücher und Papiere... 2L, 7S, 10 d" (Ward 1928, 33).« (Mark Anderson, NSJ 1, 100)

Shakespeare benutzte Plutarch als Quelle für *Antonius und Cleopatra* und die anderen »Römerdramen« *Julius Cäsar* und *Coriolanus*. Dies wird niemand bestreiten; für *Timon aus Athen* (s. unsere Edition) oder gar *Ein Mittsommernachtstraum* (AE 56) gilt das schon nicht mehr, aber das muß hier nicht diskutiert werden. Plutarch-Kenntnis war um 1550 Teil der höheren klassischen Bildung, und Shakespeare hat an dieser Bildung teilgenommen, ja wurde von ihr so sehr angeregt, daß er eine Serie von Dramen zu klassischen Themen schrieb. Diese einfache Grundannahme zieht weitere Fragen nach sich, bei denen die verschiedenen Sichtweisen auf Shakespeare (Stratford/Oxford) zu verschiedenen Antworten gelangt sind, die hier kurz angerissen werden sollen.

Eine Grundannahme für das stratfordianische *Antonius und Cleopatra*-Bild ist, daß sich Shakespeares Plutarch-Kenntnisse auf Thomas North' Übersetzung aus dem Jahre 1579 stützen, nicht auf das griechische Original oder die französische Version von 1559, denn dies wäre mit dem Axiom eines mehr

oder minder autodidaktischen Naturburschen nicht kompatibel. Fundamental ist ebenfalls die chronologische Vorgabe, daß das Stück um 1607 entstanden sein muß; daher werden noch weitere (schwache) Einflüsse wie Mary Sidney (1592), Daniel (1594) etc. postuliert. Vom immanenten Werturteil einer passiven, imitatorischen Aneignung wird niemals abgewichen – trotz aller Würdigungen der selbständigen Aneignung etc. in den werkimmanenten Interpretationen der langen Nachworte und anderen Textsorten.

Eine oxfordianische Sicht auf das Werk (die allerdings noch recht rudimentär ausgebildet ist) würde die Schwerpunkte anders setzen können. Da Oxford die französische Sprache beherrschte und zumindest auch Griechischkenntnisse besaß, wäre North und damit 1579 nicht der Startpunkt der Auseinandersetzung. Man sollte die Plutarch-Auseinandersetzung parallel zu der mit der englischen Geschichte (Hall, Holinshed etc.) sehen; zwei Seiten einer bis in die Jugendjahre zurückreichenden parallelen Abarbeitung an historischen Stoffen in literarischer Form. Ich sage bewußt nicht »in dramatischer Form«, denn Lyrik und Versepik mag am Anfang dominiert haben; die dramatische Form wird sich ebenfalls über längere Zeit entwickelt haben, und am Ende kommt unbestreitbar ein episches Element hinzu in Form des Lesedramas, zu der das zu Shakespeares Lebzeiten womöglich niemals aufgeführte Langdrama *Antonius und Cleopatra* auch gehört, zumindest in der vorliegenden Fassung. Eine Quellenbewertung ist also ohne den Kontext eines Gesamtverständnisses von Werk und Verfasser kaum möglich.

Datierung

a) Spuren vor 1623

Es ist kein wirklich zuverlässiges Indiz dafür bekannt, daß das Stück vor 1623 auf irgendeine Weise öffentlich wahrgenommen werden konnte. Von einer Aufführung am Hofe ist nichts bekannt, und eine auf den öffentlichen Bühnen widerspräche dem Geist des Stückes:

> Die schnellen Komödianten spielen uns,
> Und zeigen Alexandria bei Nacht:
> Antonius tritt betrunken auf, und mich
> Seh ich von irgendeinem Jüngling kreischend
> Als Hure dargestellt.

Mary Sidney Herbert, Countess of Pembroke (1561-1621), Schwester von Philip Sidney, sehr eng verwandt mit Edward de Vere und neuerdings sogar auch eine Kandidatin für die Verfasserschaft des Shakespeare-Werks, schrieb 1592 einen Antonius (nach französischer Vorlage von 1578), der »genügend verbale Parallelen« (AE 62) zu Shakespeare aufweist, um einen Einfluß nahezulegen – allerdings wieder einmal in beide Richtungen. Daß der notorische Abschreiber Samuel Daniel (Malim 287) nun 1594 sein der Gräfin Pembroke gewidmetes Cleopatra-Stück auch von Shakespeare inspirieren ließ, ist demgegenüber zweitrangig: »Hätte Shakespeare Daniel und die Gräfin Pembroke nicht gelesen, wäre *Antonius und Cleopatra* wahrscheinlich genauso so wie es jetzt ist« (AE 63). Umgekehrt könnte gefolgert werden, daß das, was Pembroke und Daniel von einer möglichen Shakespeare-Aufführung am Hofe aufgeschnappt haben könnten, wohl nur ein grober, indirekter Eindruck war.

Dasselbe gilt wohl auch für die »enough detailed similarities« (AE 66) zur (eher apokryphen) *Dido, Queen of Carthage* von Marlowe und Nashe (Druck 1594), von denen es keine bis in die Fußnoten der Arden Edition geschafft hat. Chiljan (349) führt eine Parallele zu I, v, 83 auf (»man of men«). Die Referenz zu Thomas Nashe von 1593 (vgl. zu V, ii, 363) ist da schon gehaltvoller: Nashe war Mitglied des literarischen Kreises um Edward de Vere.

Die einzige von der Arden Edition erwähnte Daniel-Parallele (AE 103) ist eher weit hergeholt, so daß die Spekulationen, daß Daniel vor der revidierten Ausgabe seines Dramas im Jahre 1607 mit Shakespeares Drama bekannt wurde (AE 72), unbegründet sind.

Am 20. 5. 1608 wurden vom Shakespeare-Drucker (damals eher Raubdrucker) Edward Blount zwei Stücke ohne Verfasserangabe im Buchhändlerregister eingetragen: *The booke of Pericles prynce of Tyre* und *Anthony. and Cleopatra* (Gilvary 415). Während *Pericles* 1609 noch erscheinen konnte, wurde *Anthony and Cleopatra* zurückgehalten oder unterdrückt – wie alle weiteren Shakespeare-Stücke bis 1622.

b) Historisierende Zuschreibungen

Während sich stratfordianische Interpreten bei ihren Datierungsversuchen einzig auf interne Zuordnungen stützen können, eröffnet sich für Oxfordianer das Feld der biographisch-historischen Zuordnung, das allerdings nicht immer frei von unhaltbaren Spekulationen ist. So sind alle Einordnungen, die den Namen Eva Turner Clark tragen

(Gilvary 418ff.), kaum zu begründen. Mark Anderson, der einzige Oxfordianer, der bisher versucht hat, dieses Stück in einen historischen Kontext zu stellen, geht da umsichtiger vor und stützt sich auch auf die konventionelle Shakespeare-Forschung, die den Zusammenhang zwischen Elizabeth I. und Kleopatra thematisiert hat. Zu der Passage III, iii, 17ff. paßt eine Äußerung Elisabeths, die sich auf Mary Stuart bezieht: »She is too high, for I myself am neither too high nor too low« (Anderson 57). Zu Fulvia wird Anne Cecil assoziiert (227), zu den Seeschlachtszenen die Armada-Ereignisse von 1588, an denen Oxford auch direkt beteiligt war (228). Bei Gilvary (418ff.) wird aus diesen Überlegungen zur »Internal Oxfordian Evidence« gefolgert, daß es eine frühe Version des Stückes aus den Jahren 1579-80 gegeben hat, die später umgeschrieben wurde. Diese stufenweise Entstehungsgeschichte kann für die meisten Shakespeare-Stücken postuliert werden; bei *Antonius und Cleopatra* spricht die überlieferte homogene Textfassung jedoch nicht für eine stufenweise Entstehung.

Literatur

(AE) Wilders, John (Hrsg.): Antony And Cleopatra. London 2006 (1. Ausgabe 1995) (The Arden Shakespeare, Third Series)

(Anderson) Anderson, Mark: ›Shakespeare‹ By Another Name. New York 2005.

(Chiljan) Chiljan, Katherine: Shakespeare Suppressed. San Francisco 2011

(Gilvary) Gilvary, Kevin (Hrsg.): Dating Shakespeare's Plays: A Critical Review of the Evidence. Tunbridge Wells 2010.

(Malim) Malim, Richard: The Earl of Oxford and the Making of »Shakespeare«. Jefferson, North Carolina, London 2012

Uwe Laugwitz

Steckels Shake-Speare
Editionsplan

The Life of Tymon of Athens/Timon aus Athen (2013)

The Tragedie of Macbeth/Die Macbeth Tragödie (2013)

The Tragedie of Anthony and Cleopatra/Antonius und Cleopatra (2013)

A Midsommer Nights Dreame/Ein Mittsommernachtstraum

The Tragedie of King Richard the second/Die Tragödie von König Richard II.

The Life and Death of King John/Leben und Sterben des Königs John

The Raigne of King Edward the third/Die Regierung des Königs Edward III.

The Tragedie of Cymbeline/Cymbeline

Twelfe Night, Or what you will/Die zwölfte Nacht oder Was ihr wollt

The Tragœdy of Othello, the Moore of Venice/Die Tragödie von Othello, dem Mohren von Venedig

Loues Labour lost/Verlorene Liebesmüh

The Tragedie of Hamlet, Price of Denmarke/Die Tragödie von Hamlet, Prinz von Dänemark